CULTURAL ENCOUNTERS

CULTURAL ENCOUNTERS

Essays on the interactions of diverse cultures now and in the past

Edited by
ROBERT CECIL and **DAVID WADE**

With a foreword by
ROBERT CECIL

THE OCTAGON PRESS
LONDON

**Published by The Octagon Press Ltd. for
The Institute for Cultural Research.**

ISBN 0 863040 50 0

Published in 1990

Photoset, printed and bound by
Redwood Press, Melksham, Wiltshire

CONTENTS

PART III:

ENCOUNTERS IN THE MODERN WORLD

PART IV:

GLOBAL IMPERATIVES

THE AUTHORS

ROBERT CECIL, C.M.G.
Was Chairman of the Graduate School of Contemporary European Studies at the University of Reading from 1976–78 and is Chairman of the Institute for Cultural Research

THE HON. SIR STEVEN RUNCIMAN, F.B.A., F.S.A.
Fellow of Trinity College, Cambridge and formerly Professor of Byzantine Art and History at the University of Istanbul, he is a leading authority on the history and culture of Byzantium.

KATHARINE VIVIAN
Translator of several Georgian classics, notably Rustaveli's *The Knight in Panther Skin*, Orbeliani's *Book of Wisdom and Lies* and a section of *The Georgian Chronicle*. She has also contributed to symposia on the literature and culture of Georgia in London, Bari and Tbilisi.

SIR ROGER STEVENS, G.C.M.G.
Was British Ambassador to Iran, Deputy Under-Secretary of State at the Foreign Office and then until 1970 Vice-Chancellor of Leeds University. His book, *The Land of the Great Sophy*, deals with the dawn of relationships between Persia and Europe.

NIRAD C. CHAUDHURI, F.R.S.L.
Born in Bengal, he was formerly First Assistant Editor of *The Modern Review* (Calcutta) and later secretary to Sarat Bose, leader of the Congress Party. He is the author of several distinguished books, of which perhaps the best known is his *Autobiography of an Unknown Indian*.

IRIS BUTLER
Born in India, she lived and worked in the country for thirty-seven years. She is the author of several historical studies, including *Rule of Three* (a life of Sarah, Duchess of Marlborough) and *The Eldest Brother* (The Marquess Wellesley).

PROFESSOR G.M. CARSTAIRS, M.D., F.R.C.P.E., F.R.C.Psych.
Born in India, he was formerly Professor of Psychiatry at Edinburgh University. From 1973 to 1978 he was Vice-Chancellor of the University of York, before returning to India to continue his social and scientific work. His books include *The Twice Born* and *The Great Universe of Kota*.

PETER BRENT
Author of many books, among them a major biography of Darwin (*Charles Darwin: A Man of Enlarged Curiosity*); also two studies of the mystical and religious traditions of the East (*Godmen of India* and *Healers of India*) of which the paper given here was a forerunner.

RICHARD HARRIS
Born in 1914 and brought up in China, he became a specialist in Chinese and general Asian affairs and was for many years Deputy Foreign Editor of *The Times*.

DR PETER WADE
From 1985 to 1988 Research Fellow in anthropology at Queens' College, Cambridge where he made a special study of black culture and ethnic relations in Colombia. He is now joint lecturer in Geography and Latin American Studies at the University of Liverpool.

DAVID WIDDICOMBE, Q.C.
An eminent Queen's Counsel, he has worked and travelled widely in South-East Asia and the Far East where he has developed an extensive interest in the field of race relations.

DR MARTIN HOLDGATE, C.B.
Formerly Deputy Secretary, Environment Protection and Chief
Scientist at the Department of the Environment, he is now Direc-
tor-General of I.U.C.N. – The World Conservation Union.

EUGENE GREBENIK, C.B., M.SC. (ECON)
Principal of the Civil Service College (1970–1976), he was President of the British Society for Population Studies (1979–1981) and
is currently Managing Editor of *Population Studies*.

DR ALEXANDER KING, C.M.G., C.B.E.
Founder-member and now President of the Club of Rome, he was
for many years Director-General for Scientific Affairs at the
O.E.C.D. and from 1974 to 1984 Chairman, The International
Federation of Institutes for Advanced Study.

EDITORS' NOTE

The essays contained in this volume, with one exception, began as public lectures. They were delivered under the aegis of the Institute for Cultural Research in 1970 (Brent); 1974 (Holdgate, Grebenik, King); 1976 (Runciman, Stevens, Chaudhuri, Butler, Carstairs, Harris); and 1987 (Wade, Widdicombe). All these subsequently appeared as monographs, but Katharine Vivian's essay (1982) appeared in that form only. As will be apparent, a number of the texts are close transcriptions of the lectures as spoken.

In several instances events have overtaken the original texts and where this has happened the authors have generously undertaken either to add an afterword or to revise and rewrite, sometimes very substantially. Such revisions are indicated in notes accompanying the texts.

The editors are very grateful to all those who have contributed to this volume and especially to those who have supplied afterwords or otherwise taken trouble to update their work.

All maps drawn by Virginia Smith.

FOREWORD

Robert Cecil

What is culture and where does it start? We may perhaps detect its first signs on the walls of caves, in the detritus of buried cities or in tumuli dedicated to nameless heroes. These, however, are no more than the dry bones of culture; it takes a poet, like Homer, or an historian, like Herodotus, to put flesh on the bones and bring to life the antique figures of a vanished age. For culture, fundamentally, is about people; how they lived and how they made contact with one another. We specially need poets, because, as Sir Steven Runciman reminds us in the opening essay of this volume, 'the historians of the past were not on the whole deeply interested in cultural affairs'. Historians may have left us scant account of the rise and fall of the mediaeval kingdom of Georgia, but we can learn much about its people from the epic poem, *The Knight in Panther Skin*, which has been translated into English by Katharine Vivian, author of the second essay. In our admiration of the poets and myth-makers of the past, we should not lose sight of the literate travellers and traders, like Marco Polo. One of these was the anglicised Huguenot jeweller, Sir John Chardin, whose book about Persia under Shah Abbas has been a major source for the essay of the late Sir Roger Stevens on *Europe and the Great Sophy*.

When this has been said, the fact remains that the early cultural encounters of different peoples is an elusive subject and may well be regarded as one of history's missing dimensions. We have some record of how in all ages cohesive bodies of men and women, variously depicted as tribes, races, states or nations, have entered into some form of communication with one another, marked often by trade, by treaty and, all too often, by war. With these public events historians have largely concerned themselves; they have been less concerned with the cultural contacts of individual men

and women, which have taken place in the interstices of the more
public occasions. When contacts of this kind were interrupted by
war, this sometimes entailed the subjugation of a relatively weaker
group by a stronger one. When subjugation took place, however, it
was not necessarily accompanied by the assumption on the part of
the stronger group that success on the battlefield meant superiority
in the field of culture. On the contrary, the opposite assumption
was sometimes made. Imperial Rome, for example, whilst demon-
strating her superiority in political, economic and military organisation, was willing to concede the superiority of the Greeks in art,
letters and philosophy. Similarly the invasive tribes which brought
about the fall of Rome, borrowed not only the imperial idea but as
much of the culture of the defeated as they could absorb.

It was among western Europeans of the 16th and subsequent
centuries that the belief took root that their incursions into the
lands of alien peoples with different cultural traditions marked the
dominance of a superior culture over an inferior one. The voyages
of Spanish and Portuguese mariners coincided with the resurgence
of Catholicism in the counter-reformation, and missionaries held
that their presence and their preaching vindicated the brutality of
the conquistadors. The British and Dutch seamen, who followed
after, were more interested in trade and bullion; the French, as
colonisers, came midway between these two groups of imperial
nations. Imperialism thus became linked with navies and maritime
trade and was most easily recognised in this aspect. This has been
called 'the saltwater fallacy' and has prevented later imperial
powers from admitting the force motivating their expansion. Thus
as the USA moved west and south in the 19th century, Americans
termed the process 'manifest destiny'. As Imperial Russia moved
south and east, Russians regarded their progress as equivalent to
the '*mission civilisatrice*' of France. The Russian revolution, despite
Lenin's earlier strictures on the tyranny of Great Russia over
subject nationalities, served only to provide an ideological justifi-
cation for the domination of Moscow.

European insistence that colonisation represented not only the
triumph of the ironclad and the maxim gun, but also that of a
superior culture met with relatively little opposition in Africa and
South America. In Asia confrontation and contradiction soon
emerged. These developments are treated in the group of essays

dealing with British India. At the heart of the misunderstanding that arose between Indians and their British rulers was religion. This is sufficiently shown by the steady deterioration that set in after 1813, when the East India Company (EIC) was authorised to admit missionaries to its territories and a bishopric was instituted at Calcutta. There had been Christian missionaries in India before that date, but they had either had to settle in Danish enclaves, like those mentioned by Iris Butler, or they came disguised as EIC chaplains, like Henry Martyn. The first Governors-General, like Hastings, Cornwallis and Wellesley, had actively encouraged vernacular education, including study of Sanskrit, the language of Hindu theology. They believed that missionaries would be regarded by the indigenous peoples as threatening their traditions and long-established practices, thus making the rulers' task more difficult. Changed thinking was due to the growing strength of the Evangelical influence, represented in India by Charles Grant and Sir John Shore (later Lord Teignmouth) and in London by William Wilberforce and the so-called 'Clapham Sect'. The Church Missionary Society (CMS), founded in 1799, was a powerful pressure group. Charles Simeon, the Cambridge Evangelical and patron of Martyn, is recorded to have said, 'I used jocosely to call India my Diocese.'

The early missionaries in India, as Iris Butler insists, were saintly men with a profound concern for Indian wellbeing. Martyn, who translated the New Testament into Arabic, Persian and Urdu, was an accomplished linguist, who engaged in learned discussion with Brahmins, Mullas, Sufis and other religious teachers. The trouble originated in London, where it was necessary to overcome the lingering objections of those who believed that missionary activity would cause disturbance in India and hinder trade. The Evangelicals, in order to achieve their objectives, exaggerated the scale on which suttee (immolation of widows) and infanticide were practised and ascribed every disorder in India to religious depravity. Wilberforce, for example, ignored the grandiose concept of Brahman and asserted, 'In the adventures of the countless rabble of Hindoo deities you may find every possible variety of every practicable vice . . . their religion is one grand abomination.' Grant, who in 1794 had become a Director of the EIC, took a slightly different tack. He maintained that, if ever the Indian people were to be entrusted with a greater share of responsibility for the administration of their country, a thorough-going reform of their whole way of life would be necessary; they would have 'to become acquainted with the truth and excellence of Revelation, with the improvements and the rights of man.' This line of thought culminated in the Governor-Generalship of Lord William Bentinck (1828–35), who abolished suttee, established English as the official language and defined the aim of education in India as 'the promotion of European literature and science among the natives.'

There is, of course, a case to be made out for this policy and Nirad Chaudhuri eloquently makes it. It could only have worked harmoniously, however, if accompanied by a real attempt on the part of the rulers to understand how Hindus thought about their culture and their history. Few made the attempt; the majority, whilst conscientiously carrying out their duties, treated Indians and their way of life with indifference degenerating at times into contempt. A more understanding attitude would, admittedly, have taxed even flexible and imaginative minds, such as British overseas administrators rarely possessed. For, in order to understand India in the 19th century, they would have had to turn their backs upon the faith underlying the whole Victorian ethos, namely the belief in progress and the conviction that change must necessarily be change for the better. The British held that, in bringing to India the immediate benefits of economic growth and the long-term hope of democratic self-government, they must evoke the support of all who had the good of India at heart; sustained opposition could hardly be more than obscurantism.

Here Peter Brent's essay on the guru and his disciples can enlighten us, because it reveals the inward-looking nature of the most respected of Hindu religious traditions. For the guru, the external world, in which the British administrators functioned so confidently, was the world of Maya or Illusion. The disciple was required to focus his attention on the inner world and grapple with the individual karma that held him bound to the cycle of rebirth; changes in society, or in the economic order, were at best irrelevant distractions. In any case the basic social order had been laid down in the laws of Manu many centuries ago and change would be change for the worse. Such thinking, sanctioned by religion, led inevitably to political inertia.

Before condemning it, however, we would do well to recall that our concept of history as a linear and upward progression is of no great antiquity. The Pharaohs of Egypt saw no virtue in change; the restless ones were the Jews, who were seeking their Promised Land. Their Messianic creed infused into primitive Christianity its heavy stress on Christ, the anti-christ and the millennium. Jews and Christians have never been content with the world as it is; Marx was not the first Jewish philosopher to conclude that his aim should not to be to interpret the world, but to change it. Neither the Greeks nor the Chinese looked upon history as linear development in one direction. Richard Harris begins his essay with the Chinese observation that dynasties followed a regular cycle of budding, flowering and decay. Aristotle would agree; he traced how aristocracy degenerated into oligarchy and democracy into ochlocracy, or mob-rule, from which the state would be rescued by the authority of a tyrant, after which the cycle would begin again. As our twentieth century draws to a close, the concept of linear progression looks less convincing than it did to our Victorian grandfathers and great-grandfathers. This may be one reason for what Professor Carstairs in his essay refers to as 'the lively interest shown in many aspects of Hindu culture by young people in the Western world.'

A further reason for the alienation of young people from the culture in which they have been reared is the one expounded in the final group of essays concerning ecology, pollution, energy, exhaustion of raw materials and uncontrolled expansion of population. One of the Christian beliefs, firmly implanted in the Western world, is that Man is the centre and crown of the universe; it was created for his benefit and he has been given dominion over the fruits of the earth and the beasts of the field. The more ancient religions of the East present a very different picture of man's place in the cosmos. The Judaeo-Christian dynamic, combining with zeal for self-improvement, led to exploitation of the world's resources, mineral, vegetable and animal, for man's advantage. In the early part of the 19th century Malthusians believed that inadequacy of food supplies would restrain growth of population and affluence. As technological advances began to suggest that no such limitations need occur, optimism about the joyful destiny of the human race broke out, especially in Europe and North America.

Young people today reproach their grandfathers with failing to foresee the astronomical growth of population, to which Eugene Grebenik's essay refers, and the enhanced demand for energy and raw materials that has followed, let alone the impact on the environment of unrestrained consumerism.

Those of us who have lived through two world wars may not see the first two-thirds of our century as a period of much stability or amenity. To those born more recently, however, we take on the role of asset-strippers, producing and consuming with little regard for the future or for the world-wide human community. Energy produced by nuclear fission is a case in point: in order to satisfy ever-rising demands for energy, we have generated substantial volumes of atomic waste, for which we have yet to find secure means of disposal. We have conspiciously failed to strike a balance between quantitative increments to our standard of living and the quality of life. Thoughtful observers, seeing the countryside sacrificed to more and more motorways, car-parks and airports, must wonder whether perpetual motion is a true recipe for human happiness. Where trees remain, their foliage is damaged by industrial emissions; where there are beaches, these are polluted by oil-slicks. Poets are not the only ones to complain.

CAN OF WORMS

Watching the workmen drilling down
Through asphalt, concrete, cables and gas mains
I saw they'd come to earth, which used to grow
Green grass, as Granpa said,
And never bore the weight
Of tower-blocks, motorways and used-car lots.

I gathered a handful of this earth
Crumbling it in my fingers. Granpa said
Earthworms lived in it, just as fish
Once lived in rivers, finding room beside
The condoms, tyres, gin bottles and tin cans.

I wish I'd found some worms –
I could have told my son.

If there is a feeling that man has arrogated too much to himself and raised his head too high above the parapet, this is still a

minority view; for the great majority the search for affluence and
'the good life' continues unabated and must evidently grow apace
in the deprived areas of the world. If this trend accelerates, as
seems probable, the ever-swelling population cannot fail to exert
increasing pressure on resources of food and energy and conflict is
bound to arise between 'haves', trying to hold on, and 'have-nots',
trying to stay alive. These essays do not examine in detail the many
political implications; but Alexander King, who as co-author of the
Club of Rome report of 1972 foresaw so many of the trends that
threaten us, makes the depressing point that 'political leaders are as
yet far from admitting, to say nothing of facing up to, the situation.' He insists that what is needed is a collective approach to our
problems, 'based on enlightened and common self-interest.' Unfortunately there are few signs of such an approach; on the contrary
there are in many countries fissile tendencies, leading to social
disorder and either open or latent violence. Two developing countries that suffer in this way are treated in Peter Wade's essay on
Colombia and David Widdicombe's essay on Malaysia. We cannot
flatter ourselves, however, that such dangers arise only in countries, such as these, which were formerly colonies. Europe is not
exempt from internecine violence, as troubles in Ulster and the
Basque country sadly show.

Pressure of population and erosion of the environment pose a
threat to democracy, which everywhere, except in Western
Europe, North America and Australasia, is no more than a tender
plant. In theory, it is possible for people in a democracy to school
themselves to curb their appetites and demand less from their
environment; but, as Dr King stresses, this requires a high degree
of abstinence and restraint. The democratic system, as we know it,
has long involved political parties in holding out to the electorate at
regular intervals the prospect that with a new set of leaders it will
get more out of the pork barrel. It is not hard to predict the fate of a
contemporary party campaigning on a programme of restricting
each family to one child and one car. It is significant that only China
with its authoritarian system has so far dared to impose a strict limit
on the size of families. In the West we are still encouraging unnatural pregnancies and aid to infertile females. What, one must ask,
are the prospects for family limitation in such Roman Catholic
countries as Italy and Brazil? This is not the place to pursue such

speculations; but it may be as well to recall that democracy is not the only thread in the rich tapestry of ancient Greece. A very different and less buoyant model for controlling our affairs could be found by examining Plato's *Republic* and the role of his 'Guardians'. This volume offers no such drastic solution; but it does serve to invite attention to the gravity of the problem.

I

EARLY EASTERN CULTURES

1

Constantinople and Baghdad: Cultural Relations

SIR STEVEN RUNCIMAN

Throughout the middle ages, until the end of the twelfth century the city of Constantinople was without question the greatest and most splendid city in Christendom, and the Imperial court of Byzantium outshone all other Christian courts in its magnificence and majesty. The Emperor, in his own eyes and in the eyes of his subjects and his vassals, was the supreme Christian monarch, the Viceroy of God on earth. Other Christian monarchs, though he might not be able to exercise suzerainty over them, were his inferiors. Although for a time the Byzantines had conceded an Imperial title to Charlemagne and his son Louis, and they were therefore raised by protocol to parallel but junior status, that was a temporary aberration. Later Western Emperors were allowed no more than a kingly title, which did not interfere with the Emperor's nominal authority over the Christian oecumene. But there was one monarch whom Byzantine protocol treated as being the equal of the Emperor. This was the Viceroy of God of another faith, the Caliph of Islam. The Moslems might be infidels, and there never could be complete understanding between them and the Christians. But the Byzantines realistically recognized that the Commander of the Faithful was in a similar position to their own Divine Emperor. He must be treated with similar respect. No ambassador was received with such honour by the Court of Constantinople as the envoy of the Caliph, and the Court of Baghdad returned the compliment. This mutual courtesy lasted so long as the Byzantine Emperor and the Caliph of Baghdad were the two most august monarchs in the world, and it was reflected in the general relations between Constantinople and Baghdad.

When the Moslems first emerged from the desert, the Christian world, which was used to the proliferation of heresies, regarded

3

Islam at first as an extreme Christian heresy. They came before
long to realize that this was a different religion; that though it was
infidel, it was not heathen. The Moslems themselves regarded
Christianity and Judaism as 'religions of the Book', that is to say,
religions legitimate in their time, though now they failed to accept
the final revelation of the Prophet Mohammed and the word of God
written down in the Koran. Unlike the Zoroastrian Persians, with
whom Byzantium had recently been fighting and who looted and
destroyed Christian shrines, the Moslems treated Christian Holy
Places with respect, so long as the Christians there submitted to
their authority peaceably. Only those who opposed them by force
were given the choice of conversion or the sword. It is true that the
Christian subjects of the Moslems became to some extent second-
class citizens. They were not allowed to build more churches
without permission. They could not marry Moslem women, and
any attempt at proselytism was punishable by death. But, while the
secessionist churches in Syria and Egypt lost many of their number
to Islam and the remainder accepted their new masters because
they had no option, and had in any case resented Byzantine rule,
the Orthodox congregations, which were still numerous in Syria
and Palestine, were in a rather different position. The Moslems
were ready to identify national status – if one may anachronistically
use that expression – with religion. Just as all Moslems were
subjects of the Caliph, wherever they might live, so Orthodox
Christians were all subjects of the Emperor. The Orthodox in
Moslem lands therefore were more or less in the position of resi-
dent aliens. They had to obey the Caliph's laws and pay him taxes,
but they were known as the Melkites, the Emperor's men (from
malik, the king). If they were maltreated, the Emperor could
legitimately intervene on their behalf. On the other hand, if the
Caliph wished to put pressure on the Emperor he might threaten to
persecute the Orthodox.

For about a century after the Arab irruption from the desert the
vast and expanding Islamic world was ruled by Caliphs of the
Ummayad dynasty, based on Damascus. The Arabs brought very
little culture with them beyond their literary tradition, but in Syria
they found a still thriving Christian-Hellenistic civilization, which
they adapted to their needs. Indeed, till the end of the seventh
century the Caliph's treasury was staffed very largely by Christians

who kept their records in Greek. Even in the mid-eighth century, when Arabic had come to be generally used for the administration, we still find Christians in government service. Saint John of Damascus, the eloquent defender of Orthodoxy against Iconoclasm, had worked as a Treasury official under the Moslems. The art and architecture of the Ummayad period may be classed as Syrian-Byzantine, slightly adapted to suit Moslem needs and tastes. The Ummayads even imported Byzantine mosaic artists from Constantinople to decorate their mosques and public buildings. It was Syrian art that Ummayad princes and governors carried westward with them and eventually established in Spain.

In the mid-eighth century, after a series of rebellions, Ummayad power collapsed in the East, and a new dynasty, the Abbasids, took over the Caliphate and made their headquarters in Mesopotamia, or Iraq. Babylonian and Assyrian traditions lingered on there and, more recently, the Sassanid Persians had fixed their capital, Ctesiphon, in the province. All these elements were absorbed into the new civilization of Islam. Owing to the political power of the Abbasid Caliphate, this civilization spread not only eastward, into Central Asia and to the borders of India, but also westward, over the old Hellenistic world of Syria and Egypt, and into the Maghreb. It was in this atmosphere that the new Islamic capital of Baghdad was founded. Thenceforward there were two great centres of civilization in the Near East. There was Constantinople, with its Roman, Hellenistic and Judaeo-Christian traditions, and there was Baghdad, with its mainly Mesopotamian and Persian traditions, enriched by the Syrian culture of Ummayad times. The cultural rivalry between these two centres was undoubtedly for the good of them both.

Unfortunately the historians of the past were not on the whole deeply interested in cultural affairs. They took their own civilization for granted, and only a few rare writers like Herodotus or, in Byzantine times, the Emperor Constantine Porphyrogenitus paid any attention to other cultures. We usually have to make our own interpretations of cultural influences, and we may often be wrong. However, to illustrate the cultural rivalry between Constantinople and Baghdad, a certain number of anecdotes survive, of doubtful historical accuracy but of general significance, which help to supplement the somewhat meagre known facts.

The Arabs always felt a deep respect for Constantinople. It was the great city, New Rome, the symbol of Empire, and the Prophet himself had enjoined that it must be conquered for the Faith. The Ummayad Caliphs had made two great attempts to carry out the Prophet's orders, but both had ended in bitter failure, and the Abbasids, though their armies raided deep into the territory of the Christian Empire, never repeated the experiment. Warfare remained endemic on the frontier between the two Empires. In the wilder districts there were on both sides clans of border barons who went their own way, paying little attention to their respective sovereigns, unless the sovereign brought his army into the area. For the rest of the time they raided each other's lands, but occasionally they would meet on a friendly basis to go hunting together or for jousts and tournaments. Now and then one of them would change his allegiance and even his religion, and there was occasionally intermarriage across the border. It was a heroic life, but a life without many of the refinements of civilization. Along the more populous stretches of the frontier responsible government officials faced each other, and though raids were plentiful there also, they were more orderly and, paradoxically, they resulted in closer understanding between the two civilizations.

This worked on two levels. The constant wars were interrupted now and then by truces where high officials from each Empire met each other at some spot on the frontier and discussed the exchange of prisoners taken in the raids and, if one side had a surplus of prisoners, to agree about the sum of redemption money. These meetings seem to have been conducted on a friendly basis. We know that the Byzantine government liked to choose as its representative someone who could speak Arabic, and it is likely that the Caliphate sometimes acted equivalently. Indeed, it seems on one or two occasions to have employed a Christian official for the negotiations. Then, at slightly longer intervals, there would be a high-powered embassy sent from Constantinople to Baghdad or from Baghdad to Constantinople. These were splendid occasions. The ambassadors were always treated honorifically, and in their stay in the other capital they were given the opportunity to visit the chief local sights and to talk freely with the people whom they met.

On another level there were the prisoners of war. Many of these had miserable lives, being sent to work in mines or in factories, with very little hope of regaining freedom. The better educated usually were taken off to become slaves in a private household. If they were intelligent and their master a man of culture, they were well treated, and they were usually given a chance of liberation; a certain number on each side seem to have stayed on in the other dominion, sometimes rising to posts of some prosperity there. The more distinguished prisoners were treated very well, almost as guests. They were, after all, valuable political hostages, and their goodwill might be useful in the future.

Nearly all the stories that we have telling of cultural contacts between Constantinople and Baghdad are connected with embassies or with prisoners. At first Constantinople, being the older city, contributed more to Baghdad than Baghadad to Constantinople. When the Caliph Mansur in AD 762 decided upon the site of Baghdad for his new capital – largely because the Nestorian monks who had a monastery there assured him that it was a cool spot, and remarkably free from midges – he adopted the plan of a circular city, four miles in circumference, surrounded by an outer moat and three concentric rings of walls. One area was reserved for the market. But, so we are told from an Arabic source, while the city was being built, an ambassador arrived from the Emperor Constantine V. The Caliph Mansur showed him round the new city and asked him for his opinion. 'I have seen splendid buildings,' the ambassador replied, 'but, O Caliph, I have seen that your enemies are with you within the city.' He explained that it was dangerous to have the markets within the walls, as foreign merchants could so easily act as spies or even traitors. Mansur was impressed by this advice and moved the markets to a suburb south of the city.

There was also a great water-mill in a western suburb which was called the 'mill of the Patrician'. Again it is the Arabic sources that tell us that when the Caliph Mahdi succeeded Mansur in AD 775, an ambassador called Tarath, who had the rank of Patrician, arrived from Constantinople to congratulate the new Caliph on his accession. The ambassador had been trained as an engineer and, hearing that the Caliph was interested, he offered to build him an efficient water-mill for the sum of 500,000 dirhams – about 20,000 gold pounds – assuring him that the revenue from the mills would reach that sum very year. His offer was accepted; his arithmetic was correct and the grateful Caliph thenceforward sent this revenue yearly to Tarath in Constantinople so long as he lived. It has been suggested that the mills were really called after the Patriarch of the Nestorians, whose residence was in that area. But there is, I think, no need to disbelieve the story. Indeed, the Arab source identifies the Patrician Tarath as being descended in the fifth generation from the Emperor Maruk. Tarath is the Byzantine name Tarasius, and the Emperor Maruk is Maurice, who had died some 150 years, that is roughly five generations, previously.

Unlike Ummayad architecture, Abbasid architecture as we know of it in Baghdad and in·the temporary ninth century capital Samarra – where, in contrast with Baghdad, some of the old buildings remain – owed little or nothing to Byzantium. Its inspiration was essentially Persian. On the other hand in the ninth century Byzantine architecture owed something to Baghdad. The Iconoclastic Emperors of Byzantium, with their ban on religious figurative art, were interested in the decorative art of the Moslems. Byzantine artists who saw Arabic inscriptions written in the Kufic alphabet were impressed by their decorative value and began to introduce similar patterns into their designs; several other of their decorative patterns seem also to have come from Arabic sources.

In the middle of the ninth century the Iconoclastic Emperor Theophilus openly admired Arabic art. Of the buildings built by his architects nothing now remains, but it seems that the *Triconchos* (or Triple Shell), the Palace hall was his especial pride. The design of a three-apsed building was not unknown in Constantinople, though it was certainly of Syrian origin. This one, however, was actually inspired by a building in Baghdad or Samarra; its *mysterion*, or place of whispers, on the lower floor of the *Triconchos*, with its curious acoustic qualities, was definitely a copy of a similar whispering gallery in one of the Caliph's palaces. Theophilus filled the Palace with mechanical devices: the golden plane tree with its gold and silver singing-birds which stood in the throne room was probably imitated from a similar tree in Baghdad, as were the golden lions and griffins that stood round the throne and roared when required, and the mechanism for raising the throne itself while the Emperor sat on it. Byzantine technicians were capable of manufacturing such things themselves, and they almost certainly constructed the great organ that played during audiences – they were better organ-builders than the Arabs – but the desire of Theophilus to possess such glorious toys shows that he wanted to keep up with the Caliphate. He liked to give the pavilions that he erected in the Palace names such as 'The Pearl' as there was a Pearl Pavilion at Baghdad. But the most impressive proof of his admiration for Arabic art was the Palace of Bryas, which his architect Patrices built for him in the suburbs, on the Asiatic shore of the Sea of Marmora. The designs for the Palace and its decoration were said to have been brought from Baghdad by the ambassador John the Grammarian, whom Theophilus had sent there to announce his succession in AD 829. This Palace apparently was an almost exact copy of one of the Caliph's palaces, the only major difference being that Theophilus inserted a private oratory next to the Imperial bedroom and a smallish three-apsed church in the courtyard.

Theophilus, who died in AD 842, was at war with the Caliphate during most of his reign; yet this was the period when cultural relations between the two empires were at their closest. One reason for this is that it was only after the Caliphate was established in Baghdad that the Arabs began to take an interest in ancient Greek learning and the Caliphs began to order the translation of Greek books, particularly on the sciences and medicine, into Arabic. This was doubtless due to the new intellectual Persian influence on the Abbasids, and the first great patron of the translators was the Caliph Harun-al-Rashid himself, encouraged by the viziers of the Barmecide family. The first translators were nearly all of them Nestorian Christians, whose academy at Jundi-Shapur was not far from Baghdad, and in particular members of the Nestorian family of the Bukhtyishu, a family with a long tradition of friendship with the Barmecides. There were many Greek scholars amongst the Nestorians, and there was apparently a good library of manuscripts at Jundi-Shapur; Greek texts could also be found elsewhere in the Caliph's dominions, especially in Syria. But more texts were needed, and Harun and his successors usually required of any ambassador sent to Constantinople that he should come back laden with as many Greek manuscripts as he could buy. The Byzantine Emperor discovered that the gift which the Caliph appreciated most was the manuscript of some important Greek scientific classic. Such a gift was not always suitable for other parts of the Moslem world. In the tenth century (in AD 949), the Emperor Constantine Porphyrogenitus sent to the Caliph of Cordova an illuminated manuscript of the botanical work of Dioscorides. The Caliph Abdarrahman III thanked the Emperor cordially but had to admit that there was no one in Cordova who could read Greek. Would the Emperor kindly send out a scholar who could interpret the book? In AD 951 a monk named Nicholas arrived from Constantinople. He was a good Arabist who translated other Greek works and lectured in Arabic to the Court of Cordova about Greek science. It was he who laid the foundations of Greek studies in Moslem Spain – the area from which they were to reach Western Europe.

To return to Baghdad: not only books but also Greek scholars were welcome there. Theophilus and his successors followed the wise practice of using men of learning as ambassadors. John the Grammarian was a distinguished scholar, whose rather daring views caused him to be suspected of indulging in black magic. He seems to have spoken Arabic, and not only his magnificence and lavish generosity but also his learning made a deep impression on his hosts. The great scholar Photius went as ambassador to the Caliph's court, probably at Samarra, a little later, and he too seems to have learnt Arabic and made many Moslem friends, but not all scholars were ambassadors. Amongst the most distinguished men of learning in Constantinople while Theophilus was Emperor was a certain Leo, later surnamed the Philosopher or the Mathematician. He supported himself by running a small school; but, though his pupils usually did well, he himself was ignored by the authorities. One of his pupils became secretary to a general and went with him on a campaign against the Arabs, during which the youth was captured. He was sold as a slave to a rich man in Baghdad who treated him well and who told him one day of the Caliph Mamun's interest in geometry. 'Oh,' said the boy, 'I should like to hear him and his masters discuss the subject.' His owner managed to have the Caliph informed. Mamun eagerly summoned the Greek slave to his presence. The youth discovered that while the Arab mathematicians knew their Euclid well they had no comprehension of geometrical reasoning. After he had given a demonstration of his own powers, the Caliph asked eagerly if there were many scholars such as himself in Constantinople. 'Many pupils like myself,' he answered, 'but we are not masters.' 'Is your master alive?' asked the Caliph. 'Yes,' the boy answered, 'but he is poor and little known.' Mamun at once sent the young scholar laden with gifts to Constantinople, with a letter inviting Leo to come to Baghdad, promising him riches and honour. Leo had no wish to leave Constantinople, but he wisely showed the invitation to a friend of his at the Imperial Court, who informed the Emperor. Theophilus was alarmed at the thought of losing a distinguished scholar whom he had hitherto neglected; he did not at all like the idea of a 'brain-drain'. Leo was appointed a public teacher at a good salary and given a school attached to the Church of the Forty Martyrs, near the Forum of Constantine. Mamun was greatly disappointed. He corresponded with Leo, who answered various mathematical problems for him. But the Caliph's offer to the Emperor of eternal peace and a sum of 2,000 gold pounds if he would order Leo to go to Baghdad was refused. Instead, Leo was appointed Archbishop of Thessaloniki, where his devotion to Classical literature was to distress local monastic circles.

In Byzantine eyes, at least, Arab ambassadors to Constantinople came to learn rather than to teach. We hear of one embassy having to listen to Constantine the Philosopher, the future St Cyril, apostle to the Slavs, lecture to them on theology. Constantine seems to have known Arabic – he was a very gifted linguist – and his lecture was probably delivered in that tongue. But, as with the Byzantines, some of the best cultural ambassadors came as slaves. Amongst the Moslem prisoners who were exchanged in a truce in AD 845 was a devout Moslem named Al-Garmi, who had been for many years in captivity but had been treated very well, being allowed access to libraries and having the opportunity of talking with many Imperial officials. On his return home he wrote down all that he had learnt about Byzantium, showing (apart from conventional curses on all infidels) real good-will towards his hosts, whom he had observed very closely. Later Arab geographers, in particular Ibn Kurdadhbah, derived much of their information from him.

Throughout the whole period merchants passed to and fro. The Arabs imported merchandise from the Far East, usually by sea to the ports on the Persian Gulf, though some still came by the great land caravan-convoys. Syrian merchants then conveyed it to Constantinople, usually overland, though some goods might be shipped from Trebizond or from the Syrian ports. Constantinople was the market for distribution in Europe. For the convenience of

Moslem merchants a mosque was built in Constantinople and the Arabs could worship freely there, to the shocked disapproval of visitors from Western Europe. In the Caliph's territory the presence of Christians of so many persuasions meant that Christian visitors could always find a church, but in Byzantium the only Moslems were the merchants and the captives, and an occasional diplomat; so it was felt right that the authorities should maintain a mosque for their benefit.

So long as Baghdad and Constantinople were the two great capitals of the world, this friendly intercourse continued. Wars continued, too, and the difference in religion made a real alliance impossible. But there was a genuine mutual respect, from which both sides benefited. At this time one can say that it was the Moslems who benefited the more, because it was from Byzantium that they could obtain the texts of the old Greek scientists, in whose works they were now so deeply interested, and they could meet scholars who were well versed in this ancient learning: whereas at this time the Byzantines did not learn much more from the Arabs than new artistic ideas and new mechanical devices (whose makers were almost certainly not true Arabs but Syrians or Persians). Some centuries later, in the declining years of Byzantium, the position was reversed. By that time the Moslems of the Caliphate had developed their own sciences on the base of Greek science, and the later Greeks came to them for their knowledge of the newest developments in medicine, for the new science of algebra, and indeed to learn about the revolution in mathematics caused by the invention of the figure zero, which seems to have come into the Arab world from India. In return, Byzantine artistic and mechanical devices were now of interest to the Islamic world.

By that time the two great cities had fallen on evil days. The Abbasid caliphate began its decline in the tenth century, when provinces seceded and the rival Fatimid Caliphate was set up in Egypt, and the Caliph in Baghdad was more and more the prisoner of his Turkish mercenary Palace Guard. By the mid-eleventh century Turks were pouring in from Turkestan to join their fellow Turks within the Caliphate, coming in such numbers owing to the desiccation of their homelands. They overran Syria and Palestine, adding to the racial confusion there, but more ominously, they advanced into Asia Minor, at the expense of Byzantium.

Meanwhile from the West, Byzantium had to face a general resurgence amongst the Western Europeans, and, more immediately dangerous, attacks from the restless Northmen or Normans, who robbed Byzantium of its foothold in Italy and longed to expand further. The Turkish invasions, which upset pilgrimage and threatened the whole eastern frontier of Christendom, the growing sense of power amongst the Western Europeans and the ambitions of the Normans all combined to launch the movement of the Crusades. Byzantium, which the Crusade was intended to benefit, when Pope Urban II preached it, was in the end the chief sufferer. In 1204 an army of Crusaders, with greedy Venetian allies, chose not to go to fight the infidel in Palestine but instead stormed and sacked the great city of Constantinople. Byzantium was to recover its capital half a century later, but was never a great power again; her civilization had suffered an irreparable loss, with the Crusaders pillaging the churches and burning the libraries, destroying everything except the works of art that the Venetians hastened to appropriate for themselves. The Moslem world was not nearly so hard hit by the Crusades. After the initial shock it revived under such leaders as Nur ed-Din and Saladin. The death-blow to Baghdad came from the East, with the invasions of the Mongols. Baghdad was sacked by the Mongols in 1258, and there the devastation was far more awful even than it had been in Constantinople in 1204, for the Mongols were far more thorough than the Crusaders, and there were no Venetians to rescue things of beauty. It is true that the Mongol Khan gave orders that scholars were to be spared, but by the time that a scholar was identified he was usually dead.

Constantinople lingered on in decline till it was taken by the Ottoman Turks, when it became for four and a half centuries the splendid capital of a vast Empire. Baghdad revived at last to be a provincial centre and now the capital of a sovereign state. But the great days of both those great cities were over a thousand years ago, when they vied with each other to be the imperial home of civilization, and civilization was enriched by their rivalry.

2

Christian Georgia and Sufism

KATHARINE VIVIAN*

Georgia in Transcaucasia, a small mountainous country, through-out its history has been bounded by mighty empires. It lies south of the Caucasus range, with the Black Sea to the West and in the South the marches of Turkey, Armenia and Azerbaijan. To the South-East is Iran and to the East, between Georgia and the Caspian Sea, the Republic of Daghestan. Today a republic of the Soviet Union, until 1801 the country was a monarchy. For long periods it was split into two kingdoms, Eastern and Western Georgia, the ancient Iberia and Colchis.

These two divisions of the country had always lain within different spheres of influence. From remote antiquity, there had been Greek settlements in the western Kingdom of Colchis, which later came under the sway of the empires of Rome and Byzantium. The eastern kingdom, Iberia, lay on the border of the Persian empire. Thus Greece and Rome in the West, and Persia in the East, played an extensive part in shaping Georgia's destiny, as did the Arabs, Turks and Mongols, who came to invade the country in repeated waves of conquest. In the Xth and XIth centuries, successive kings laid the foundations of unity between the several provinces of East and West, until the political unification of the nation was estab-lished by the great King David IV, the Restorer (also called the Builder), who reigned from 1089–1125.

Christianity came to Georgia in 337. According to a contempo-rary historian[1] the Queen of Iberia, who was seriously ill, was cured by a Christian woman captive. In consequence she became con-verted to Christianity. The King, sceptical at first, was on a hunt-

* This text is an enlargement and revision of one originally published in 1982 as *Sufic Traces in Georgian Literature* (Institute for Cultural Research Monograph Series No 18).

14

ing expedition when suddenly he found himself in total darkness –
in what appears to have been an eclipse of the sun. Lost and
separated from his followers, the King swore that if this Christ of
whom the captive woman had spoken would deliver him from his
predicament, he would embrace the Christian faith. Immediately
after this it grew light again. The King was converted and proclaimed Christianity the State religion. The Georgian Orthodox
Church, with its own Catholicos-Patriarch, was closely associated
with the Church of Byzantium.

From the time of the Arab conquest in the VIIth century there
was continuous pressure on the Georgians to adopt the Moslem
faith. In spite of this religious conflict, however, there are passages
in the Georgian Chronicle[2] – as elsewhere – to indicate that beneath
the surface of political opposition there often existed close and
friendly relations between Christians and Moslems.

Pavle Ingorokva gives valuable data on the place of Moslems in
medieval Christian Georgia, as for example that Moslem poets of
the XIIth century composed odes in honour of Queen Tamar and
other Georgian sovereigns.[3] The reign of King David IV, great-
grandfather of Queen Tamar, is of particular interest in this
respect. A superb military commander, he drove the Arabs out of
the capital, Tbilisi, after four centuries of Arab rule and recovered
it for the Georgian crown. In the following year he liberated the
Armenian capital of Ani from the Turks and annexed it to Georgia.
These and other military successes were due in part to his reorgan-
isation of the army, with emphasis on training and discipline, and
largely also to his statesmanship, completing the long task of
unifying the Georgian provinces and bringing the Church under
the authority of the State.

Although Georgia was a Christian country, there were a number
of Moslems among the population. Under David's rule,

... Moslems were by no means subject to persecution. King
David spared their clergy, protected their merchants and
formed ties of friendship with Moslem poets and philosophers.
There were many Moslems living in the capital of Tbilisi, and
David IV granted them various privileges. He forbade the
Christians to do anything which might offend the religious

sensibilities of their Moslem fellow-citizens, or disturb them in the practice of their religion . . .

The King was well versed in the teaching of Islam, and took part in theological discussions on themes from the Koran with the Qadi of Ganja. On Fridays, attended by the Crown Prince, he would go to the great mosque, listen to the prayers, the reading from the Koran and the sermon, and distribute alms to the clergy. He built a community centre for Moslem and Sufi poets and provided the means to maintain it.[4]

Thus it appears that David IV, as later King Vakhtang VI in the XVIIIth-century renaissance of Georgian literature, was in friendly relations with Sufis. It is not certain, however, what is meant by this term, which is still even today widely identified with Islamic mysticism. What place then could Sufism have in a Christian country with a powerful priesthood? – in one, moreover, where the Christian religion has always been a rallying point in the people's struggle for national independence.

As the Sufis' own writings make clear, their tradition is not confined to any one religion; and they do not regard mystical experience as an end in itself, any more than the flow of blood through the body is halted after its purification in the lungs. They are in the world to serve humanity, to show people the Way to transcend ordinary limitations and realise their potential.

It is as well, therefore, to know what a writer has in mind in using the word *Sufi*. When the Georgian King Vakhtang VI was held captive in Persia, the Persian Shah was referred to in a letter as 'the Sufi'; there the word may have meant simply 'the Moslem' or 'the Persian'. In the case of the academy built by King David 'for Moslem and Sufi poets', it seems probable that his chronicler used it in a wider connotation, closer to that of an XVIIth-century scholar: 'The Sufis are poets and lovers. According to the ground in which their teaching grows, they are soldiers, administrators or physicians . . .'[5] They do not always declare themselves, and their work takes form in accordance with the precept, 'Speak to each in accordance with his understanding.' It is characteristic of them to act not at random, but from understanding of a situation and knowledge of the results. This approach is suggested in an article on Georgian music:

Georgian master builders constructed their edifices to accord
with different 'registers of perception'. In ancient churches the
register of hearing plays an important part. The way the building is constructed sets in motion a harmonic progression of
indefinite nuances, part of a whole in which every movement
(every rhythm) extends to the 'inaudible' – perceptible perhaps
for one who can learn to 'hear with the inner ear of the heart',
and then discovers a new time which brings him 'face to face
with the present'.[6]

Examples of Sufi diagrams can be found in the designs which
adorn many Georgian buildings, from cathedrals and churches to
country dwellings and modern craft work.

Georgia has a literature with a long history, constantly enriched
by contact with the great civilizations on its frontiers. The first
known works date from the fifth century, and even before the
Georgian alphabet was formed the people possessed a store of
learning and legend brought from Greece and Persia. These ancient myths and tales were transformed and developed into a vast
body of folklore. Some of the most popular legends are those
centred on the hero Amiran, a Georgian Prometheus. For his crime
of stealing fire from Heaven and bringing it to men, he is chained to
a rock on Mount Elbruz in the Caucasus where an eagle tears
perpetually at his liver. According to the writer Grigol Robakidze,
the liver is the seat of the force which controls the transition from
the waking state to sleep. The Georgian words for *liver* and *vigil* –
ghvidzli and *ghvidzili* – are almost identical. Thus in attacking
Amiran's liver the eagle causes it to become enlarged and keep him
constantly awake. He can never sleep: a possible explanation of his
curious punishment.

The date of the earliest known inscriptions is about AD 150, and
the first literary work of note – the *Passion of St Shushanik* – dates
from the fifth century. Literary activity in the beginning was
confined to Christian religious subjects – hagiography, liturgical
poetry, commentaries and translations of sacred texts. Gradually it
extended to history, with a chronicle of the conversion of Georgia
to Christianity, followed by annals of the Georgian kings. These
were collected and revised at the end of the seventeenth century
under the title of *The Georgian Chronicle* or, literally, 'the life of

Georgia'. In the Middle Ages the scope of literary work was greatly
enlarged through the influence of the Greek renaissance, and the
establishment of a number of centres of learning by that enlightened monarch, David IV.

There were two periods in the history of the Georgian kingdom
when literature of outstanding quality appeared. The first was the
Golden Age, the twelfth and early thirteenth centuries, epoch of
the Sufi poets of Persia and the troubadours of Western Europe. At
the end of the twelfth century Shota Rustaveli, a poet at the court of
Queen Tamar, composed his epic *The Knight in Panther Skin*, one
of the treasures of world literature.[7] There followed a long period of
invasion and internal strife, until late in the seventeenth century
came a new renaissance of art and letters, the so-called Silver Age.
Illustrious literary figures of this period were the scholar statesman
Sulkhan-Saba Orbeliani and a number of poets. One of Orbeliani's
principal works was a Georgian lexicon; another was the collection
of stories, jokes and sayings translated as *A Book of Wisdom and
Lies*.

Georgian writers have always drawn deeply on the national store
of tradition and legend, as well as events in their long and eventful
history. There is a story of the Creation which provides a backcloth
to the scene of our present study, an introduction to the country
and the people:

When the Creation was finished the Lord God called together
representatives of all the countries of the earth, to allot to each
his own territory. They assembled to wait in the ante-room –
among them, naturally, being four Georgians. These were the
last to arrive, fond as they were of idling in the sun. Finding that
they would have long to wait, they went off to visit one of the
charming little inns to be found in the Georgian countryside.
When they returned the antechamber was empty. They
knocked at the Lord's door. He opened, and looked at them in
dismay.

'I have distributed all the land on earth,' he told them. 'There
is nothing left for you.'

Far from giving way to despair, the Georgians set themselves
to charm and delight the Lord. They sang, they danced, they

beat out the liveliest measures on their drums, until the Creator could hold out no longer.

'You sing and dance so well, you are so full of joy in life – I cannot let you go empty-handed! Take this corner of the earth that I was keeping for myself, settle here, be fruitful and multiply!'

So it was that the Creator took up his abode in the heavens, and the Georgians found themselves in possession of Eden.[8]

This story may come to mind on a visit to Gelati, where King David IV founded an academy which became a *studium generale* where literature and philosophy, theology and the sciences were studied. The buildings, a monastery and cathedral, stood on a wooded mountainside outside Kutaisi, the ancient capital of Western Georgia (a part of them is used today for academic conferences). Studies were carried out there under the direction of a Neo-Platonist scholar Ioane Petritzi, a Georgian educated in Athens and at the Mangana Academy in Constantinople, whom David installed to work there.

Petritzi's best-known work is his translation of Proclus' *Elements of Theology*, with an extensive commentary. He translated many philosophical works, principally Neo-Platonist, with the aim of reconciling the ideas of the great classical thinkers with the central message of Christianity. His broad humanist outlook was in advance of his time and brought him into conflict with the Georgian Church orthodoxy, until David IV eventually established him at Gelati. He was versed in rhetoric and geometry, astronomy and metaphysics, and set down some of the most important elements in Georgian grammar. One of his few original works is *The Ladder of Virtues* – thirty steps towards Faith, from the first step of Renouncing the World, through Repentance, Poverty, Silence, Wakefulness, Self-Knowledge and other attainments. Both in his philosophy and his literary style, Petritzi – 'sun of the Georgians', 'wise in all things' – had a lasting influence on Georgian thought and literature, especially marked in the eighteenth century. He founded one of the three schools of Georgian translation – an art in which his fellow-countrymen have distinguished themselves throughout their history. There can have been few, if any, important works of literature or learning not known to them in their own language. Today in the Department of Translation in Tbilisi University both the theory and practice of the art are studied.

David IV freed his country from foreign domination and laid the foundations of an era of peace, order and prosperity. On those foundations his great-granddaughter Tamar, who reigned from 1184 to 1213, raised the kingdom to a height of military and economic power, territorial expansion and cultural development unsurpassed in its history. At the end of the twelfth century the territories subject to the Georgian crown extended from Trebizond on the Black Sea to Derbend on the Caspian coast, and later included Armenia and Azerbaijan. Georgia maintained close relations with Byzantium; there was intermarriage between the royal and imperial houses. Queen Tamar is a figure now clothed in legend, but underlying it is a body of facts which point to a powerful civilizing force at work in her time. We see the paradox in her reign already noted in that of her ancestor, David IV – a contrast between the martial vigour that she inspired in her people, and the gentleness she is reputed to have shown in her personal life and in her administration.

In *The Georgian Chronicle* it is recorded that the army, under the command of Tamar's consort David Soslan, fought continuous campaigns both offensive and defensive to secure their country's independence and military supremacy. As in the reign of David IV, their achievements called for a high degree of diplomatic as well as military ability, to control the feudal lords and the Orthodox priesthood, who wielded considerable power. At the same time, Tamar's chronicler records that 'she did not become angered with her viziers or her soldiers, showing the favours of a parent to those who merited them',[9] and that during her reign no one was flogged or executed at her orders. She is said to have been pious and devout; such expressions however were often no more than a convention in the annals of a sovereign's reign.

The prosperous and stable conditions of Tamar's reign were fertile soil for the growth of art, literature and scholarship. Among the circle of poets at her court was Shota Rustaveli, composer of Georgia's greatest classic *The Knight in Panther Skin*. At the same period, Chakhrukhadze was at work on his famed *Tamariani*, a lyric anthology of odes to the Queen and her consort – a virtuoso performance, a sparkling display of erudition and poetic talent.

There are points of likeness between the two works, such as allusions to Greek philosophy and legend, and to the Persian romances *Vis and Ramin* and *Layla and Majnun*.

Both poets write from a religious outlook far broader than that of Christian orthodoxy. They work in different metres – one is a lyric poet, the other epic – and both display brilliant technical accomplishment in their versification. Within exacting confines of rhyme, stress and assonance their verse flows in a glorious cascade of sound which often conveys the sense even when the words are obscure. 'Not with random step shall the lover pursue his calling,' Rustaveli says in his Prologue,[10] and the impression made by these poems does not appear to be produced at hazard. Like other young men of rank, Rustaveli and Chakhrukhadze would have had a thorough grounding in the classics – the literature and philosophy of Greece – either in Athens or at one of the academies in Georgia. Allusions in the poems show that they were also familiar with works of Persian and Arabic literature, many of which were translated into Georgian. It may have been part of their education – as it has until recent years with classical scholars in the West – to study the technique of versification.

After Chakhrukhadze had composed the *Tamariani* he left Tamar's court and travelled to every part of the then known world. He 'appeared in Iran and the Arabian countries as a wandering minstrel, reciting his verses in Iranian and Arabic.'[11] It is not known what impelled him to take up that way of life; but from his writing and what is known it appears that he lived and worked as others did who followed the Sufi path, carrying out whatever task he was given to the best of his powers, and learning from it what he needed to learn.

Unsurpassed in Georgian literature is Shota Rustaveli's *Knight in Panther Skin* – a work having many features that a student of Sufism will recognize. The poet observes the often stated Sufi principle of 'time, place and people' in speaking to his fellow-countrymen in terms that all could understand. His story is based on their own conditions of life and allusions to Georgian history and the various religious beliefs extant among them, in a form which would enable it to survive through oral transmission, as well as in manuscripts vulnerable to loss or destruction. This magnificent work is widely known and quoted and its influence felt up to the present day – almost eight centuries after it was written. It has been translated into all the major languages of the West, and also into Japanese and Arabic.

The story opens in a kingdom called Arabia – thought to represent Georgia – where the aging King Rostevan sets his daughter Tinatin on the throne, just as Tamar, the reigning queen of Georgia, had been enthroned by her father as co-regent in his old age. Rostevan and his young commander-in-chief Avtandil are engaged in a shooting contest when they see a mysterious stranger, who disappears before they can discover who he is. He kills a number of Rostevan's men when they try to pursue him, and the king is distracted with grief. His daughter Tinatin summons Avtandil, who cherishes a secret love for her. She charges him, as her knight, to set forth and find the stranger, promising to wed no other until he returns.

Leaving his faithful squire Shermadin in charge of his affairs Avtandil sets out, and after a long and wearisome search at last comes up with the knight clad in panther skin. The strange 'knight' proves to be a prince of India, Tariel by name. He is roaming the world in search of his beloved, the princess Nestan-Darejan, who has been carried off by demons. Avtandil swears an oath of friendship to Tariel, in the Georgian tradition of 'sworn brotherhood' – an important element in the story, as it has always been in the lives of the Georgian people. He returns to Arabia to report his discovery to Tinatin and King Rostevan, and again sets forth – after failing to obtain the king's leave – to rejoin Tariel and aid him in his search. After many adventures the captive princess is found and set free and the two royal couples marry amid great rejoicing.

Other characters in the story are portrayed with vigorous realism. The first clue to Nestan-Darejan's fate is given by a third and lesser prince, Nuradin Pridon, who has seen her for a brief moment; he joins Tariel and Avtandil in their quest. They learn more of her from a merchant's wife, the amorous Phatman, who falls victim to Avtandil's charms – an episode that recalls the legend of Jason and Medea in Colchis.

All Rustaveli's personages are clearly drawn, recognizable in their features. While the story moves in the realm of allegory, it is given a dimension of actuality by links with the everyday world.

The central theme, stated in the Prologue, is that of the troubadours of Western Europe in their lyrics of courtly love: 'I speak of
the Love that is highest ... Love that exalts and gives man wings
for upward flight.' 'What is the knowledge of the Sages worth,'
Avtandil asks in the noble phrases of his Testament, 'if we do not
act on it? The purpose of their teaching was to perfect our nature
and raise us to the order of the heavenly beings ..."Love ennobles
us!" '15 He is speaking here of friendship as a form of the love that is
the way to self-perfection. Rustaveli also praises love in other
forms, human love as leading to the divine. The Sufi Way has been
called the way of love.

Although the poem is infused with religious feeling – Avtandil's
invocation to the Sun, the Moon and the five planets is one of its
finest passages – Rustaveli makes no concession to Christian orthodoxy. There are two or three quotations from the Bible but no
mention of Christ or the Virgin Mary, or of any Christian ritual.
This suggests a possible explanation of the much-discussed line
in the Prologue: 'This Persian tale I found in the Georgian
tongue.'13

Reference to an anonymous source which could not be identified
was a device sometimes employed for protection, giving a writer
freedom to express advanced or unorthodox views that might lay
him open to attack by Church or State. Other explanations have
been suggested, one being that it was the fashion at the time to do
things in the Persian manner, much as it was in England later to
copy Italian styles of architecture and French *couture*. In spite of
lengthy research, no single Persian tale has ever been found as
Rustaveli's source. A writer, however, may take material from a
variety of sources and create from it something that is new, individual and his own. In the Middle Ages, moreover, the concept of
original creative work had not the importance attributed to it
today. The great stories of the world reappeared in different dress
over an immense range of time and space, adapted and reworked to
suit the circumstances.

A Georgian scholar, Gaioz Imedashvili, observes that Georgian
culture and thought have always had a double orientation, facing
towards the empires of Greece and Rome in the West, and Persia in
the East. After the advent of Christianity the bias swung towards
the West, and Professor Imedashvili concludes that one should

look westward rather than eastward for the inspiration of *The Knight in Panther Skin*. However, as we have seen, there was much interchange between the two cultures, and the gulf between their respective viewpoints is probably less wide than is sometimes assumed.

Many features in this poem are characteristic of the literature of chivalry and courtly love that appeared before and during Rustaveli's lifetime in Western Europe. There is a notable likeness between the influence of the King Arthur cycle of legends on the civilization of England, and that of Rustaveli's poem in Georgia.

One of the qualities in Rustaveli's list of those that a lover should possess is youth – *siqme*, an old Georgian word corresponding to the Provençal *jovens*. In a study of the relations between Rustaveli's ideas and those of the Provençal troubadours, the Russian scholar S. Serebryakov points out that the concept expressed in both words is that of the Arabic *futuwwa* – 'all noble qualities in a young man'.[14] According to A. J. Denomy, this was a Sufi concept that originated at the birth of Islam in ancient Arabia. There is now much evidence to connect the poetry of the troubadours and minnesingers – like the many fables and tales beginning to circulate in Western Europe at the beginning of the thirteenth century – with Arabic sources in Moslem Spain. In philosophy, science and medicine Arab learning led the field. The first of the troubadours of Provence, William VIII, Duke of Aquitaine, knew Arabic well and introduced Arabic poetry and ideas of romantic love into southern France. The Georgians – who had always been accomplished translators – were accustomed to translating direct from Arabic, and the work of leading writers and scholars of the Arab world was thus accessible to them. The thought of such writers as El Ghazzali penetrated to Georgia as it did to the West.

Among works of Western medieval literature contemporary with Rustaveli's story of Tariel, one that compares with it closely is the story of Parzival and the Grail. Wolfram von Eschenbach's *Parzival* appeared not long after *The Knight in Panther Skin*, a story with a background of court life and feudal society much resembling those of the period in Georgia. Both works tell of knighthood, feats of arms and noble aspirations. Both refer to an unknown source.

The two poems are alike in another aspect. For the first part of their lives the heroes Tariel and Parzival are blessed with good fortune; they have the world at their feet. Then comes a moment in which they are found wanting. Thenceforward a train of sorrow and disaster ensues for both. The occasion is one when speech is called for, and each of the heroes fails to speak. Parzival, dazzled by the sight of the Grail, fails to ask how it can be used. Tariel, horror-struck at the proposal to marry his beloved to the Persian crown prince, says nothing to oppose it.

Both young men behaved in obedience to a command. Parzival as a boy was fond of asking questions, until his tutor taught him that it was discourteous and unbecoming in a knight. Tariel had been charged by the king's daughter, in accordance with the code of lovers, not to reveal his love for her. They obeyed; yet their neglect to speak when speech was needed proved culpable, a sin to be expiated before they could attain their desire.

Like a composer of music, Rustaveli often repeats a theme with variations. Later in the poem the vizir Sograt, unwilling to bear a message from Avtandil to the king, quotes Ecclesiastes, reiterating the idea that 'there is a time to keep silence and a time to speak.'

In poetry all over the known world in Rustaveli's lifetime a single theme was dominant: the power of love to ennoble men. Not only courtly love but all kinds of earthly love were regarded as a ladder to the spiritual, a concept going back to Plato. This found expression in different languages, in countries far apart, like the traces left by an unknown being in its passage over the earth – or a scatter of stars all taking their light from one invisible sun. What was that sun, where was that source of light? From what we know of the Sufis an answer may be sought in their tradition, which 'between about AD 700 and AD 1500 was based upon love, operated through a dynamic of love, had its manifestation through ordinary human life, poetry and work.'[15]

Persia at that epoch had entered a period of literary renaissance. The language was regenerated from Pahlavi, and a school of Sufi poets came into being to do work of unsurpassed brilliance. Two Persian poets in particular appear likely to have influenced – possibly to have been influenced by – Rustaveli. There are features in the story of the hero Rostom in Firdausi's *Shah-Nameh* which are found also in the story of Tariel: the panther's skin, the faithful maidservant, the disguise of a merchant. Motifs such as these would naturally have been familiar, through copying and translation, to poets and writers in many countries.

A Persian epic translated into Georgian in 1188, the year in which it was composed – a few years earlier than *The Knight in Panther Skin* – was a version of the love story of *Layla and Majnun*. This allegory of love, widely known throughout the East, was again put into verse in the fifteenth century by Jami, one of the great exponents of Sufi ideas. The earlier version was by Rustaveli's contemporary Nizami of Ganja, a Persian born on Georgia's Persian frontier. There is little doubt that this poem, if not the poet himself, was known to Rustaveli. The two works – *Layla and Majnun* and *The Knight in Panther Skin* – are in many respects alike, in others dissimilar. In one version of *Layla and Majnun*, quoted in the Sufi Suhrawardi's *Gifts of Knowledge*, the lover Majnun faints when he catches a glimpse of Layla's skirt through the raised flap of her tent; and Tariel likewise swoons away when he first beholds Nestan-Darejan through the curtain of her pavilion. The same incident occurs in the Persian *Visramiani*, one of the earliest works to be translated into Georgian, when the curtain of Vis' litter is blown aside in a gust of wind, revealing her to Ramin's gaze. Such similarities suggest that Rustaveli was familiar with the conventions common to love poetry of the period.

Layla and Majnun, in Nizami's version, probably comes closer than any known work to that 'Persian tale found in the Georgian tongue' of Rustaveli's Prologue. He states in another verse that *mijnuri*, the Georgian word for a lover, is derived from the Arabic *majnun*, love-maddened. In Sufi poetry, the highest spiritual concepts have often been expressed in the symbolism of earthly love.

'The path of the dervish is in qualitative exactitude,' wrote the poet Hafiz of Shiraz. The impression given by *The Knight in Panther Skin* is that of a work composed to produce a specific, foreseeable effect. The story and versification are such as to please people of all sorts and conditions. The verse, easier than prose to memorize and less open to distortion than the outline of a story, ensured its survival among a people of whom few, when it first appeared, were literate. It was a casket marvellously fashioned to guard and transmit the jewel of the doctrine of love.

Close on the Golden Age in Georgia there followed an age of

darkness. Not many years after the death of Queen Tamar in 1213
the country was invaded by the Tartars from Central Asia, and
subsequently by the Mongols, first under Genghis Khan and again
under Tamerlane. These shattering blows were followed by centuries of war with the Turks in the West, and the Persians in the
East; and it was not until the seventeenth century that the nation's
internal economy was sufficiently restored to make possible a
revival of cultural activity. A minor renaissance then took place,
chiefly under the aegis of Vakhtang VI, one of the most enlightened
of the Georgian kings. He gave encouragement to the arts and
sciences and did much to revive the country's ruined economy; he
introduced important innovations and reforms, drew up a legal
code, installed the first printing-press in Tbilisi, and collected and
edited the annals of the Georgian kings. He received the throne of
Georgia at the hands of the Shah of Persia – the same who was
referred to in a letter as 'the Sufi'. He was later invited to the
Persian court at Ispahan, and received with great ceremony. The
Shah pressed him to embrace Islam. On his refusal, he was kept in
captivity in Persia. As a captive, he seems to have enjoyed considerable freedom, being active in diplomacy, studying chemistry and
making translations into Georgian, among them the *Tales of Bidpai*
known as *Kalila and Dimna*.

One of the most celebrated Georgian writers, Sulkhan-Saba
Orbeliani, was Vakhtang's uncle, tutor and lifelong counsellor.
His *Book of Wisdom and Lies* is a collection of fables, proverbs and
precepts related to the education of a king's son. Since Orbeliani
was tutor to Vakhtang in his boyhood, it may well be that he made
the anthology to use in the course of his instruction. The Georgian
word *araki* for these tales has the meaning of allegory, and also of
teaching-story. Several of them are found, with variations, in
collections of Sufi tales: *The Man and the Snake*, *The Ploughman*,
the Weaver and the Tailor, *The Caliph and the Arab* and others.
Some are of purely Georgian origin. The teaching story is part of
the Sufis' method of teaching. In its original, pure form it connects
with the innermost part of a human being and 'establishes in
him or her a means of communication with a non-verbalised truth
beyond the customary limitations of our familiar dimensions.'[16]
Orbeliani, a nobleman and a courtier, had spent some years as a
monk and lived in poverty and hardship. He well understood the

preoccupations of the common man, and his stories are full of earthy incident, comedy and melodrama.

Orbeliani was sent to Europe on a diplomatic mission to obtain the aid of the French King Louis XIV and the Pope to liberate King Vakhtang from captivity in Persia. It was on that occasion that he used the word 'Sufi' in a letter. The word does not occur in *A Book of Wisdom and Lies*, although the book undoubtedly contains Sufi ideas – not only in the stories themselves but in their setting and presentation. They are told by five well-contrasted characters, each of whom might represent a facet of human nature. The vizir, who at first appears as the wisest, does not hesitate to offer the mysterious stranger Leon his own position at court, apparently recognizing Leon as in some way a superior being. The relations between the five – the king, his son, the vizir, the prince's tutor and the eunuch change and develop in entertaining and often startling interplay, as a background to the tales.

Many stories like these are found in Georgian folklore. There is one which tells of a man who lent his friend two silver coins. He insisted on repayment; his friend refused; and they went on stubbornly holding their ground even after they had discovered a hoard of gold and shared it out between them.[17] It's not a story with a moral, but it does, in the characteristically Sufi way, hold up a mirror of caricature of the kind of behaviour which can be an obstacle to developing higher perceptions.

One of a group of talented eighteenth-century poets was David Guramishvili, whose work was largely devoted to events in the history of his country. He wrote of the reign of Vakhtang VI in the early part of the century with a profound sense of the tragic fate that Georgia had suffered in the past and might in the future meet again. In his poem *Georgia's Adversities* he urges his fellow-countrymen never to forget the value of knowledge:

> Hear, oh seeker after knowledge!
> Learning is yours until your dying day.
> All that you learn remains with you for ever:
> No one can take it from you,
> Nothing can part you from it.
> Other possessions can be snared
> And snatched away.

A man who has not knowledge
Will suffer in this transitory world.

This verse is aptly quoted on the first day of the school year. The phrase 'this transitory world' or 'this fleeting life', in Georgian a single word, is much used by Rustaveli in an older form: a concept now almost forgotten in the West, but part of a common world-picture in earlier times.

As well as these main landmarks in Georgian literature there are other literary forms that suggest an orientation towards an ancient tradition of wisdom. Until printing was introduced in Georgia at the beginning of the XVIIIth century, books were a rarity and dwellers in mountain regions, in remote and isolated villages, would have relied much for entertainment on travelling story-tellers and bards. Georgian folklore with its wealth of stories and legends is an oyster-bed yielding many pearls. Variants can be found of stories known all over the world. The story of Cinderella has its counterpart in the well-loved romance *Eteriani*, the subject of an opera by Zakaria Paliashvili. Foxes, snakes and donkeys figure largely in popular tales: Mulla Nasrudin, the Sufi comic figure, and Uncle Remus are very much at home in Georgia, if under different names. The story of the peasant's son who stumbled on a gathering of giants and, paralysed with fear, yet turned everything that happened into a chance to outwit them until they believed that he was stronger than they and fled from him in terror – this has echoes of Nasrudin's adventures as a courtier.[18]

Other stories belong to the country itself and are grounded in a particular region. One such legend is the subject of *The Snake Eater*, a poem by a highly popular nineteenth-century poet, Vazha Pshavela, who lived and worked in the mountains 'in a part of the country where the tribes continued to live as they had in ancient times, in timelessness or rather in a sort of absolute present where the absent have their place, yet without any effacing of the difference between the here and the hereafter . . .'[19] The same story in a different version is also retold by the late Konstantine Gamsak-hurdia. In this the hero, Mindia, is carried off by the Patron of Beasts, a Pan-like figure who 'scratched his goat-like beard with his hoof', to the Land of the Cuckoos.[20] There he is given a brew of white snakes, and after eating it acquires wisdom and is entirely transformed. He has become a being who casts no shadow. 'The sky, the earth, the forests begin to speak to him . . . He realizes that every living and every inanimate being has a language.' Sickened by the bloodshed and savagery of tribal warfare, he finds himself unable to kill or harm any living creature, even to hunt for food. He refuses to eat meat – the staple diet of his tribe. The young men, his companions, jeer at him . . . and his fate works itself out.

This intuitive sense of unity with nature is deeply characteristic of the Georgians and is expressed in many ways in their literature. The first chronicler of Queen Tamar relates that she had 'a magnetic power of attraction for wild beasts. One day the Shah of Shirvan sent her a lion cub that he had reared, already well grown . . . it laid its head on the Queen's bosom and caressed her with its tongue.'[21] In the lives of early Georgian monks and hermits, incidents involving animals and birds are described. Professor D. M. Lang quotes one with a typically Georgian touch. A dragon infesting the cave of a saint and his disciple is consumed in flames by a thunderbolt from the hand of God. The saint 'protests vigorously to Heaven against this violence to one of his own protégés, and has to be pacified by an angel sent specially by the Almighty Himself.'[22]

Many themes in Sufi tales are found, in different forms, in Georgian. Somebody meets with unexpected good fortune and something is gained from him in return; a person is offered advice – often by an animal or an old woman – to meet a difficulty he has not foreseen; universally familiar features occur such as swords to be pulled out of stones, magic carpets and rings, captive princesses.

There is a saying in the East that a guest is sent from God. A guest at a Georgian banquet may be asked whether his parents are still living and, whether they are alive or died long ago, a toast is drunk to them. The story is told of a young man of blameless life who died and went to Heaven. There, looking about him, he saw groups of people drinking, seated among the clouds. One group who invited him to join them turned out to be his ancestors. After a time he asked: 'How is it that however much you drink your wine jug is always full?' Whenever somebody on earth drank to them, they told him, the jug was refilled: an echo of the Prophet's saying, quoted by the Sufi El Ghazzali in *The Alchemy of Happiness*: 'The prayers of children profit their parents when the latter are dead . . .'

The ritual of toasts at a Georgian party, although it cannot be called a form of literature, is in direct line of descent from an early literary form. That is the *keba*, a speech or poem of praise, thought to be derived from one of the earliest forms of Arabic literature. Both Rustaveli and Chakhrukhadze repeatedly use the phrase, 'It would need the eloquence of the Sages and the harp of David to praise her!' In *The Knight in Panther Skin* the leader of a merchant caravan, described as an educated man, greets Avtandil with an encomium 'according to custom'. On another occasion there is a lyrical passage when Pridon breaks into a paean of praise on hearing Tariel's name. Today, occasions such as New Year's Day, the beginning of the academic year or the first fall of snow are celebrated in a Georgian newspaper with a page of poems, many by unknown writers.

The custom also survives as a feature of banquets and feasts, both at formal gatherings and in a circle of family or friends. A toastmaster, the *tamada*, is appointed – somebody other than the host. He proposes toasts to peace, friendship, Georgia, the guests' native lands; and it is also his task to give a toast to each person present. At a large party this might become something of an endurance test; but it is often interspersed by fine polyphonic singing in a highly developed style; and when it grows late the principal guest may use a formula of thanks to bring the proceedings to an end. The *tamada*, sometimes adopting a special ritual intonation, makes a point of bringing out people's qualities and achievements, in the way that we reserve for an obituary notice. Here, however, the guests are present in the flesh and able to enjoy hearing about themselves. Apart from being an entertaining way of performing introductions and getting through a great many bottles of wine, the custom has other beneficial effects. Everyone goes home not only well wined and dined, but having had nourishment of another sort – attention. Faces that were tired, listless, anxious or sad light up, sometimes to unexpected beauty, when for a few moments they are the focus of attention as the *tamada* recites their praise, even though everyone knows it is no more than a formality. It can, of course, have a different effect when somebody hears himself extolled for qualities he knows he does not possess.

The speeches and replies help to keep alive the art of rhetoric, of expressiveness in speech. The Georgians have a profound and ardent love for their language, which in the words of a tenth-

century song 'contains all kinds of mystery in its depths.'[23] As one
Georgian put it, 'Language is the nature of man.' Many are natural
poets and adorn their speeches with quotations and impromptu
verse.

Georgia with her double orientation has been no stranger to the
ideas and culture of East and West. Indeed, the principal currents
of thought from various directions flowed strongly through her
territories at a time when Sufi teaching was widely diffused in
Europe and Western and Central Asia. *The Knight in Panther Skin*,
the masterpiece of Georgian literature, although deeply rooted in
its homeland's history and tradition, is not a work of solely national
interest but part of the whole body of medieval literature. A
traveller in Georgia may gain the impression that here is a country
where the blessing of an influence from another dimension than
any in ordinary life has once been manifest. Traces of it can be
found in literature, as also in music, architecture and the arts. Its
imprint is in some ways impalpable as a taste of honey in the air: it
is in people's attitudes and expressions, manners and customs,
turns of phrase, unexpected notes of gentleness or laughter. In this
brief survey we have tried to indicate what appears to be clear
evidence of Sufi thought in Christian Georgia, particularly in literature, which plays a more active part in everyday life than we are
accustomed to see. Beyond what is apparent, this literature has
other features that point to Sufi influence, suggesting that at some
time in the past the doctrine of love held sway, with a power that
can still be felt. In terms of the present day, its effect could be
described as skill in the art of living.

REFERENCES

1 Rufinus, *Histoire ecclésiastique*, Leipzig, 1908.
2 *Kartlis Tskhovreba*, The Georgian Chronicle, Tbilisi, 1959.
3 P. Ingorokva, *The Knight in Tiger Skin*, Introduction, Tbilisi, 1938.
4 *Idem.*
5 I. Shah, *The Sufis*, New York, 1964.
6 Y. Grimaud, *Georgian Vocal Music, Bedi Kartlisa*, vol. XXXV, Paris, 1977.

7 Sh. Rustaveli, *The Knight in Panther Skin*, tr. K. Vivian, London, 1977.
8 K. Salia, *History of the Georgian Nation.* Paris, 1962.
9 *Kartlis Tskhovreba, op. cit.*
10 Sh. Rustaveli, *op. cit.*
11 P. Ingorokva, *op. cit.*
12 Sh. Rustaveli, *op. cit.*
13 *Idem.*
14 S. Serebryakov, *Rustavelidan Provensal Trubadurebamde*, From Rustaveli to the Provençal Troubadours, Tbilisi, 1973.
15 I. Shah, *op. cit.*
16 I. Shah, *Caravan of Dreams*, London, 1983.
17 G. Buachidze, *Contes populaires géorgiens*, Paris, 1988.
18 I. Shah, *Exploits of the Incomparable Mulla Nasrudin*, London, 1983.
19 K. Salia, *op. cit.*
20 K. Gamsakhurdia, *Mindia, the Son of Hogay*, Moscow, 1965.
21 *Kartlis Tskhovreba, op. cit.*
22 D. M. Lang, *Landmarks in Georgian Literature*, School of Oriental and African Studies, London, 1966.
23 Sh. Dzidziguri, *The Georgian Language*, Tbilisi, 1969.

SUGGESTED FURTHER READING

W. E. D. Allen, *A History of the Georgian People*, Kegan Paul, 1932.
C. M. Bowra, *Inspiration and Poetry*, Macmillan, 1955.
D. M. Lang, *A Modern History of Georgia*, Weidenfeld & Nicolson, 1962.
H. D. Luke, *Cities and Men*, vol. II, Geoffrey Bles, 1953.
F. Maclean, *To Caucasus*, Jonathan Cape, 1976.
S. S. Orbeliani, *A Book of Wisdom and Lies*, Octagon Press, 1982.
I. Shah, *The Elephant in the Dark*, Octagon Press, 1974.
   The Way of the Sufi, Octagon Press, 1968.
K. Vivian, *The Knight in Panther Skin*, The Folio Society, 1977.
O. Wardrop, *The Kingdom of Georgia*, Luzac, 1977.
R. Wood, *Kalila and Dimna*, A. A. Knopf 1980 (available Octagon Press).

3

Europe and the Great Sophy

SIR ROGER STEVENS

First of all I ought to offer a word of explanation about the Great Sophy. The word Sophy is a corruption, primarily an English corruption I believe, of Safavid which was the name of the Persian dynasty which ruled from 1500 to 1722 when it came to an end as a result of the Afghan invasion. Sophy may also be derived from Sufi, which means a hermit or holy man; that word was also associated with groups of beggars and very poor people in Persia at that time. The result was that travellers to Persia were thoroughly confused by this name: some called the Shah the Sophy, or in the case of Abbas the First, the Great Sophy; others said this must be wrong because the Sophies were people who begged after alms. But it is a convenient and picturesque phrase and that accounts for its use in the title of this lecture.

The scope of my subject is the period beginning in the late 16th century and ending with the Afghan invasion which I have just mentioned. This is a period of great interest and great fascination in European-Persian relations, particularly if one starts at the end of the 16th century when a number of events occurred changing a situation which had been one of virtual non-communication.

Until the end of the 16th century there was little contact between Persia and Europe; the Crusades acted as a barrier to any understanding between the Christian world and Islam. There was some communication through Turkey and India; you will find a picture in the National Gallery by Holbein, containing a Persian carpet, which dates from about 1480. There was a certain amount of trade in silk and other things from Aleppo, while the Portuguese occupied the Gulf ports and were present in India from about 1515 onwards – although that served to block rather than to encourage

34

contact between Europe and Persia. However, towards the end of the 16th century all kinds of things started to happen.

First, rather paradoxically and in some ways the most import-ant, was that the Spanish and Portuguese crowns came to be united. That meant that the Portuguese hold on India, on the Indies generally, including the Persian Gulf, was weakened. Second, a missionary interest which had developed first in India began to be applied to Persia. Third, in 1587, a most remarkable Shah came to the throne, Shah Abbas, and Iran and Europe found themselves united by an interest in fighting the Turks. Finally, in 1600 the English East India Company was formed; in 1602 the Dutch East India company was formed and trade with India de-veloped very quickly into a sort of cross-trade which included Persia. This is the period when these two civilizations suddenly found themselves confronting each other almost for the first time. It was an exciting moment, with Europe just past its Renaissance flowering and with the golden age of Persian poetry and miniatures and painting and architectural decoration virtually unknown in Europe; as I have said, Europeans already knew something about carpets and silks, but about very little else.

One of the results of the factors I have mentioned was that, beginning about 1600, quite a large number of Europeans started coming to Persia and it is with their work and their experiences that I am chiefly concerned.

These visitors were not primarily interested in Persia's artistic achievements; they were not really in a position to appreciate them. They were more struck by the idiosyncracies of the political scene, by the impact of Islam in its Persian manifestation, which is primarily Shi'a rather than Sunni, by differences in customs and manners and by peculiar Persian characteristics. For this reason, I shall not be dealing with the artistic influence of Persia on Europe or vice versa. That is a subject which calls, in any event, for an art historian. I am much more concerned with the question of cultural confrontation between Europe and Persia in personal, in social and in political terms.

Now before considering that, I would like to say a word about the nature of these European visitors. To begin with there were the missionaries, first Augustinians from Goa who were Portuguese, then Carmelites sent by the Pope who were mainly Italian; thirty years later Capuchins who were mainly French and in the middle of the century, Jesuits. They all had a very important contribution to make in terms of records and some of them remained as long as fifty years in the country. Next there were the admirers of Shah Abbas like the Sherley brothers who were English and the Italian, the Roman patrician, Pietro della Valle. There were also the official missions: for example, a mission of about 1618 from Spain which was intended to cover Portugal as well. It was led by a seventy-year-old Spaniard and took four years to get there; it then waited a year and a half to see the Shah, took four years to get back and the Spaniard died on the way. The first British mission in 1628 was a very unhappy one: there were two ambassadors both of whom died in Kazvin under circumstances about which I will say a little more later. There was an absolutely ridiculous mission from the Duke of Holstein; Russians would pour in at intervals. Whenever people travelled and recorded their travels they seemed to meet Poles en route. In fact the amount of running around and travelling that was done in Persia was quite extraordinary. One Frenchman, about 1660, actually met a Spanish monk who said he was on his way to Peru. The French in fact were in rather a special category and I will say more about them later too. Finally, of course, there were the traders: the representatives of the English and Dutch East India companies – the English from about 1615, the Dutch from about 1623 – while towards the middle of the century we find a great burst of French jewellers who are the most valuable people of all as far as keeping records is concerned.

My main sources for what I am going to talk about are, very briefly: Pietro della Valle, the Roman patrician whom I mentioned earlier and who has written some 400,000 words in the form of letters to a friend;* the chronicler of the Spanish Ambassador whose name was Don Garcia de Silva y Figueroa; Thomas Herbert who came with the English ambassadors I referred to earlier but did not die and got away; the Carmelites; a German called Olearius who came with the Holstein mission; the jewellers Tavernier and Chardin; another Frenchman called Thévénot; Father Raphael du Mans a Frenchman who lived in Isfahan from 1644 until 1694; an

---

* This is a colossal book and only available in Italian at the moment, though a very good précis of it was done by Wilfred Blunt some years ago.

English East India Company doctor called Dr John Fryer; a Dutch artist called Le Bruyn and a Polish Jesuit called Kruzinski. I will not attribute things to them individually but those are my sources.

Let me start then by saying something about the Persian political scene. Until the end of the 16th century Persia had been a highly centralized monarchy, clearly identified with the Shi'a branch of Islam, traditional and enclosed. But in Abbas I, Abbas the Great, she suddenly found a monarch who was curious about the rest of the world; he was up to a point outgoing in character, a mixer, a bit of a tease, unpompous. At the same time he was militarily ambitious, a brilliant organizer and an outstanding town planner. I think one can safely say that his personality made a significant contribution to the influx of Europeans, leading to the greater mutual knowledge which is the subject of my talk.

It was first of all the Shah's putative interest in Christianity, about which I will have more to say in a minute, which attracted the missionaries and these gathered – I dare not say like flies – in hoards in the early part of the 17th century. It was Anthony Sherley who discovered Abbas' capacity for quick friendship. Sherley was a friend of Essex, Queen Elizabeth's falling favourite, a swash-buckling, self-appointed emissary to Shah Abbas without any authority to come there at all. He arrived in Kazvin in December 1598 with a party of 26 including his nineteen-year-old brother Robert; he was royally entertained, he struck up a warm friendship when riding in company with Abbas from Kashan to Isfahan, he proposed an alliance against the Turks and he was sent back to Europe to try and fix it up with the Christian princes. He was given a letter which would be more impressive if one did not have the very strong suspicion that he wrote it himself and that Abbas may never have understood it, but this is how in part it read:

> All you princes that believe in Jesus Christ, know you that He hath made friendship between you and me. It was none that came to make the way and remove the veil between you and us but only this gentleman. While he has been in these parts, we have eaten together from one dish and drunk of one cup like two brethren.

Pietro della Valle heard about Abbas from afar and, as he records, wanted to get to know the brave and famous king who was putting the world in uproar. Word also went back to Europe about the magnificence of the new Isfahan. This is not the place to extol the beauties of Isfahan, but it was a remarkable piece of town planning, largely on the fringe of an old town which consisted of a warren of streets. The Shah built great avenues, an enormous Maidan or parade ground, gardens, pavilions. This attracted many people.

Unfortunately, however, there was a certain disillusionment at close quarters with Abbas personally. It was realized that he was double-faced, that he was ruthless, and he had a very unpleasant habit – which was partly based on a law which prevented anyone who was blind from coming to the throne – of putting out the eyes of his heirs so that they could not ascend the throne, all except for one chosen, who would not get any competition. He was also criticized for his dissolute life and for his superstitiousness; and della Valle who went fighting with him even had some doubts about his courage in the field. So one finds a very considerable degree of disillusionment. Poor Robert Sherley, when his brother went on that mission, was left behind as a kind of hostage; he soon got fed up and four years later he was writing pathetic letters to his brother in which he says of Shah Abbas, 'He entrapped us with deceit and flattery, his intention being only to serve his own turn.' Pietro della Valle said, 'Where the affairs of this king are concerned, no one can believe in any external appearances whatsoever.'

On the other hand there is no doubt that he was an extremely efficient, firm and effective ruler. Rather a different type of comment but very characteristically British, I think, came from an early representative of the East India Company who was talking about how tyrannical Shah Abbas was. But he then went on to say this which made me laugh, 'If he should die before his subjects have experience of the honest intents of the English, they would much fear woeful times.' What a splendid piece of self-confidence! In fact the situation under his successors became worse because they shared his faults but not his ability. Chardin wrote: 'When this great Prince ceased to live, Persia ceased to prosper.' I might in passing just mention that Chardin became a British subject and is buried in Westminster Abbey. He was a Huguenot and found France rather uncomfortable after 1685.

Travellers to Persia were also horrified by the way in which the royal young were brought up. I must just quote one passage on this from Le Bruyn, a Dutchman, because this expresses very eloquently what it was like to be an heir to the Persian throne:

> Born in the Seraglio, guarded by black eunuchs within and white eunuchs without, the Shah is brought up without education or the least knowledge of what is going on in the world. When he reaches a certain age a black eunuch is deputed to teach him to read and write and instruct him in the Moslem faith, his head is filled with the great deeds and miracles of the twelve Imams and with an implacable hatred of the Turk and the Great Mogul. But they do not teach him history or politics or fire him with a love of virtue; on the contrary they abandon him to women and indulge him in every kind of sensuality from his most tender years. They make him chew opium and drink poppy water into which they put amber and other ingredients which incite to lust and for a time charm with ravishing visions but eventually cause him to sink into an absolute insensibility. On the death of his father they seat him on the throne and the court throw themselves at his feet in submission. Everyone tries to please him but no one thinks of giving him any good advice; it pays them to keep him ignorant and to pander to his pleasures, much more attractive to a young and inexperienced prince than puzzling his brain with affairs of state. So, these princes dream away the first years of their reign without the least concern for the welfare of the country or their own glory.

That was written in about 1706. The influence of the harem was undoubtedly a very serious one on the upbringing of the princes.

It was very difficult for foreigners to get into the harem, they had to pretend to be painters or go in with painters who were redecorating or something of that kind. It was also very difficult for the women in the harem to get out. In order to get out you had, apparently, to make love to the Queen Mother and try and get her to marry you off to some officer: that sort of thing. There would be periodical raids recruiting new candidates for the harem, but it was a great problem keeping something like 300 women including the wives of deceased Shahs content and happy when they hardly ever went out. So the habit developed, particularly later on in the century – and this is a subject of a great deal of description by

Europeans – of taking them for excursions through the town and out into the country, but it was absolutely forbidden for any male person to look on a member of the harem. The result was that the streets had to be cleared, not only the main streets down which they were passing but the side streets; people would be turned out of houses, curtains would be hung up in the middle of the side streets, people were put to great inconvenience sometimes for days on end. And this not unnaturally was regarded by the Europeans as an extremely barbarian practice and was very fully described. They refer also to the increasingly powerful role of the eunuchs who, by the way, were both white and black as my last quotation illustrates, the so-called black ones coming apparently not so much from Africa or Abyssinia as from the Malabar coast.

Ministers too had a pretty hazardous life; Chardin recalls one who said to him, 'Every time I leave the Royal presence, I look in the mirror to make sure my head is still there.' There is no doubt that the atmosphere of suspicion and rivalry both within the family and between the Royal family and the advisers, the viziers and so on, was terrible.

On the other hand there were certain things that could be admired. First, the extreme informality which applied particularly to Shah Abbas and in a lesser degree to his successors. Abbas would walk through the bazaar, sometimes incognito, sometimes in disguise, chatting with everybody. There is an account in one place of him frying fish in the open air with his own hands and at the same time drafting a despatch. And he made a particular practice of this kind of thing and at one point referred very caustically to those Catholic monarchs who spent all their time sitting on their thrones in their palaces and never came out to see the people.

At the other end of the scale, one has to remember that the monarchy had a divine origin and this meant, not so much that the king could do no wrong, but that he could do as much wrong as he liked with impunity. There was a great deal of comment on the fact that the Persian people were so docile; there were few murmurings, there was no revolt during the whole period I'm talking about and coupled with that to some extent was the most extraordinary prevalence of law and order particularly on the roads. French visitors in the middle of the 17th century would say, 'It's absolutely

amazing that we can move about this country without worrying
at all about robbers or anything like that. Such a contrast to
France.'

Chardin tells a delightful story of how he was riding with a party
somewhere in the south between Shiraz and Bandar Abbas on the
Gulf. As he rode he read a book and he got absorbed in the book.
Suddenly he looked up and found that all his companions had
disappeared. It was getting dark and he did not know what to do so
he went into a cave for the night. The next morning he went into
the nearest village and was immediately surrounded by a sort of
highway guard called *rahdah* who wanted to know who he was,
what he was doing there, where his party was and so on. They had
the whole thing absolutely cut and dried: they took him to where
his party was in order that he might identify himself, and would not
leave him until he had satisfactorily done so. Law and order was
extraordinarily well organized.

I come now to the question of religion and here again the
personality of Abbas played a very important part in arousing the
expectations of the missionaries. It was fashionable among Oriental monarchs at this time to profess an interest in Christianity. I
discovered recently that the Emperor Jahangir who was roughly a
contemporary, used to see how long he could stand with his arms
outstretched in the form of a cross; and Abbas did rather similar
things. Once riding into Isfahan with an Augustinian monk in
attendance he said, 'Do let me try on that necklace of St James's
relics and ride into Isfahan with it.' The father said he hoped that
Abbas might become a Christian and the Shah cast his eyes heaven-
wards and said, 'God might bring it about!' Then he turned to his
followers and said, 'If I become a Christian, you must do the same.'

On another occasion at a banquet he asked the Augustinian friars
to demonstrate how to make the sign of the cross and he had his
whole court kneeling down on the carpet copying them. Then they
went on to other conversation; he said he recognized the Pope as
the universal head of the Christian church and he would like to see
all mosques converted to Christian churches and much in the same
vein. After dinner he said, 'Before you go you must show me how
to do that sign of the cross again.' And so it went on.

There was another occasion when he got into a fascinating
conversation, again with a Portuguese Augustinian who was asked

to explain to him the doctrine of the Trinity and the mystery of the virgin birth. After he had done so and the Shah had commented on it, this father said that it only remained for Abbas to become a Christian fully to comprehend these matters; to which he replied, 'How do you know I am not a Christian at heart?'

But I am afraid, however, that all this was done with a political end in mind. Abbas was hoping to enlist the help of Christian monarchs against the Turks and he was prepared to flirt with Christianity, just as he brought in a lot of Armenians who were Christians to the same end. He very soon changed when he found that the Emperor had made peace with the Turks and he became suspicious that the Catholics were trying to convert the Armenians to Rome: they owed their allegiance, you see, to a patriarch in Armenia. The same Augustinian who had had such a pleasant experience with him as I have just described was within a few days after that publicly insulted, being offered a courtesan to sleep with. He gave her a lecture on chastity and she turned her head away as much as to say, 'What do you think you are?'

Abbas was always as it were making use of differences between Christians too. Fourteen years later he arranged a kind of conference between the Carmelites and a party from the East India Company which included an English chaplain. He arranged for them to meet, oddly enough, in the harem and he asked them questions like this: Did the English make a sign of the cross and have images and saints? Were Catholics not idolators? Having heard their divers answers to these questions, he then proceeded, so we are told, to deliver a sermon lasting three-quarters of an hour, at the end of which the English in their downright way said they would like to go off to the Caspian and buy silk. To this he said reprovingly that it was quite improper for them to raise such a question in front of these holy men. He then asked whether there were three or four nails on the cross and this led to a heated argument between Protestants and Catholics about the number of Christ's wounds and so it went on. Rather surprisingly they appeared to leave the party in which, I think, Abbas had been the victor, on fairly amiable terms with each other. But he obviously enjoyed sparring in this way; he was, as I have said, a tease. Yet it was in this same year 1621 that a Carmelite was able to write, 'We are in the country of the greatest tyrant the church has had, the

methods he adopts are taken from hell.' It is not surprising perhaps
that the monks were a little disillusioned by this time; all these
missions remained there but in dwindling numbers and they had
no success with conversions. A Carmelite reported in 1673 that he
had been in the country for 26 years and he hardly knew of a single
one.

That brings one to ask oneself: what did the Europeans who
were in Persia think about Islam? My impression is that they had
very little curiosity about it; there was certainly no attempt by the
missionaries to ask themselves why it was that conversion was so
difficult, what was the source of Islam's strength. They were so
convinced of the rightness of their own ways of life and their own
purity that it never occurred to them to look at it from that point of
view. They tended rather to pick holes in what they could see, they
talked about the hypocrisy of the mullahs, the priests, to whom
they referred as whited sepulchres. Chardin who was not particularly devout quotes a Persian as saying, 'Watch the face of a
woman, the back of a mule and all sides of a mullah.' Christians
also got very upset because good Moslems thought them unclean
and would move away from them across to the other side of the
road or the street. In 1609 we find a Carmelite telling how a Persian
touched by a Christian considered himself polluted and would go
off to the baths to cleanse himself.

At the same time many laymen, especially, were impressed by
certain things about Islam. First, by the readiness of Persians to
engage in philosophical, religious discussion and enjoy it; there are
many accounts of that, particularly from those who stayed there a
long time like della Valle. Second, they were impressed by the lack
of sectarianism between Shi'as and Sunnis; although Shi'aism was
the official religion of the state and the majority of Persians were
Shi'as there were also a considerable number of Sunnis; for
example, all the Kurds were Sunnis. And the third thing that
impressed them was the extraordinary stillness and devotion of the
worshippers in mosques. Foreigners did not, of course, often get
into mosques but when they did they were always impressed by the
intensity of the worship.

As regards customs and manners generally we have many different descriptions of many kinds of feasts. There was rather an
unpleasant one which involved sacrificing a camel and the bits of

the camel were carted all over the town by various competing sections of the town. There was an annual washing ceremony in the river; there was a fantastic ceremony also once a year, in which everyone went down to the river with buckets in their hands and threw water at each other and they had a tremendous splash and an awful lot of fun.

I mentioned earlier the enormous Maidan which had the bazaar at one end and the Royal Mosque at the other. At night it would be illuminated with 50,000 earthenware lamps and charlatans, marionettes, jugglers, reciters of verse and prose and even preachers would appear instead of the vendors' stalls which would be cleared away. If there was to be a ceremony in the Maidan, the avenues would be closed, everybody would be turned out, it would be watered a day or two beforehand and swept, says Chardin, 'like a great room for a ball.' We have many descriptions of the most wonderful ceremonies which are seen from the Ali Kapu, a sort of grandstand of a building which was also the entrance to the Royal Palace. It is difficult to know how best to describe the extraordinary scenes that went on; there would be fights between wild beasts and bulls, there would be tilting and javelin throwing. But I think I cannot do better than just quote to you Chardin's description of . . . perhaps you can guess what:

> In this exercise the gamesters divide themselves into two equal bodies; several balls are cast into the middle of the square and everyone has a mallet given to them. To win, the balls must be made to pass between the two opposite pillars which are at the end of the square and serve as goals. This is no easy matter because the adverse party stops the balls and drives them towards the other end. They are laughed at that strike while their horse is upon a walk or stopped; the game requires that it should be struck only on the gallop and those are reputed the best players who riding upon full speed know how to send back the ball with a dry blow when it comes to them.

A very good, simple description, I think, of polo.

Then there were the banquets. Now banquets can be very tedious; as one who has some experience of diplomatic life I feel this very strongly. These Persian ones were no less tedious than banquets today. There was always a long wait. You did not have chairs, you were made to squat on the ground. Some of the more elderly ambassadors, like the Spaniard I referred to, became very impatient, particularly if they got hot in their thick uniform. But there were many favourable comments about the superb organization of the banquets, the charm of the music off-stage, the beauty of the open air setting. Europeans comment on the total absence of napkins; they were given flat bread instead and some of them assumed that this was not to eat but just to wipe their mouth with. Everybody ate with his fingers. A number of people commented on the fact that when you at last got into the meal, the Persians particularly bolted their food, absolutely chucked it down and never talked. Then they realized that the reason for this was that they only had about twenty minutes to eat it because after that everybody broke up. Departure was completely informal; you did not say goodbye to anybody, you did not bow to the Shah or anybody, you just walked out and you generally had great trouble in the cloakroom where you had left your shoes behind. So banquets in those days were not perhaps so different from what they are today; at any rate these are the things that visitors noted.

Their comments on feeding are also rather interesting. Normally there were only two meals a day and the French say that they thought they ate very little and everybody else thought that they ate rather a lot. That perhaps says more about the French than about the Persians. 'They take only two meals a day,' said Chardin, 'one of fruits, sweetmeats and cheese at mid-morning and the other of meat about seven at night. At this meal, if guests are present, the host with a great wooden ladle puts rice and meat on little plates which the servants pass round. The guests fall to taking out rice by handfuls and the meat with their fingers, sometimes they mix curdled milk with their rice and meat making up a lump of all together as big as a tennis ball, and put it all in their mouths at the same time, which is the reason they never sit long at table.'

There were many comments too on how superstitious the Persians were: how, for example, Royal audiences and Royal visits could be affected by the words of the soothsayers. You always consulted the omens before going on a journey. People had a superstition about living in the house in which their father had died; they would refuse to do so and the house was allowed to fall down. We are also told that it was very fashionable to talk

astrology, it was something of a craze. The curious credulity of the
Persian mind and its complications come out very clearly in a
number of cases. I will tell you one story which I think is perfect.

Don Garcia y Figueroa who, as I say, was 68 or 70, was offered
some ladies as was the local custom when he was at Shiraz. He
thanked them and said he was really too old for that sort of thing. In
the course of conversation he displayed rather a profound knowledge of Persian history because he was, in fact, a very educated and
civilized man. So the rumour started that he had been there as
ambassador before, since without that how could he have known so
much Persian history? So people made calculations and they came
to the conclusion that he must be about 120. He was cross-exam-
ined about his earlier visit and he said that he really did not have
any clear recollection of it. Then they concluded that he was so old
he must have lost his memory, but they watched him and it seems
that he was very good on horseback, whereupon they put it about
that he had maintained his strength by supernatural means. I think
this illustrates the complications of Persian thinking very well
indeed; life is full of ambiguities.

An early visitor, earlier than any I have mentioned before, was
sent by the Muscovy Company, which was a British company, in
1566. When he was somewhere in the north, he met a couple of
men, one of whom said that he was a duke and the other that he was
a great friend of the Shah's. These two promised to ensure that he
got an audience and all the rest of it; they did not do a thing for him
in fact, but he did get an audience. That audience is quite interesting because the then Shah, who was rather an unattractive character, wanted to know where he came from. He said, 'England' –
talking, I suppose, through an interpreter. The Shah turned and
said, 'Where's that? Have any of you heard of England?' They all
said no. So then he thought he would try something else and he
said, 'Inghilterra.' At that the penny dropped: one of the courtiers
said, 'Ah, Londra,' and then they understood. Apparently London
had quite a reputation already at that time.

Having said a good deal about what the Europeans thought of
the Persians I am tempted to ask what the Persians must have
thought of the Europeans. Of course there is very little evidence for
that; there is not much Persian documentation of this period; most
of it was destroyed in the Afghan War; but in any case this kind of

personal reminiscence would not be recorded. One can only say, trying to put oneself in Persian shoes, that some of these Europeans were very odd indeed; they were an extraordinary lot and I would just like to give you a few examples. I have already talked about the Sherley brothers; Robert Sherley, the younger brother, who stayed for nearly ten years in Persia, was then sent to Europe by the Shah who I suspect wanted to get rid of him. He came back ten years later and was sent off again within six months, apparently on a mission to the King of Spain. As far as I can see, and I have looked at this fairly carefully, the Shah and Sherley ceased to maintain communication with each other, but eight years after he left Persia, he landed up in England and proceeded to make some very specific proposals to James I about sending out barges which would be assembled on the Persian Gulf and providing military assistance and so on, none of which I think he had any authority to make.

Shortly after that a Persian called Naqd Ali Beg arrived as ambassador in London, and Robert Sherley went to call on him and be polite. The most extraordinary scene ensued: Naqd Ali Beg picked up the dispatch, the credentials that Sherley was carrying, pulled them out of his hand, tore them up, hit him in the face and said, 'You are an impostor, you have no right to go round representing the Shah.' This caused considerable flutter at the Court of St. James. Charles I was on the throne by this time and he decided that he must send an ambassador to Persia and he chose an old boy called Sir Dodmore Cotton. It was rather a comic party because Dodmore Cotton and Robert Sherley and Naqd Ali Beg, the Persian, were all to go back together and try and sort out the truth of things, but they were on such bad terms that it was decided to send them in separate ships in the same convoy.

They were delayed for a year which did not help anybody's temper and when they finally got to India, Naqd Ali Beg took an overdose of opium, which may have been suicide, so his evidence was not available. And Dodmore Cotton and Sherley did finally get one audience with the Shah who was extremely cryptic about it all. Some people have read what he said to mean that he was standing up for Sherley but I personally do not think so; I think the explanation is that he was very doubtful whether Sherley really had credentials. However, both Sherley and Cotton were so upset by their reception that they got ill and they both died. That was the first British mission to Persia, and one can well see that the whole Sherley business must have made rather an odd impression on the Persians. The Sherleys were undoubtedly adventurers of a high order.

At about the same period, 1602, or thereabouts, there were a couple of Portuguese, one layman and one monk, who got a remit from the Pope to go to Persia and try to assist the conversion of Shah Abbas. They quarrelled on the way, the monk stole the layman's clothes, the layman put the monk in chains. When finally the layman got to see Shah Abbas he took his letters from the Pope out of his breeches pocket and made the Shah stand up to receive them. Apparently the Shah said to him, 'If you had brought it with the respect due and not from your behind I should have gone out to receive it.' As it was he was pretty annoyed.

Another example was an extraordinary counsellor from Hamburg who went with the Holstein mission and who made himself difficult at every turn. He refused to accept two horses because only one had been named in a letter; he misbehaved with Armenian girls, he had a passion for letting off guns at parties which greatly disturbed the Shah; he had a row with a member of his own delegation who took refuge in the Ali Kapu which was sanctuary; he plotted to get him out and get him arrested. Finally he beat to death a soldier who refused to stable his horse. He was, I may say, hanged when he got back to Hamburg, but that sort of thing must have made rather a curious impression too.

A most astonishing visitor to Persia was Henry Bard, Viscount Bellamont. He was a fellow of King's College, Cambridge, and was sent out by Charles II, then in exile, to try and raise some money for the Royalist cause. This, as far as I know, is the only occasion on which any Briton has been to Persia to try and raise money until very recently. He really behaved quite abominably; first of all he said that the Persians owed a lot of money to the British because the British had helped them throw the Portuguese out of the island of Hormuz, which was not very tactful. In response – and I really think I must quote this, which to my mind is the perfect English-Persian confrontation – in response the Persians said that they attached value to the King of England's friendship (he was not actually king of course) and efforts had been made to afford him assistance but alas they could not send cavalry or troops, the

distances were too great. In short they refused the impossible and
that is a good way to start negotiations such as these; they had not
got a fleet and they could not even purchase vessels from the Dutch
or the Portuguese.

Bellamont listened to this long speech with signs of impatience
and then observed that this was not the kind of assistance he was
expecting. What he wanted was much simpler, it was money, but
obviously the Shah had no intention of paying his debt. The Grand
Vizier replied smilingly that the Shah wished to pay but to carry
such large sums through many countries or even by sea would
entail great risks and require many beasts of burden – which is a
beautifully Persian way of putting it. Bellamont replied 'with a
certain show of emotion' that if they gave him the money, he knew
quite well how to take care of it and remove it in safety. In a mild
voice the Vizier remarked, 'Necessity is not the most perfect of
judges.'

Bellamont also asked that all the English traders be expelled
because they were not supporters of Charles II. The Persians said
that they could not meet the king's request to expel the English
traders; if Bellamont wanted to do this with his own forces (which
he had not got) they would not interfere. Finally 'being wearied
out', the ambassador said with a certain amount of passion that he
had not looked for such an answer from a king of such fame in the
world, especially after the Persian Kingdom had received aid from
the King of England at great cost to the latter. The Grand Vizier,
however, kept his cool and offered to help Bellamont if he was in
any difficulty with expenses. All this was recorded by an Italian,
Marucci, who accompanied Bellamont and who concludes, 'I admired the way in which the Grand Vizier was able to evade the
aggressive answers of the ambassador without betraying any sign of
ill-humour.'

In addition to the British, there were the Russians. Now the
Russians were rather a problem; they brought large quantities of
vodka on one occasion to present to the Shah; Shah Abbas said, 'I
think you had better keep your vodka, you are more in need of
spirits than I am.' Another party arrived in 1664 with 800 followers
and they tried to smuggle in large quantities of goods without
paying duty. They were the ones, I believe, who used their fur caps
when they were in their cups as drinking goblets, which was all

right up to a point but then they forgot and put the caps on their head with the wine still inside. They were reported by the Persians to be smelly and rather dirty and generally drunk.

One of the most remarkable visitors of all was a French lady called Marie Petit. She was the mistress of rather a disreputable Turkey merchant called Fabre who in about 1705 was appointed by Louis XIV as ambassador. He was badly in debt and he could not finance his own trip; she was quite well off so he borrowed the money from her, but she made a condition that she should be allowed to come too and have a say in the planning of the trip. They arrived in Erivan, which is now Turkey, where she obviously caught the fancy of the governor, and there something happened, although it is not quite clear what because there are varying accounts of it; one says that she threw an orange at an Armenian soldier and another says that she poisoned her husband. At all events, her husband died and she was left in a very mixed party, a couple of priests and I forget who else. She decided to go on, to be the French ambassadress and she said that she had a mission from the French princesses to the Persian princesses. She got locked up, or as the chronicler says 'put on deposit,' at Tabriz; she managed to talk herself out of deposit and her friends had the greatest difficulty getting her out of the country. When she returned to France, she was tried but, remarkably, she was acquitted – this is many years later – partly as a result of the intervention of the widow of Fabre himself.

Now that was a very odd story and the Persians must have been very puzzled by all this. Doubtless they were also puzzled by an earlier French party of which three members were officials of the French East India Company and the others were diplomats of a sort who wanted, I suspect, to conceal their identity a little bit. They were described as 'gentlemen having an inclination to travel', and what Chardin says about this is very worth noting. 'The Persian ministers,' he says, 'were quite incredulous; the very words could not be put into the Persian language without an air of absurdity. They asked if it was possible that there should be people who would travel 2,000 or 3,000 leagues with so much danger and inconvenience just to see what we Persians look like.'

To end, I should like just to tell you what impressions visitors in general formed of the Persian people. They regarded them as handsome, well-built, healthy unless given to drugs. They thought that the rich were less subject to sickness than people in Europe and that this accounted for there being few doctors and only two hospitals in Isfahan. They admired the climate and thought such good health must be due to the fine air. They observed too that the Persians were exceptionally careful about personal cleanliness; they did not allow any stains on their clothes; the rich changed their linen every day; a man was valued for his neatness and good clothes. They noted further a great lack of skill in mechanical arts; Persian people were content to import goods rather than to make them; there was hardly a native of the country who could mend a watch and, in fact, there were a number of Swiss watchmakers in Persia from about 1630 onwards.

There were no printing houses; those had to be introduced by Europeans. Yet, Chardin notes: 'It is marvellous what they were able to achieve with the minimum of tools. They sit on the bare ground,' he said, 'in the corner of a room on an old carpet, and in a moment you see the board up and the workman sitting on his breech at work, holding his work between his feet and working with his hands.' For anybody who knows Persia that is a very familiar picture.

Vistors were impressed by the Persians' beautiful manners; by their kindness to strangers; by what they call 'their lively, quick and fruitful fancy, their easy and copious memory, their natural ingenuity.' As to their artistic achievements, these only get qualified praise, which is why I do not think there is very much reward in giving European views on Persian art and architecture. In John Fryer's view, 'Building is one of the noble deeds for which they merit to be extolled.' Tavernier, who is normally so critical, lists carpet-making, flowered and linen cloth, damasking with vitriol on cutlery, making bows and arrows, bridles and saddles, earthenware, silks and velvets among things they do well. But on the whole Europeans did not think much of Persian painting; they referred to their figures as lascivious, and whether they were lascivious or not they were poorly rated. Della Valle saw some artists doing a portrait of Abbas in the gardens at Ashraf on the Caspian, and observed, 'It bears about as much resemblance to him as I do to my godfather.' Le Bruyn, who was an artist himself, visited a number of studios. He liked the paint, finding Persian ultramarine the finest blue in the world but thought less of the painters. For example, a royal artist whom he visited knew nothing of light and shade, although there were a number of European artists operating in Persia at that time and they were beginning to start European methods of painting.

However, I think it is the light and shade of the Persian character which in the end the foreign visitor found most puzzling. There was so much charm, so much sophistication, so much desire to please, so much, I quote, 'art and insinuation'. As Le Bruyn says succinctly: 'The tongue and the heart never travel together.' Chardin tries to sum it up in balanced terms: 'The Persians are the most kind people in the world; they have the most moving and engaging ways, the most complacent temper, the fluidest and most flattering tongues, avoiding in their conversation stories or expressions which may occasion melancholy thoughts.'

II

PERCEPTIONS OF INDIA

4

The Influence of British and European Literature on Hindu Life

NIRAD C. CHAUDHURI

The subject matter of my talk not only comes within the scope of the series in which it has been included and lies within the field of investigation which is the particular concern of the Institute for Cultural Research, but it also tells in part the story of one of the most outstanding examples of cultural interaction seen in human history. The whole phenomenal acculturation, to employ the formidably academic but convenient word, is paralleled by only two others among civilized peoples, namely the impact of Greek culture on the Romans and of the Revival of Learning on modern Europeans. The impact of European culture through the agency of the English language on the life of the Hindus brought about a far-reaching revolution; it renovated their minds and resuscitated their culture.

What I have to say at the very outset is that the cultural traffic was wholly one-sided, that is to say all the influences flowed from the West to the East; the process reversed the old tag 'ex oriente lux'. In fact, those who were carrying on the cultural revolution were perfectly aware of this one-sidedness and were not ashamed of it. When the process of Westernization of the Hindu mind had got into its stride, it was subject to attacks both from the front and the rear. The local British and the traditional Hindus combined in calling those Bengalis who were westernizing themselves 'imitative monkeys'; they did not mince their words. Bankim Chandra Chatterji, whom I regard as the greatest intellect in modern India, who was the most powerful westernizer and at the same time the creator of a new Hinduism and a new nationalism, took up the challenge and defended imitation as a stage in the creation of cultures. In an article written in Bengali and published in 1887, he first of all declared that in the creation of cultures, imitation in itself is not to be condemned. Among the examples of cultural creation by means of imitation, he singled out above all the influence of the Greek culture upon the Roman as the most important; he wrote (I am translating from the Bengali): 'When the Romans came upon Hellenism they began to imitate the Greeks whole-heartedly. The result of the process was Cicero's eloquence, Virgil's epic, dramas by Plautus and Terence, lyrics by Horace and Ovid, Papinian's jurisprudence, the ethics of Seneca, the political philosophy of the Antonines and the architecture of the Imperial era.' In the Bengali text all the key words are in English. Chatterji went on to specify the legacy of Greece and Rome to modern Europe; he wrote: 'Italian and French literature are modelled on the Greek and the Latin; European law is based on Roman jurisprudence; European government is also an imitation of the Romans: somewhere or other one finds the same imperators, the same senate, the plebs and also the same forum and the same municipium.' Again all the key words are in English in the Bengali text.

He formulated certain general principles in the evolution of cultures. His first conclusion was this: 'Certain societies become civilized by themselves and create a new culture; others take over from others. The first process takes a long time but the second is relatively quick.' His second conclusion was: 'When a relatively uncivilized people come in contact with a people of higher civiliz-ation, the natural law is for the less civilized to imitate the more civilized, even to the extent of total imitation.' His third conclusion was: 'Imitation in itself is not harmful for it confers important benefits and after the preliminary phase of imitation, independent creation begins.'

So Chatterji declared without any shamefacedness that given the existing state of Bengali society, that is as it was in the 19th century, it could not be said that the impulse to imitate was wrong. 'The Bengali,' he continued, 'sees that the Englishman is superior to him in culture, in education, in strength, in wealth, in happiness, in fact in every respect; why should not the Bengali then want to be like the Englishman? Any people in like circumstances would have done the same thing. Imitation becomes harmful only when it becomes mechanical, uncreative, unadaptive and unstimulating.' He was referring to a kind of indiscriminate imitation and in 19th century India this cultural disease had not become common. It is a phenomenon of today and is seen everywhere in an exhibition of debased Europeanization, an imitation of the fashions of the lowest in the West.

The extent of the mental revolution became clear within a decade of the foundation of Calcutta University in 1857 and the most emphatic testimony of it came from an Englishman who was one of the foremost intellectuals of Britain in those days. He was Sir Henry Maine, a great legal historian, a member of the Viceroy's executive council during the time of Lord Lawrence and also Vice-Chancellor of Calcutta University. Addressing the Bengali graduates at a Convocation of Calcutta University in 1864, he said: 'It is impossible that there should be one in this room to whom the life of a hundred years ago would not be acute suffering if it could be lived over again.' And again: 'It is impossible to imagine the condition of an educated native with some knowledge and many of the susceptibilities of the 19th century – indeed perhaps too many of them – if he could re-cross the immense gulf which separates him from the India of Hindu poetry, if indeed it ever existed.'

In 1871, when giving a course of lectures at Oxford, he said: 'I have had unusual opportunities of studying the mental condition of the educated class in one Indian province (he meant Bengal), though it is so strongly Europeanized as to be no fair sample of native society; taken as a whole, its peculiar stock of ideas is probably the chief source from which influences proceed which are more or less at work everywhere. Here there has been a complete revolution of thought, in literature, in taste, in morals and in law. I can only compare it to the passion for the literature of Greece and Rome which overtook the Western world at the Revival of Learning.'

The main instrument of this cultural activity was of course a new type of mind; Maine drew attention to this as well. 'The new generation of Bengalis,' he said, 'saw in the intellectual life of Europe a force to extend their own mental horizon!' There was a reaction from the traditional intellectual life of the Hindus; as Maine put it: 'Finding that their own system of thought was embarrassed in all its expressions by the weight of false physics, elaborately inaccurate, careless of all precisions and magnitude, number and time, the educated Bengalis were turning to Western thought, especially in its scientific form.' He concluded: 'To a very quick and subtle-minded people which has hitherto been denied any mental food but this, mere accuracy of thought is by itself an intellectual luxury of the very highest order.'

But the new mental outlook was not confined to science alone; it embraced every department of human thought, emotion and feeling. The new generation of educated Hindus not only would not approach the original philosophy in the original spirit, by the end of the 19th century they could not even understand it if it was explained to them in the traditional manner. This was stated by the new Hindu reformer, Bankim Chandra Chatterji; in offering a commentary of his own on the Gita, he wrote: 'The problem is that the new educated class of Bengalis cannot easily understand the explanation of the ancient commentators even if translated from Sanskrit into Bengali, just as the pundits who depend on the traditional explanation of Hindu philosophy would not understand an explanation of that philosophy by Western scholars even if it were translated into Bengali or another Indian language. This is not blaming anyone,' Chatterji added; 'Western modes of thought and Hindu modes of thought are so different that translation of language is not a translation of ideas. We must adopt Western methods of exposition and seek the help of Western ideas.' Chatterji made these comments in writing his incomparable commentary on the Gita for Bengali Hindus.

In dealing with the recasting of the Hindu mind under the influence of the English and of English literature, it is very important to understand that this was entirely due to the English language and to books in English which we Bengalis read but which were not read to us by the Englishman in India. I myself had published my first book both in London and New York before I had had six hours conversation with an Englishman in my whole life. I had never learned English from Englishmen and I could not even understand English as spoken by them until 1952, when I was fifty-five years old. This was because we knew they were hostile. Government policy was to give education in English, but it was not given any chance by the lower functionaries. Apart from this, the British civil servants in India in general nursed the most ferocious hatred of Bengalis who spoke and wrote English. This is not the place to put forward examples of this but, with the exception of some very far-seeing men, from Macaulay to Sir Michael Sadleir, who visited the universities in my young days, the rest were absolutely hostile and there was hardly an insult which was too gross to be hurled at us.

I quote as proof the opinion of Kipling, the greatest English writer on India. In 1913, the year in which a Bengali had brought the Nobel prize for the second time to England after Kipling, the latter wrote: 'Well, whose fault is it that the Babu is what he is? We did it, we began in Macaulay's time; we have worked without intermission for three generations to make this Caliban; every step and thought on the road is directly traceable to England and English interests.' Perfectly true, England acted on us despite the local English hostility. This hostility to cultural proselytization remains the greatest crime of the British people against their own civilization. This is the crime of British imperialism, not the political subjection of India. The English totally failed to realize that no empire can last unless it is ready to propagate its culture. The Romans realized it, the French realized it in part, today the Soviet Union realizes it. In any case, that was the British failure.

In contrast we Indians, particularly the Bengalis, were magnaminous, generous. We never showed any hostility to English life, civilization, literature and language, even though we were insulted day in, day out by the local English. We kept the two things separate, just as during the Second World War you probably kept the music of Mozart and Beethoven separate from Hitler. Indeed I did the same thing, for during the war the music of Haydn, Mozart and Beethoven was my mainstay when I went vicariously through your sufferings of 1940.

In the same way we could brush aside the contempt of the local English for the sake of the English civilization. We could take the beastliness of the local English by a kind of cultural generosity which is not usually found in nationalism; our nationalism was able to make a distinction between the two things, politics and mental life.

I will now give some examples to show how far this Anglicization, this Westernization permeated our life around the turn of the century, in 1900. I was born a year or so earlier in 1897, so I really belong to the 19th century. My mother did not know English, yet it was she who told me the story of the Iliad, she told me the story of King Lear and she told me about Marcus Aurelius.

Let me give you another little piece of information: a year or two after my birth, probably, a picture was brought and hung in our hut, with its mud floor, tin roof and walls and ceiling of matting. It hung there as far back as I can remember; it was the picture by Raphael, the *Madonna della Seggiola*, and my father and mother used to say, 'That is the Madonna della Seggiola by Raphael.' That was how I came to know the name of Raphael, though I cannot remember when I first heard it, just as I cannot remember first hearing many other names, for instance Shakespeare, Homer and, of course, Queen Victoria and Prince Albert. For me they all date from my protomemoric age.

I myself recited Shakespeare at home and from the school stage at the age of ten, in 1908, a bit of *Julius Caesar* in which I took the part of Cassius. We read English poetry and immensely enjoyed it; I could still recite the poems I learned in 1908 and in fact on writing them down and comparing them with the text, I found that not one word had been wrongly remembered. So that when I first arrived in England in 1955, the first thing I did on the morning after my arrival, at six o'clock on a March morning, was to walk down to Westminster Bridge to compare the scene with Wordsworth's description.

And this is not my case alone. My wife is twelve years younger than I am; as a small girl she read first of all, strange to say, not Wordsworth's but Herrick's *Daffodils* which says:

> Fair daffodils, we weep to see
> You haste away so soon.

She was very much puzzled because she had seen daffodils in Shillong, a hill town where daffodils grow, and she said, 'Daffodils last for many days, why did Herrick write that daffodils fade away at the end of the day?' It was only on coming to England that we learned that he was speaking of the wild daffodil not the garden variety.

This kind of interest of the heart itself, not of the brain, in English literature is disappearing in our society, but even so it still persists. Before I came over in 1970, a young Bengali girl wrote to me that she was living in a village in the midst of a jungle far away from Calcutta and she told me that she did not know English well. We developed a correspondence and she wrote to me of her depressions as well as of her exultant moods. Suddenly in the middle of her letter she quoted these lines:

> Although there were some forty heavens or more,
> Sometimes I peer above them all;
> Sometimes I hardly reach a score,
> Sometimes to hell I fall.

It was from George Herbert that she was quoting. Astonished, I wrote back, 'Where did you read this?'; she replied, 'I don't know, somewhere.'

So you see this persists. One of the extraordinary things is that the residual literary culture derived from the English is not to be found among the Anglicized upper-middle class today, but among such people, those who

> ... live amongst the untrodden ways,
> Besides the springs of Dove,
> Maids whom there are none to praise
> And very few to love.

They are still cherishing this language and literature because they are not exposed to the blight of the cities, false Anglicism, false hatred of the British and so on and so forth. They still retain that freshness of approach to English and to English literature which I had in my boyhood.

The impact of Western culture through the English language and literature was felt in all departments of our thinking, feeling and life; it completely renovated not only our mental life but our own intellectual activities. The instrument was, of course, English literature and the English language, but also translations of French and Italian literature. I will mention later what we read, but for the moment notice that all the old elements in our mental life were transformed and renovated. For instance, the idea of God, the old idea of God was replaced completely by a new idea of God; the religious life turned from ritualism to devotion, and devotion towards a personal God, an aspect which is not very pronounced in our religion. Intellectual life had been hidebound, something that is the curse of scholasticism, dogmatic and narrow; it was extended and became free.

In literature, prose was created for the first time in India through the influence of English because before that, except for workaday purposes, all literary expression was in verse; even philosophy was put into verse. Moreover poetry itself was completely transformed.

Architecture of the European type was introduced. In India, architecture had not remained Hindu but had become Islamicized so that up to the end of the 18th and the beginning of the 19th century many types of building were Islamic in style. But all of a sudden, all around Calcutta, Georgian and Palladian buildings began to spring up. Bishop Heber went to India in 1823 and drew a picture of a Bengali house near Calcutta; one can see the temple in the background but Corinthian columns support the porch to the flight of steps down to the river. I have myself visited many of these houses; they are all falling in ruins, of course, today.

But the wholly new ideas were these: first of all, individualism, that man individually matters. Hindu society is a regimented society; it hardly allows any individuality in its members. They have to conform to a very strict code of behaviour and that code of behaviour is mercilessly imposed. Nobody who disregarded the code could ever live in Hindu society, he would be ostracized. The sanctions were terrible; for example, the bodies of such men and of their families would not be cremated by the neighbours.

Of course to begin with individualists had to suffer a good deal, but they stuck to individualism. And what was this idea of individualism? Strangely, it was the idea of the Renaissance man, as explained by people like Pico della Mirandola – *uomo universale*, the universal man, many-sided, not a specialist, having all kinds of interests, so that he was a full man. I myself am bringing up the rear of that movement, for nowadays specialization exists even in India.

Then, the response to nature. Curiously enough, although some of the grandest scenery in the world is in the Himalayas, and although there is also very impressive scenery in the plains and beautiful scenery in the central Indian hills, we modern Hindus had completely lost the sense of the beauty of nature. We had become totally insensitive to natural beauty, in complete contrast to the ancient Hindu, whose adoration of natural beauty was in no way less than that of a European. Under English influence the feeling was re-created, but curiously, we thought that natural beauty was to be found only in Europe or in the Himalayas, never in Bengal. It was very late in life that I realized that natural beauty appertains as much to Bengal as it does to England, but this was a kind of transition made by me personally; my fellow Indians even today would not find any beauty in the landscape of the plains.

I am not going to deal with all this in detail, but rather with one aspect of Westernization which has completely escaped notice. This is the impact of the life of passion as revealed through European literature on Hindu personal life, on the man–woman relationship in Hindu society, especially in Bengal. The revolution was far-reaching; it jettisoned almost completely the old relationship. This is the main subject of my talk, though I have had to introduce other topics in order to place it in its proper framework.

First of all I must take a subsidiary point: can literature and particularly the literature of love, whether poetry or fiction, really mould love life or does it only portray love life? Even in Europe it is not realized how much literature has contributed to the notion of love. Some writers realized that from the beginning; one of the most charming love stories in Western literature was written in the second or third century AD, the famous story of Daphnis and Chloë by Longus. The man knew what he was doing, for he wrote, 'I dedicate this story to Eros, to the nymphs and to Pan, but it will be prized by others too; it will cure sickness, console persons who have become a victim to disappointment; he who has loved in the past will have memories revived; those who have never loved before will find in it their initiation, but there never has been nor will be anyone who can escape love so long as there exists beauty on earth and eyes to see it.' This was the writer's point of view, but for himself he desired immunity from involvement in love; he said: 'As for ourselves, may God grant, if events cannot save me from love, that we may tell the story of love while remaining wise ourselves.'

The Greek view of love and of falling in love was either very erotic or it was that love was a tragedy, a source of suffering for human beings, not of happiness. This is the entire teaching of classical civilization in regard to the man–woman relationship. Romantic love is really the creation of the Middle Ages, above all of Dante and Petrarch; after *courtoisie* and chivalry and all that, Dante in particular developed the idea of romantic love.

With the Renaissance came another set-back in some ways, a reversion to the erotic-physical aspect of love, and by the 17th and

18th centuries again the old tragic view of love had reasserted itself.
Madame de Lafayette's *Princesse de Clèves* is a dire warning against
love; it is one of the best novels in European literature but it warns
against love as a delusion and a pitfall. And the 18th century story
of *Manon Lescaut*, by the Abbé Prévost, also depicts the suffering
of love. However, love in its romantic aspect was rehabilitated in
the 19th century by romantic individuals all over Europe and in
England particularly.

We, of course, got the idea of romantic love from the romantic
novelists and poets and we in India share too the romantic admiration for Shakespeare, who was even greater in Bengal than he was
in England. Strangely enough, in spite of his *Venus and Adonis*, in
spite of his sonnets, in spite of certain things which you find
enshrined in his plays, he was specifically described by Bengali
critics as the exponent of Aphrodite Urania, sacred love, not of
Aphrodite Pandemos, of profane love. Why was this? The same
Bengali critics said that Byron, on the other hand, was an exponent
of profane love; they drew a distinction between Byronic love and
Shakespearian love. The man who really introduced the concept of
romantic love into the Bengali mind and also in some ways established it in life, wrote about certain aspects of Shakespeare. He was
Bankim Chandra Chatterji, who was quoted earlier on. In 1876 he
wrote, in a critique of *The Tempest*: 'Every student of Calcutta
University has the love dialogue between Romeo and Juliet in the
garden by heart, but,' he said, 'the dialogue between Ferdinand
and Miranda is in no way inferior' and he quoted, among other
passages, this one:

> Hence bashful cunning!
> And prompt me, plain and holy innocence!
> I am your wife, if you will marry me;
> If not, I'll die your maid; to be your fellow
> You may deny me; but I'll be your servant,
> Whether you will or no.

And he even compares Sakuntala, with whom Goethe fell in love,
unfavourably with Miranda; he says, 'She is more erotic, in a good
sense, more coquettish, while Miranda gives expression to a far
purer and holier love.'

Even Shakespearian symbolisms entered into our lives; there is a story, a tragic story of love and of a woman's death, in which the woman's nephew built a temple to her memory; in the garden around the temple there were no coloured flowers, only the white, sweet-smelling Indian flowers, like jasmine and so forth; apart from these there were rows of cypresses and willows. The willow never grew in Bengal and cypresses would not grow easily, yet in the story they are placed in the garden of a Bengal village. Do you realize where the inspiration came from? The 'Willow Song' in *Othello*, and the cypress from *Twelfth Night* – these two Shakespearian plays provided the inspiration.

This influence grew stronger, particularly at the end of the century. Among the poets, Tennyson and Browning were the favourites, and Browning, strangely enough, more than Tennyson. Tennyson was somewhat too English; Browning was sufficiently pompous, I believe, to appeal to the priggish Bengali mind. So in those days a young man who had the good fortune to come in contact with an educated, modern girl, which was not at all easy, on the contrary almost a windfall, would try to cultivate her, not as a girl-friend but as something absolutely different. He would, for example, eventually take a volume of Browning in a padded binding and respectfully present it to the girl. These padded bindings are no longer made, but I have seen many of them and I did manage to procure one of them second-hand from an Oxford bookseller.

Among the novelists Scott was a great influence, as were also Dickens and Thackeray, but, strange to say, not so much the Brontës and Jane Austen as, above all, George Eliot, because again the Bengali mind was priggish and there are few English novelists more priggish than George Eliot. Again, among her novels, it was not *The Mill on the Floss* and books of that type which were preferred, but *Middlemarch*, a book which I have never been able to read, and *Romola*, which of course I have read.

Among the Europeans, Victor Hugo was naturally a great favourite. I remember by the time I was thirteen I had *Les Misérables* almost by heart; I read *Toilers of the Sea* and *Notre Dame* before I was seventeen. Apart from him, somehow Maupassant was read but not Flaubert, Gautier was read but not Paul Bourget. Anatole France was read after the First World War. Russian writers were much in fashion; Tolstoy, Turgenev and Dostoevsky; Chekhov came very much later. Also we were fond of both Ibsen and Strindberg, of all people. All these works were read quite widely by 1914 and so we knew a great deal about these things and this generally moulded our outlook.

Although the study of love in European literature had its influence on actual life, it is extremely difficult to get any documentation of love life among Bengalis because letters and biographies like the English ones simply do not exist. No love letters survive from any real person, but there are novels and they give an idea of what it was probably like. It is very curious how sudden was the impact of this romantic love on Bengali society; actually it can be dated from a particular year, 1865, with the publication of a romance. Then in three successive novels published in 1867, 1869 and 1872, love was fully established in literature and correspondingly in life. I say in life inferentially, though direct evidence does not exist, because of the immense popularity of these novels and also the value that was set on them in our ordinary life. During my childhood, if I went to the house of a relative, I would find these novels by my pillow; no doubt they had a shrewd idea as to who liked to spend their time reading novels and they were put by the bedside; probably at night they were shared between the husband and wife, who knows?

In 1872 was published the first novel dealing with contemporary Bengali life (all the other three were romances) and this publication swept Bengali society off its feet. An English newspaper wrote: 'There is no parlour in Bengal where this book has not been continuously discussed' and this was certainly true. I have myself written a whole book on the impact of European love on our man–woman relationships. I cannot convey the whole book to you but the standpoint of the book will be appreciated if I say only that its motto is from Pater; it starts with a quotation from Pascal and ends with a line of music by Schubert; this is Schubert's famous setting of Schiller's ode to the Greek gods, *Die Götter Griechenlands*. I have documented fully the changes brought about by the romantic influence, how it was acclimatized, how it was put into Bengali. I can only give the broad, bare facts of this transposition.

I am not bringing ancient India into this at all; ancient Indian sexual life and man–woman relationships are altogether of a different order. They were physical but physically of an order which is not easily understood in the West. If I were to be very frank, I would say there is nothing I resent more than the present Western interest in our erotic literature and art. It is an insult to that erotic literature, it is almost sacrilege; I would sooner have our gods kicked by Westerners than our erotic sculpture treated as it has been in the West. That comes from a different world of sensibility altogether; it is a glorification of the body in a manner which only Greece and Rome probably understood.

But I am speaking, not of ancient Hindu India, but of conditions as they were before British rule was established, say before 1800. Man–woman relations affected three different aspects of society: first, within marriage; second, illicit relationships, very common as in all society – there is nothing wrong with it, it happens, it is natural; third, prostitution, a very different matter.

Let me take first of all, married life: what was married life like? In marriage only three elements existed: first, a social relationship for procreation, in which hardly any feeling entered. The children did not belong to the father and mother but to the grandparents; so the children were the property of the family and the young husband was something like a stud bull, that is all, from the social point of view. He was not supposed to take any interest in the birth of his children or anything else; it would have been the height of immodesty. Second, affection gradually grew up but was not as common as you might expect because until the young man was about thirty years of age, he could hardly meet his wife except late at night, after dark; up to about 1910, husband and wife could not meet in the daytime.

I am going to tell you an authentic story, an incident which happened during my childhood. Though the circumstances are not normal, but rather exceptional, it is a good illustration. One day a young lady of twenty-five to twenty-seven years of age (by that time she would have three or four children) was standing in the inner courtyard of her house, supervising the bringing in of logs for burning in the kitchen (we had no coal). The men who brought the wood were untouchables by caste and could not therefore enter the woodshed, which was next door to the kitchen, so they said: 'My lady, will you ask someone to take these logs into the shed by the side of the kitchen?' She looked up and saw a man coming in who looked trustworthy and said, 'Ask that fellow', whereupon the woodmen exclaimed, 'What are you saying, my lady! That is the master!' She had had four children by him but could not recognize him in the daytime. It is not as absurd as you may think; it was highly immodest to go to bed with one's wife before ten or eleven o'clock at night; when the husband came into the bedroom a little oil lamp would be burning on a stand and all the beds had mosquito nets because of the mosquitoes; then, since the walls – I am speaking of East Bengal – were made of matting and all the eaves-droppers and peeping Toms might be on the other side, the hus-band had to put out the light before he got into bed, under the mosquito net. How could the poor woman recognize the face of her husband in such circumstances?

The first element then was a purely sexual, bodily relationship without any emotion at all. Nor could any romantic feeling come in, naturally, in either illicit relationships or in prostitution, and in the society of those days going to a prostitute was not at all frowned upon. They would no more have thought of depriving a man of the right to go with a prostitute than of taking the safety-valve off a locomotive. This was the way things had to be done because one could get no proper sexual satisfaction in wedlock, nor even in illicit relationships. Hence the prostitute was always there. The extreme attitude on the physical level was this: whenever one saw a beautiful woman, the whole idea would be 'Every woman is se-duceable; shall I send a procuress to her, tempt her with money, with other things?' and since mostly these young women were married in childhood, they would be sick of their husbands by the time they were seventeen or eighteen and would probably pine for a change. So that sort of thing was expected to exist in society and I have complete documentary proof of it in newspapers and novels; it is all discussed.

As to the description of people, it is very curious how crude it is. There is a very famous Bengali poem, a romance written about 1753. In it the heroine, a princess and a great beauty, is described in these terms, starting from top to bottom, an elaborate item by item description: first of all, her plaits shamed the snakes so much that they went into their holes; her face put the moon absolutely into the shade; no mountain peaks could be harder than her breasts, out of envy of which the pomegranates burst; Mother

Earth herself felt crushed to dust by the size of her posterior; the poet could not be so explicit about the other parts, but he said whoever had eyes could guess what lay in front of her hips, it was so fair and fine. I could easily recite to you the Bengali poem from which I have culled all these details. I have also read another poem, which runs as follows: 'I have been to a lake to bathe and saw one marvellous beauty, her face blooming like a lotus, a figure of wonderful rhythm, her body shone through her blue sari like lightning through the clouds.' Very beautiful, very romantic but what is the practical conclusion? 'May God in his mercy send me an efficient procuress, whom I can send to her to offer her as much money and ornaments as she wants, if only she would come and spend a night with me.' This is a very famous Bengali poem.

Now a revolution took place almost overnight. First of all, a new idea of feminine beauty, something to be adored and worshipped, never to be looked upon with any kind of uncleanness. I could put before you scores and scores of descriptions concerning the beauty of the body in the new literature but I will quote only one, dating from 1883: 'Her youth was like that of a lotus in full bloom; she had no adornment, no proper clothes, not sufficient food even, yet her refulgent beauty radiated through her tattered sari; that beauty was in its full development; there was something ineffable in it like music among all sounds, like genius in the mind and like happiness in death, indescribable sweetness, indescribable love and indescribable adoration.' The word which I translate as 'adoration' should really be translated by the Greek word *agape*; that is the level which the admiration of beauty had reached.

And what of the concept of love? The young Prince has been told that a girl whom he looks upon as a sister is a young widow; he suspects that she has a lover and does not like this very much; he says it is not good for a widow to have love affairs and he must therefore remonstrate with her. The girl takes the young man to the bank of the Ganges, where they are staying in a villa and she says, 'Ask the Ganges to flow back to the mountains.' This is irresistible. Then again she says, 'I must not underrate love; love is not confined to the individual; it starts with the individual and spreads to all mankind.' The young man asks, 'But would you love a sinner?' and she says, 'Yes, even a sinner is to be loved because love is independent of anybody's merits, it is like God's love, whole love. Everybody loves the virtuous but nobody loves the sinner, yet it is the sinner who requires our love the most.' Then again the young man himself complains about the girl he loves and uses the word in the past tense, 'I loved her'. She says, 'Don't say "I loved her"', say you still love her' but the man says, 'No' and she replies, 'No? Do you think you have ceased to love simply because the object of your love has offended you? Who has given you this false consolation? Don't give in to self-deception.'

The whole concept was well defined in various books and poems in this way: from love between man and woman we ascend to divine love; it is like the love between Dante and Beatrice, starting from human love and going up to divine love. This took hold naturally in life. In society it would not take quite that idealistic form but from my own experience I would say that it had a very ethereal quality in which the physical aspect, the physical element was like alcohol in very fine claret. And that basis will always remain, for only a fool or an ignoramus will say that any love can be independent of the physical basis. It was not the physical basis which mattered but what was added to that physical basis, and it certainly was added in Bengali society and gloriously embodied in poetry and literature.

But in the end some problems remained. First of all, it is very curious that in Bengali society young people could not meet, so how could they fall in love? The picture was therefore rather that of post-marital courtship instead of pre-marital courtship. Also, there were various relationships which made it permissible for a young man to meet a young woman and to fall in love; for instance brothers of sisters-in-law and sisters of brothers-in-law were allowed to be in the same house and therefore the young men and young girls could fall in love within the scope of that acquaintance.

As I have said, the whole idea of love in this romantic sense was taken from European literature, so also was the idea of patriotism and nationalism, and this created another conflict. From the end of the 19th century through the days of my youth a quite unnecessary conflict was created between duty to one's country and love of woman. Even in my young days my teachers would say, 'Don't think of marrying, devote yourself to the service of your country', as though there were a conflict between the two. But the idea was very real to us in those days. There is a whole Bengali novel of about 600 pages written on this theme, in which a young man sets his love for a girl against his love for his country and is going to sacrifice himself completely; he is saved from doing so only by a chance occurrence. There are many other stories about this same conflict, which was very unnatural but became very real, so that in our lives two things derived from Europe were quite unnecessarily at loggerheads.

I have given you what I can only call a very summary description of the changes which came about in our life through the influence of the English language and literature and also of elements which we got from European literature through the English language. I hope that one day someone may write about the whole subject as I have done in Bengali. Unfortunately, not many people among our students these days know the history and those who have had intimate personal experience of that life are dying one by one; I am one of the very, very last of them. I may not write it, but it should be written. Equally unfortunately, no European is likely to know our language well enough to be able to undertake the task. In some ways it is a story which will probably remain like some secret treasure, never to be brought to the surface.

5

The Primal Sympathy

IRIS BUTLER

While casting about for a title to this lecture, I was struck by the appropriateness of a line from Wordsworth's *Ode on Intimations of Immortality from Recollections of Early Childhood:*

> ... primal sympathy
> Which having been must ever be.

My recollections of early childhood were given form and new life by re-creation of their sources after a period of exile in what I suppose should be termed my native land. But what is a native land? Is it where one is born? Or is it the land of one's race and nation? I was born in India, and my childhood there certainly had 'the glory and the freshness of a dream'. The eleven years I spent in England between the ages of six and seventeen were shadowed, chiefly by the prison house of school. When I read, 'The Youth, who daily farther from the east must travel', I interpreted the words quite literally and lived for when I could reverse my direction. Now, remembering rather than travelling is all that is left, and I must try and remember with honesty. Professor Eric Stokes, in his brilliant essay on Rudyard Kipling, says of that interpreter of British India that he suffered from 'the foreclosure of sensibility that shut out all conflict, so that the mind could bathe in idealized images and every element and character observe a perfect fit.' Perhaps you will find my images idealized and, if so, it is because I can honestly say I was never aware of conflict. I mean conflict of cultures – cultural shock. I came across this expression quite recently and dismissed it as psychological jargon. Then I analysed it and realised that this, maybe, was what soured Indo-British relations, though the experience did not come my way.

But I must emphasize that during my adult years in India, and I am using the term to denote the whole sub-continent, I did no more than browse round the edges of its culture and history. I am in no way an expert, but an ordinary person who spent much of the leisure we all enjoyed in following up clues received in my childhood.

Nirad Chaudhuri writes that Max Müller, the nineteenth century orientalist and philologist, 'thought and said that British rule would be more understanding and sympathetic and therefore more productive of good for the Indian people if the ruling order became familiar with their culture.' Though Max Müller lived and worked in Oxford, he was German by race and education and received his inspiration from German orientalists who, in their turn, had been inspired by British scholars working in India at the end of the eighteenth and beginning of the nineteenth centuries. As the latter century advanced, British opinion narrowed and hardened until everything 'native', though allowed to be picturesque and curious, was given inferior status.

It so happens that a thin thread of circumstance linked my interest in Indian culture and history to those British scholars who blazed a trail, afterwards sadly obscured by the moral and intellectual vanity of their successors.

Warren Hastings was himself a competent orientalist, and then there were administrators – H. T. Colebrooke, Mark Wilks, Colonel James Tod, Mountstuart Elphinstone and others – who found time to study Sanskrit and Persian classics and the history of the areas they governed. They were men bred and educated in the rational, intellectually inquiring atmosphere of the late eighteenth century and thus well grounded in the disciplines of European classicism. The epics of Greece and Rome and those of the Hindus have so much in common as to form, and even in philosophy, that it was natural for men trained in the one culture to move on into the other.

In addition to the administrators there were full-time orientalists, notably Sir William Jones, who founded the Asiatic Society of Bengal in 1784 and published their work in its journal, *Asiatic Researches*. This work not only influenced German scholars but Indian scholars as well, and this latter influence was to breed political consequences in that it revived the national honour and self-respect of Hindus. It is this period of British Indian history

which has always most appealed to me, and which I studied in
depth when I was writing a life of the Marquess Wellesley. He was
a Governor-General who has often been abused for arrogance and
imperialism. In all the books about him which I read, I never found
justice done to one of his enlightened acts, the founding of the
College of Fort William at Calcutta. This was a mixture of Eton and
Christ Church designed to supplement the meagre attainments of
young 'writers' in the East India Company. A most severe curricu-
lum was imposed on the young men which included Hindu and
Moslem law. Lord Wellesley, an intellectual himself, recognized
intellect in others, no matter who they might be. He engaged what
he describes as 'one hundred learned natives' to be on the staff of
the College. When the Court of Directors of the East India Company closed it down he records his dismay at the injustice done to
the *munshis* and *pandits* summoned from far and wide to take up
honourable positions in Calcutta. The Directors were annoyed, for
they had not been informed or consulted by the Governor-General
before the College was set up, in fact not till they got the bill for it.
They established a truncated College in its place at Haileybury in
Hertfordshire, which became a public school in 1858 when the
administration of India passed to the Crown. Boys with an ambition to serve in India were sent there by their parents in the
nineteenth century. My father was one of them. This is one strand
of the thread.

Lord Wellesley further demonstrated his recognition of intellect
by appointing one William Carey, a Baptist missionary, to pro-
fessorships of Sanskrit, Bengali and Hindi at the College of Fort
William. When this William Carey and his friend, Joshua Marshman, first came to India in 1792, they were not allowed to settle in
the territories of the East India Company. Any proselytizing was a
punishable offence in those days, as it was held to be disruptive and
unsettling to the natives of the country. Carey and Marshman
moved about uneasily and finally, in 1799, took refuge in the
Danish-owned settlement of Serampore, twenty miles up the
Hooghly from Calcutta. William Carey was no ordinary missionary. He was a scholar, a philologist, an inspired educationalist. He
brought a press with him and printed in nearly forty different
languages and dialects. His primary object was the dissemination
of the Christian scriptures, but he also wrote and printed text

books for the College and opened the door to developments in
Bengali literature which ranged far throughout the oriental field.
He was a pioneer in the study of Chinese and, finally, the founder
of a newspaper, *The Friend of India*, which was later incorporated
into *The Statesman* of Calcutta, published to this day. My maternal
grandfather, George Smith, edited this paper from 1859 to 1874.
William Carey died in 1834 and Joshua Marshman in 1837, so my
grandfather never knew them personally. But no one working at
Serampore ever after escaped their influence. They formulated a
covenant which may not always, as the years went by, have been
strictly observed, but which prevailed in spirit:

> To set an infinite value on the individual soul
> To esteem and treat Indians always as our equals
> To abstain from whatever deepens India's prejudices
> To engage in every work that is for India's good
> To be instant in the nurture of personal religion
> To give ourselves without reserve, not counting even
>   the clothes we wear as our own.

Thus an atmosphere untouched by racial superiority or authoritarian prejudice descended to George Smith and to his children,
some of whom served India in various capacities. Ideas, family
legends and attitudes of mind reached my generation, though I am
the only one of that generation to have lived and worked in India.
My brother, however, piloted the India Bill of 1935 through the
House of Commons and, though this Bill was regarded as inadequate by Indian politicians, it was a beginning, even if the sequel
is not quite what was envisaged. Great-grandchildren of George
and Janet Smith are involved in Indian affairs to this day. One has
just been appointed British High Commissioner in Delhi; another
is happily married to an Indian in the Civil Service of his country.

My father and his elder brother, Harcourt Butler, were the first
of their family to have anything to do with the East, but they seem
immediately to have felt at home there. My father was a classical
scholar of some distinction and it was natural that he should be
attracted to the Hindu classics though, by the time he joined the
Indian Civil Service, there was not the same leisure for study that
his predecessors of the eighteenth century had enjoyed. I still have
his copy of extracts from the *Ramayana* and the *Mahabharata*,

collected by J. C. Oman, with his comments in the margins and a
pencilled genealogical tree of the Pandava brethren on the back
fly-leaf. One of our favourite nursery books was called *Stories of
Indian Gods and Heroes*, and it stood on the shelf next to Charles
Kingsley's Greek *The Heroes*. The Indian book was, of course,
extracts from the two great Sanskrit epics, told to the children. The
illustrations were beautiful and I loved this book and knew it as
well as I knew Hans Andersen or Peter Pan. I liked it better than
the stories of Greek gods and heroes. I remember so well the
picture of King Yudhisthira, the eldest of the Pandavas, walking
along a narrow path by an abyss, his way impeded by skulls and
bones. He had refused to enter Paradise without his faithful dog,
and had then gone to the 'abodes of anguish' to redeem his four
brothers and their joint wife, Draupadi. This is one of the oldest
versions of the doctrine of saviour and redeemer.

In his book, *Jung and the Story of Our Time*, Laurens Van der
Post says that Greek and Roman cultures 'both have their origin in
one and the same story or myth which, joined to the Hebraic theme
as set out in the Bible, was to provide the greatest formative values
of the complex of the western spirit.' The *Ramayana* and the
Mahabharata have certainly provided the greatest formative values
of the complex of the Hindu spirit. If these western and eastern
epics are placed side by side, I think they can be seen to be part of
the same archetypal myth, to use an expression employed by Jung
himself. I do not feel qualified to enlarge on this profound subject;
it is treated in depth by Nirad Chaudhuri in his book *The Continent
of Circe*, and also in his interpretation of the life and work of Max
Müller.

The purely political affiliation of the British with the Indian
sub-continent was a moment in time, as human history goes, and it
is a great pity that in the hey-day of the Empire this passing
moment was glorified at the expense of a more ancient, a holier
bond.

The cultural influences of my childhood were continued into
adolescence for, during the First World War when our parents
were in India, my brother and I spent our holidays with our
mother's brother, James Dunlop-Smith who was political A.D.C.
at the India Office. He had been in the Political Service and had a
host of Indian friends. He was born at Serampore, and suckled by

an Indian nurse. Martin Gilbert, now editing the definitive life of
Winston Churchill, published a book about Dunlop-Smith called
Servant of India. I am going to quote a piece which I wrote for it:

> The house in Ovington Square was full of India. I do not mean
> elephant head tables and Benares brass, but books and talk and,
> above all – Indians. It was war-time and on Sunday evenings
> distinguished members of the princely order came to supper, in
> uniform, with wonderful Rajput turbans on their heads, and
> Rab and I were allowed to stay up and meet them. Before the
> Indian guests arrived, Aunt Minnie, Dunlop's sister, took down
> two round bells, with spiked edges, which lived on the dining-
> room mantelpiece, and by special manipulation she made them
> ring plaintively, giving long, mournful echoes. She said they
> were temple bells and would ring in the right atmosphere. Uncle
> Dunlop and his guests always conversed in Hindi. Deep, soft,
> rich voices with that gently thunderous throaty note which
> English speakers can hardly every produce. Uncle Dunlop had a
> particularly beautiful voice and read aloud to us from Kipling's
> Indian books, and he had known Kipling well in India and could
> explain who many of his famous characters really were.

Incidentally, my uncle was the original of Colonel Forsyth Sahib,
from the story 'In the Presence'.

Aunt Minnie had a friend called Gabrielle Festing who wrote
books for young people. One was called *The Land of Princes*, which
was a précis of Colonel Tod's *Annals and Antiquities of Rajas'than*.
From this we could picture how –

> All night long the Barons came
> The Lords of the Outer Guard
> All night the cressets glimmered pale
> On Ulwar sabre and Tonk jezail
> Mewar headstall and Marwar mail
> That clinked in the Palace yard.

Memories of our childhood in Rajas'than were evoked, memories
restored to life when I went back to that enchanted part of India
after I left school. Then there was a book called *Prince of Dreamers*,
about Babur, the first and most endearing of the Moguls. But my
favourite of all was *The Adventures of Akbar* by Flora Annie Steel – a

somewhat fictional account of the childhood of the greatest of the
dynasty. This book was magnificently illustrated by Byam Shaw,
who must have been to India to demonstrate so vividly the influence of Mogul architecture and Mogul painting.

Flora Annie Steel invented a character called Roy the Rajput.
When Akbar's father Humayon and his wife and baby son were in
flight from his rebellious brothers, across the burning deserts of
Jaisalmer, they came upon a boy dying of exposure and rescued
him, so that he lived and became Akbar's playmate and compan-
ion. I think Flora Annie brought this character into her book to
underline Akbar's tolerance of faiths other than his own and his
later marriages into Rajput families. Roy is supposed, in the book,
to have lost his memory but in due course is proved to be of a
princely house. Flora Annie makes him tell the child Akbar old
Rajput legends, notably about Rajah Rasalu who swung seventy
maidens all in one swing. Later on Akbar was imprisoned by his
cruel Uncle Kumran in the Bala Hissar at Kabul. Humayon collected an army and brought it before the city to rescue his son. The
pride of the army was a huge gun called 'Thunder of God' and this
was trained on the walls of the fortress. As the master gunner
stepped forward with a lighted fuse to fire the charge, a figure was
seen speeding across the intervening plain. It was Roy the Rajput
crying out with frantic gestures, 'The Bastion, the Bastion – the
Heir to Empire!' Kumran had hung Akbar over the walls in a cage
to be slain by his own father, but Roy saved him. This is quite an
authentic story but it is usually stated that the 'Heir to Empire' was
protected by his nurse. As a child I believed implicitly in Roy the
Rajput, and never remember the story without emotion.

When I returned in 1922 to live in Old Delhi, the new city was
only about a foot high. The countryside remained wild. If you rode
out towards the Purana Quila, the Old Fort, you would see black
buck and peafowl everywhere. The Purana Quila was where Humayon, at last firmly established as Emperor, sat in his library at
the top of a tower. Rising hastily when he heard the call to prayer,
he fell on the steep steps to his death. I climbed down those steps
very carefully, thinking of Humayon. But long, long before his
day, this area of Delhi was where Indrapasthra, the glorious city of
the Pandavas, is said to have been situated. From the top of the
ancient Qutb Minar, not so very far away, you look out over the

cockpit of Hindustan. It is not the battlefield of the Pandavas, as I was told in my youth; that—Kurukshetra—is further north at Thaneswar in the Punjab. But on the immense plain of Panipat successive invaders of Upper India came to victory or death. The Emperor Babur won a victory here in 1525; Akbar in 1556; here the Mahrattas bid for an empire and were defeated by Afghan forces which finally packed up and went away, leaving Delhi to be eventually taken by the British. Akbar made no real impact on Delhi—he is to be found at Agra and Fatehpur Sikri. Here he would sit in the Hall of Worship, on a pillar shaped like a lotus, while all around him the representatives of different religions argued about it and about, while the Emperor listened and dreamed of a universal religion, the Din-I-Illahi. This had been the vision of Kabir, an Islamic mystic of the fourteenth century. Akbar was more human; the head of his new Faith was to be himself. It is interesting to note that he was contemporary with the Reformation in Europe, and only one generation older than our King Henry VIII.

So it was, in those days, that I relived the past. It may well be asked, what impressions did you receive of the present? How did you see the future? It is difficult to convey to the modern mind how natural and normal our lives in India seemed then to be. British visitors now are, almost without exception, shocked and shaken by the contrasts in wealth, the beauty and romance on the one hand, the suffering and poverty on the other. It may be that the pervading atmosphere of acceptance, which is very strong in the East, also affected those of us who lived there. But it so happened that I went back to England for a year and did some work in the East End of London, and this awoke my social conscience but not my heart. I took both back to India with me and looked around with fresh eyes. It was not easy for anyone to initiate any sort of welfare work, as it is called today, without status or authority. I never commanded anything like that until my husband took charge of the Governor's Bodyguard in Bombay and was king in a little kingdom consisting of two troops of horse, Punjabi Mussulmans and Sikhs, many of whom had their wives and children with them. In this community we were free to initiate anything we liked. I was able to visit and get to know the families of the men. This was something which may have started as a Lady Bountiful act, but very soon I found I was learning more from these women than they learnt from me; I grew

to love them dearly and we had a lot of fun together in a simple way.
Naturally we became involved in the religious festivals of our
military 'family' and also of our servants. At Dassehra, the ten days
which celebrate the victory of Rama over the demon Ravana,
symbolic of the victory of good over evil, the finale of the *Ramayana*, all weapons of war were garlanded – sword, rifle, shot
gun, service revolver. The horses came up from the stables with
roses on their headstalls and marigolds round their fetlocks,
coloured shawls on their backs. During Ramzan we joined our
Muslim friends in watching eagerly for the new moon of the Id. I
remember when the only son of the Sikh ressaldar-major died, and
the child's mother seemed likely to die too of a broken heart. I was
asked to join in a procession to carry the Granth Sahib, the holy
book of the Khalsa, to her house and pray there. I first heard of the
Granth Sahib when I was a child. My grandfather and his friend,
Meredith Townsend, whom he succeeded as Editor of the *Friend of
India*, had a bet with each other that no rhyme could be found for
the words 'orange' and 'month'. Meredith Townsend won with
this quatrain:

> From the Indus to the Blorange
> Went the Rajah in a month,
> Sucking now and then an orange,
> Reading all the time his Granth.

There really is a river called the Blorange. It is a tributary of the
Oxus. We enjoyed this verse as children and, arising out of it, we
were told about the Indus, the Blorange and, above all, the Granth
and what it meant to the Sikh community. I made a picture in my
imagination of the Rajah. He would be in a palanquin and before
reverently turning the pages of his Granth he would wash his hands
free of orange juice. I based him on our friend the old Rajah of
Nabha who gave to Rab and me lovely Sikh dresses which we wore
at fancy dress parties.

These were simple bridges across the gulf between East and
West. More complicated bridges, so complicated as to be almost
impassable, are built of the various aspects of Hinduism, or Sana-
tana Dharma, the Eternal Way. Many western people, especially
among the young, are now attracted to some of these aspects. I see

that Professor Carstairs will be touching on this subject;* I long to know what Indian perceptions of the 'Hippy' cult can be. Nirad Chaudhuri, whom I cannot help constantly quoting because he is stimulating and provocative, says: 'There are few characters which are more painfully unattractive than the Hinduizing occidental. The Hindus have detected this weakness and have not been slow in setting their mountebanks on the West. It enables a number of my countrymen to make a comfortable livelihood.' The situation appears to me as if eastern people became 'Shakers' or 'Holy Rollers'. The outward and visible sign is often taken for the inward and spiritual grace. All the same, I must witness to a constant impression of some sort of transcendental awareness from which I never escaped in India. Indeed I did not wish to. I missed it when I returned to England. It was an atmosphere found among Moslems as well as Hindus and I am told that in these days it is much weakened. Even if this is so, this legacy of the centuries will take a lot of destroying, and I suspect that it is some desire for it, a search for it, that renders western youth 'god-intoxicated', to use Professor Carstairs' term. But it is not enough to chant *Hare Krishna* and shave your head, or even to stand on it. The real thing, in so far as I understand it, is much more difficult.

I think it was the Kailasa Cave at Ellora in the Deccan, which first made me aware of just how difficult. The sculptures of the Kailasa date from the third and fourth centuries AD when the Brahmins were disturbed by inroads on their teaching made by Buddhism and Jainism. The impression these sculptures made upon me was of a Prometheus Bound. It seemed that an elusive quality, apprehended only by the initiated, must be seized and crushed, thrust into the narrow limitations of the intellect. Life, said these sculptures, even in its basest manifestations, is worthy of worship because it is what we are, and to life we must always return; there is no end to the cycle.

The Buddhist caves at Ellora are quite different in feeling.†The Visvakarma Cave has a vaulted, ribbed ceiling cut from the heart

---

* See next paper of which the title in lecture form was *God-intoxicated Youth: Indian perceptions of European Hippies.*
† Of the 34 caves at Ellora, 17 are Hindu – Kailasa being one; 12 are Buddhist and the remaining 5 are Jain. *Eds.*

of the hill. The colossal presiding figure is that of the Buddha to come, the Lord Maitreya. The Cave is small but so perfectly proportioned that an impression of great space is achieved. The echo of a voice ripples round the roof and splashes into an immense silence. Below in the plain, the wheel goes round: you can see it from the cave mouth—suffering, the origin of suffering. Above, the vast image implies extinction of suffering, Nirvana. There is the trouble; here is the answer for those who can find it. I was fortunate enough to visit Ellora and Ajanta twice, with plenty of leisure to examine and think over all I found there. I cannot imagine how a package tour reacts to them today. Western people often recoil from the violence of Hindu symbolism, or titter at the erotic implications as if they were leafing over a sex magazine. Hindu art is an effort to give form to a sacramental attitude to the creation of life. It is not factual but symbolic.

I visited these caves when my husband was employed by the Nizam of Hyderabad in whose territories they lay. This was during the last two years before the War, and it seems significant that we spent the end of an era in such a sophisticated, elegant and yet expiring society. One could hear tumbrils in the distance. It was in Hyderabad that I broadened my knowledge of Islam, for there were opportunities to meet highly educated and devout Moslems who accepted us as friends. The ruling class were all Moslem, since the Nizam's dynasty descends from a Viceroy of the Deccan appointed by a Mogul emperor of the eighteenth century. The population was Hindu and now, like all the other semi-independent States, Hyderabad is part of India and rulers and ruled have, presumably, more in common. The British have often been criticized for favouring Moslems more than Hindus. I think, in all honesty, that this may have been so socially because Christianity and Islam have a good deal in common. We are people of one book, the Old Testament, along with the Jews. I remember hearing a moving performance of Benjamin Britten's oratorio, *Abraham and Isaac*, a few years ago in the majestic, very English setting of Blickling Hall in Norfolk. I immediately thought of the festival of the Bakr Id – which celebrates the finding of the ram in the thicket when Abraham bound Isaac to slay him in obedience to the commandments of God. Sikhism is easier for us too; the teachings of Guru Nanak, the founder, are very close in spirit to the Sermon on the Mount. We are all three very young compared to Hindu philosophy, Hindu culture. We are sometimes impatient, as the young are with the old.

The ladies of Hyderabad were very emancipated, even in those days, and I had friends in purdah as well. I have never been able to understand the fuss made by some British people about purdah – I mean in the social sense. It was certainly one reason given for lack of integration between the races. There was nothing to prevent British women from meeting and making friends with their Indian sisters behind the veil. Naturally one was expected to speak Hindi or Urdu, and very polite my friends were about my faulty speech. Hyderabadis speak a very pure, Persianized Urdu. Looking round at our permissive society, I cannot help feeling sometimes that a little purdah would not do any harm. One of my dearest friends set her face firmly against emancipation. I could see her point of view; she had status and power in her own home – in fact her household were rather afraid of her because she possessed psychic gifts. I diffidently suggested that she might lift the veil for her daughters, but she did not agree. She felt that they would be happier under her protection. Her enemies accused her of being a witch and she once asked if she might visit me to perform healing ceremonies after I had had a bad accident. She cast certain spells, which included the use of cold iron, a tray of nails, which I was bidden to touch and then they were thrown away, with the correct prayers made over them. The occult significance of cold iron is part of European legend, so I was very interested. This may have helped to make me better, though I think the real reason was that the offering was made with affection.

Ancient spells, folk lore and fairy tales should never be despised. All religions are rooted in them. In the West we have covered them up with concrete and machinery. Why does everyone struggle to keep a little bit of the garden going, even if it is only a window-box? It is because of mother earth. Some of my dearest memories of India are of jungle days. I admit we went there to shoot wild animals but this was much more controlled than is now realized, and in many cases it was done at the request of the jungle people whose precarious livelihood was threatened by predators. In the vast forests on the borders of Madras and what was then the Central

Provinces, I met tribal communities untouched by Hinduism, living as they must have done in pre-Aryan days. Their primal deity was Mother Earth. Sita, the heroine of the *Ramayana*, was born of an earth furrow. It is thus she first appears in the *Rig Veda*, which is older than the *Ramayana*. At the end of the epic she lies down to die on the ground and is received back into the bosom of her mother. The jungles I travelled in several parts of India were much as they must have been when Rama and Sita passed years of exile among them, as did the Pandava brethren when they were turned out of their kingdom. The armies of Hanuman, who helped Rama to find and rescue Sita from the demon Ravana in Lanka, were not bears and monkeys as often portrayed, but the original Dravidians, called Vanars. In the uninhabited areas of the jungle, away from encampments and fires, animal and man are on equal footing. One could understand how it would be easy to worship the one as much as the other. The animal forms in Hindu imagery are perfectly logical.

At the outbreak of war my husband returned to the Army. I decided to be a nurse in a military hospital, but there was no opportunity for this at first. We were at Ahmednagar in the Deccan at the time and one day, when wandering in the city, I came upon a Salvation Army hospital and was moved to go in and ask if I could help. I worked there part-time for a few months and it was a great experience. People in the Club said, 'The Salvation Army, good heavens, do you bang a tambourine?' The Salvation Army cares for the poorest of the poor everywhere, and in India that means something. There was no time in that hospital for anything but constant unremitting care and compassion. That was the prayer and praise offered daily. It was here I came to know Mahratta people well, though I never mastered the language properly. I enjoyed their unique sense of humour which has a banana-skin quality in that it is often exercised at other people's expense. But it carries them through appalling hardships with a smile. When I came to research the Mahratta Wars for my biography of Lord Wellesley, I was glad I had got to know them as real people. I could better envisage their system of warfare and their terrifying predatory toughness. I also did a bit of work for an American mission which ran a sisal fibre industry for untouchables. The Harijans had always soaked the sisal in the main open drain of their village and then made ropes out of it. This did not bring in much money. My friends in the Mission taught them to dye and weave the sisal into very pretty handbags, hats, sandals, mats and such like things which were sold in quite grand shops in Calcutta and Bombay. Looms were set up in the hutments and the standard of living in the village greatly improved. Thus I got to know something at first hand of the Harijans.

Of course, we Christians are all untouchables in the eyes of caste Hindus. I wonder sometimes how the *Hare Krishna* boys and girls stand in the matter of caste. When I did finally get to work in an Indian military hospital I realized the great strength of caste even among quite humble people, even some of the largely Moslem nursing orderlies. They would not do any cleaning-up work or wash and tend the few sad sweeper patients. As the orderlies had never been given any nursing training, I held blanket bath instruction sessions using a sweeper patient as victim. After a little explanation and demonstration, the barriers were broken down. But when the idiotic Colonel of the hospital removed all sweepers from every ward simultaneously for a kit inspection, chaos reigned.

These experiences were hardly cultural but they did extend knowledge and, thereby, understanding. I was so lucky to be born into a little knowledge and to be led on to a little more, but you had to step off the main routes to find it.

> A stone's throw out on either hand
> From the well-ordered road we tread
> And all the world is wild and strange.

Professor Stokes quotes these lines from Kipling to explain 'foreclosure of sensibility' – the well-ordered road is necessary to protect the dreamer while dreaming, necessary to preserve the dream. I hope my memories of India are not all dreams. I feel inclined to say to those who insist upon the hatred and fear which was supposed to come between Indians and Britons in colonial days, 'How do you know it was *all* like that? You were not there.' To which they would, I think, answer, '*You* cannot judge objectively because you *were* there.' Yes, I was there and my roots came up shrieking, as a mandrake is said to do. They have never quite settled

down since and give faint squeaks now and then. So I return to
Wordsworth where I began this talk:

> We will grieve not, rather find
> Strength in what remains behind;
> In the primal sympathy
> Which having been must ever be;
> . . . . . .
> In years that bring the philosophic mind.

6

Changes over Time in Western Perceptions of Hindu Culture

PROFESSOR G. M. CARSTAIRS

A striking phenomenon of the last fifteen years has been the lively interest shown in many aspects of Hindu culture by young people in the Western world. There was no hint of this in that eloquent articulation of adolescent mood of the late 1940s, J. D. Salinger's *The Catcher in the Rye*, nor in the nineteen year old Truman Capote's best-selling *Other Voices, Other Rooms*. The swing towards yoga, mysticism and meditation was heralded by Allen Ginsberg and Jack Kerouac (*The Dharma Bums*) in the 1950s and early '60s but it assumed full force only after the Beat Generation had been succeeded by the Hippies and their more ethereal off-shoot, the Flower People. When the Beatles displayed their fleeting adherence to the Maharishi, in the mid-sixties, this no doubt helped to swell the tide which was already by this time running strongly.

Later in this essay I shall draw attention to the impact made on Indian society, and especially on its younger members, by the influx of Hippies not only from America but also from Australia, Japan and Western Europe, who made themselves conspicuous from Cape Comarin to Kathmandu. First of all, however, I should like to recall two earlier streams of visitors from the West who also made an impact on the Indian scene during the last half-century of the British Raj; namely, the Missionaries and the Theosophists. Throughout the 18th century there were Chaplains in all the main stations of the East India Company, but religious observance was formal rather than devout: the English were uninterested in missionary activity, leaving that to the various Catholic orders, mostly Portuguese and Italians, or French. The Italian priest Roberto de Nobili adopted the life-style of a Brahmin sannyasi, and pretended to have no connection with other Catholics: but he was formally condemned by the Pope in 1744. The Jesuits in their turn tolerated many Hindu practices among their converts.

The early Protestant missionaries (Danish and German, together with some English) were viewed with suspicion, contempt and wonder by their mercantile fellow Christians. Many of them denounced native beliefs intemperately, but Christian Frederick Schwarz who worked in South India from 1750 to 1798 began his mission by making a careful study of Hindu sacred books. Unlike most of his fellows, he did not denounce Hindu beliefs while extolling Christian ones.

During the 18th century there was clear social segregation between the English, the Hindus and the Moslems alike; but little or no prejudice of superiority. Racial prejudice increased in the 19th century with the advent of the Mem-Sahibs and the development of Anglo-Indian snobbery: it was exacerbated by the great Indian revolt of 1857, with its atrocities and savage reprisals. Yet at this same period there was an upswing of Victorian piety and missionary fervour, in which my own maternal grandmother, and both of my parents took part. The former was a Miss Margaret Hunter Hardie, of Scottish extraction, but born and raised in the small town of Hawesville, Kentucky. In 1875 she embarked with a group of Protestant missionaries on a series of journeys by ship and train which were to take her to London, Paris and Rome before a final stage by bullock-cart deposited her in a mission bungalow in Mynpoorie, U.P. Throughout her voyage and early months in India she wrote letters to her friends at home and these were preserved for posterity by being published in the *Hawesville Plain Dealer*.

In a letter written a few weeks after her arrival in India, she expressed attitudes towards Hindus and Hinduism which were typical of missionaries of that period: 'These people are not savages; the native men have their homes, their wives and children whom they love dearly. They send their children to school, when they can, and beat their wives, when necessary, both for their own good. But as regards their spiritual conditions, I can hardly tell you how very low they are. Their gods are hideous, ill-smelling, disgusting objects, and their number and name is legion ... These gods are the tangible images of their poor depraved minds – low and horrible beyond description.'

Miss Hardie's missionary work was cut short by illness: during her first hot weather in India she became so ill that the Mission doctor insisted that she must not risk another one. On her way back to America, however, she met a Scottish clergyman and married him: in 1877 she was writing home from the Manse of Southend, Kintyre, and giving an account of the debauchery and depravity of the Scottish peasants which fairly put them on par with the natives of Mynpoorie!

In that same year of 1875, a different type of interest in Indian life, thought and religious beliefs was signalled by the foundation, in New York, of the Theosophical Society. Its creation was largely due to a remarkable woman, Madame Helena Petrovna Blavatsky, who was born in 1831 into a noble Russian family, in St. Petersburg. At the age of seventeen she married a much older man but separated from him within a few months. For the next few years she travelled widely, including a trip to Tibet in 1856, when she was twenty-five years old. She must have had considerable charm because she was welcomed in society both in Europe and America and took a lively interest in art, philosophy and the occult. In 1873, in New York, she joined a group of prominent people who were studying spritualism, and personally exposed some 'spirit' phenomena as fraudulent.

Still her curiosity was undaunted. In 1875, with her older collaborator, Colonel Alcott, she founded the Theosophical Society whose objects were:

1. To establish a nucleus of the universal brotherhood of humanity.
2. To promote the study of comparative religion and philosophy.
3. To make a systematic investigation into the occult, the mystic potencies of life and matter.

In 1877 she published *Isis Unveiled* which contained remarkably idiosyncratic theories about the evolution of humanity, and of religion. Two years later she travelled to India with Colonel Alcott and established the headquarters of Theosophy in Adyar, a suburb of Madras. She embraced a number of Hindu concepts into a revised programme of the Theosophical Society, including that of re-birth. She also claimed supernatural powers (which were indignantly repudiated by her former colleagues in the Society for

Psychical Research) and maintained that she was in daily communication with Buddhist *mahatmas* in Tibet. In spite of – or perhaps because of – these flights of imagination she attracted a world-wide following of over 100,000 adherents before her death in 1891.

Thanks to her, Theosophy became for two generations the main focus of Western interest in Hindu thought. At the same time, of course, Sanskrit scholarship was being quietly pursued, as it had been by some of the earliest visitors to India. Even Warren Hastings, although in some ways a typical merchant adventurer, studied Hindu codes of law and in 1785 wrote prophetically in his preface to one of the first English translations of the Bhagavadgita, that works like this 'will survive when the British dominion in India shall have long ceased to exist and when the sources which it once yielded of wealth and power are lost to remembrance.'

The Germans were first in the field of Indian scholarship, led by Friedrich Schlegel, author of *The Language and Wisdom of the Indians* (1808) and by August Wilhelm von Schlegel who became the world's first Professor of Sanskrit in 1818. Later in the nineteenth century Schopenhauer, Hartmann, Nietzsche, Wagner and Heine were all influenced by translations from Hindu and Buddhist texts by such scholars as F. Max Müller, L. von Schroeder and A. Kaegi. Their work was extended into the early years of the twentieth century by the British orientalists J. Muir (who published English translations of original Sanskrit texts in 1889), A. A. Macdonnell and Arthur Berriedale Keith, while Sri S. Radhakrishnan became the most distinguished of many Indian scholars who presented Hindu philosophy to the West.

The Theosophist movement might well have dwindled after Madame Blavatsky's death but for the appearance of another even more remarkable woman who became her disciple and spiritual successor. This was Annie Besant, a person of strong character and unorthodox ideas. She was married to an Anglican clergyman but startled mid-Victorian society by declaring herself to be a theist, and then an atheist, after which she obtained a legal separation from her husband. For some years she worked with Charles Bradlaugh, the celebrated atheist and social reformer, and became a pioneer of birth control – then a gravely scandalous concept. George Bernard Shaw made her acquaintance and converted her to

Fabian Socialism, but after a few years she joined a more extreme left-wing group.

In 1889 she chanced upon Madame Blavatsky's book *The Secret Doctrine* and underwent another conversion experience. Five years later she travelled to India for the first time and at once announced her 'discovery' that most of her previous incarnations had been Hindus. She herself became a Hindu, and an active supporter of the Swaraj freedom movement. In later years, however, she quarrelled with both Gandhi and Nehru because she found their political ideas too moderate.

In 1909 she discovered a talented child, J. Krishnamurti and declared him to be a new incarnation of Lord Krishna. She announced a new religion, the Order of the Star of India with him at its head; but in 1929 the young man broke with her and with her religion, renouncing his messianic role and repudiating his divinity. (He has remained to this day an eloquent and thoughtful philosopher whose works are widely read: but he firmly rebukes his admirers when they seek to venerate him.)

Annie Besant's long involvement with India began just at the time when late-Victorian enthusiasm for propagating the Christian faith was nearing its zenith. It was about that time – 1904, to be exact – that my father first set foot on Indian soil: he was to work as a missionary in Rajas'than for the next 30 years. His first reactions to the manifestations of popular Hinduism were as negative as those of my grandmother, thirty years earlier. Within a few weeks of reaching Rajas'than he wrote in a letter to a friend at home: 'A holy procession blocked the street today. Holy men sat on an elephant which waddled slowly templewards. Two wild-haired naked men, smeared with yellow ochre, danced in front to clear the way, brandishing naked swords. I squashed through to the clear space where they were dancing. They scowled at me but went on leaping about. Their eyes had a dull sort of glaze as if they had been drugged – I think they had. The whole thing was bestial – as bestial as the vile-looking idols at the corner of the bazaar streets . . . I had learned for certain already that there are viler things done under the Hindu religion than one cares to think about.'

And yet, only three weeks later, a different tone is apparent in his letters: 'I am gradually discovering that from the conventional point of view at least I am a bad missionary. I have friends whom I admire and like who are Hindus or Mohammedans or nothing at all, and I don't feel any smell of brimstone about them.'

Among those whom he came to admire was Mahatma Gandhi – and this at a time when the Mahatma had few admirers among the British in India. I still possess an old leather purse which contains a package of rough salt inscribed by my father's hand as a relic of Gandhi's famous Salt March of 1930, one of his dramatic acts of pacific defiance of the British Raj.

Some years later, after my father's return to Scotland, I heard him preaching in a Presbyterian church and taking as his text not the customary verse from the Bible, but a saying which he had heard pronounced by a Brahmin, giving *satsang* (religious enlightenment) to a group of listeners under a banyan tree in an Indian village. Both he and a fellow-Scottish missionary, Andrew Low, became esteemed, in their later years in Rajas'than, as men who were familiar with the moral teachings of the Bhagavadgita and the Koran, as well as of the Bible.

As the tide of missionary fervour abated, during the course of the present century, a number of missionaries demonstrated their scholarship in Sanskrit, Pali and Tibetan scriptures. Like other Western orientalists they found that they had much in common with Indian scholars in Benares, Calcutta and other Hindu centres of learning.

There have thus been three main currents of Western interest in India, the missionaries, the orientalists and the would-be yogis, or disciples of yogis. In recent years the Theosophists have been succeeded, in the third of these categories, by waves of young people from the Western countries who have been emotionally drawn towards the practice of meditation and the study of Hindu and Buddhist teachings. Since the mid-60s India has seen a new type of tourist in the person of young Hippies roaming the countryside, congregating on Goan beaches or in the outskirts of Kathmandu or visiting the more celebrated ashrams.

These peripatetic seekers after the Hindu experience are to be distinguished from the much smaller number of people who have become profoundly involved in the Hindu way of life, and have made India their home. Among these, women have outnumbered men. One recalls the woman acolytes, some young and some not so young, who formed part of Mahatma Gandhi's entourage in his later years, and there are several elderly ladies who have spent many years in various ashrams. In recent years some of the contemporary 'Seekers' have been carried away by the appeal of a particular Guru and have become his (or her) disciples: but all too often, as the writer Ruth P. Jhabvala has described in her recent works (*A New Dominion, Heat and Dust, How I Became a Holy Mother*) the involvement, initially ecstatic, ends dismally in sickness and disillusion.

For the last dozen years or more I have encountered numbers of these usually impecunious young people in New Delhi's Connaught Place, a way-station in their wanderings. I have often invited them, in twos or threes, to join me in a meal and have heard stories of their adventures and misfortunes, or rewarding experiences and sometimes bitter dillusionment. As the late '60s merged into the early '70s it seems that for more and more of them the journey to the promised land of spiritual enlightenment has proved sadly disappointing. The quest on which they had embarked was one aspect of the Western adolescent counter-culture of the nineteen-sixties, which found expression in defiant repudiation of the values of adult society in one country after another. Here one has to bear in mind that in every community 'socialization' has consisted in the transmission of the skills and insights obtained by the ancestors, together with their interpretation of the meaning of the universe, and the purpose of man's life within it. Normally the young have either willingly or reluctantly come to terms with their inheritance. Why did so many refuse to do so during the 1960s? They expressed a mood, rather than any clearly defined intentions. Throughout the decade, a persistent element in the successive manifestations of the young has been a rejection of things intellectual, a celebration of myth, fantasy and creative imagination. This has greatly alarmed many of their elders, to whom it seemed a retrograde step towards primitivism; but perhaps they took it too seriously. The young undoubtedly reproached their parents with taking many things – such as material possessions, social status, and 'success' – very much too seriously. Having rediscovered the pleasures of creativity, and of sensuous experience, young people soon realised that their parents' way of life demanded a postponement, if not a renunciation, of these new-found joys in the interest of 'getting on in the world': and in large numbers they preferred to opt out of the competitive world of study and work.

The so-called 'alienated youth' has not been politically motivated, except for forthright denunciation of social wrongs, such as US involvement in the war in Indo-China, and racial discrimination in all its manifestations; but in its early years, as a number of sociologists have pointed out, it was content to assert a mood of affirmation of non-intellectual values, of openness to experience (including the novel experiences induced by marijuana or LSD) rather than to seek clearly-defined alternative values to take the place of those of the acquisitive society. During the late 1960s and early '70s, however, there appears to have been a rather widespread hankering for some system of belief which would make sense of their existence: and for hundreds of thousands of young people certain elements of oriental philosophy seemed to meet this need. These elements are: the assertion of the superiority of spirit over matter, the latter being regarded as fundamentally illusory; the resort to techniques of meditation in order to achieve self-mastery and contact with one's own inner spiritual resources; and, as a corollary to the above, a willingness to subordinate oneself to an admired esoteric teacher, or Guru.

The social history of Western society in general, and of America in particular, has contained numerous instances of emotionally-charged revivalist Christian movements, usually inspired and led by a charismatic figure such as Aimée Semple MacPherson or Billy Graham; but these movements attracted followers of all ages. In the late 1960s, many young people found solace in becoming devotees of revivalists of Hindu or Buddhist persuasion. Today, some of these movements – such as the Hare Krishnas, the 'Divine Light' believers in the divinity of Balyogeshwar, and of course the massive following of the Maharishi Mahesh Yogi – have much larger membership in the West than in India, where they originated.

Participant observation in the activities of each of these cults reveals a quite remarkable change of orientation on the part of their Western adepts. In positive terms, they are all remarkably benign, non-violent, tolerant towards each other and even towards the unsympathetic onlookers who jeer at them; and they seem genuinely bent on exploring and realising their own inner world. Here there seems to have occurred a very widespread shift away from the predominantly extrovert, action-oriented interests of previous generations of Western youth, whose first wish was to achieve mastery over practical skills, especially those involving machinery, speed, and the control of powerful engines. Today's young people seem less concerned with practical accomplishments and instead have become inward-looking, exploring realms of direct experience of feeling, either in the collective surrender to emotion characteristic of *bhakti*, or devotional worship, or in the silent practice of meditation.

A consequence of this 'swing to the East' has been the appearance in India, during the last few years, of a new variant, among the thousands of young Western Hippies, or simple travellers: this variant could be characterised as 'Seekers', who hope to find enlightenment by adopting the life-style of a Hindu Saddhu who wanders penniless on long pilgrimages, relying on alms for his subsistence. They formed an audience ripe for the re-discovery of Hermann Hesse's brand of adolescent phantasy, which had made relatively little impression on the young people of the 1920s and 1930s. His *Siddhartha* in particular (a novel which, in emotionally over-charged narrative style, parodies the life of Gotama Buddha) has offered many young people the very model for a period of soulful pilgrimage. The Hippy-Saddhu differs from his model, however, in that he is seldom celibate, preferring to travel in company with a devoted girl-friend, or with another boy: and also, in that he is seldom completely penniless.

In India, just as in the West, the sudden appearance of long-haired, curiously garbed young Europeans who have repudiated the normal adult roles of their society, has provoked strong, and frequently hostile reactions. There are many apocryphal stories about their being dirty, disease-ridden, sexually promiscuous, dishonest and addicted to drugs: and yet when one takes the trouble to talk with them, it is usually soon apparent that these stories are exaggerated. It is true that they commonly eat, drink or smoke cannabis, as do most Indian Saddhus but, like the latter, they use the drug as an aid to meditation or in order to impart more zest to a session of hymn-singing, rather than just for kicks.

Still most Indians find it hard to take these Western yogis seriously; and perhaps this is just as well because their curiosity – and at times their mockery – has served to remind them that they are, after all, living through what Erik Erikson has called a 'moratorium', a period in which one's normal life-pattern is set aside while one tries to discover, or re-discover, a set of values which will restore to one's life its lost significance. Conversely, it can be actively harmful for a Hippy-yogi to be accepted too enthusiastically by simple illiterate villagers, whose credulity may reinforce, instead of modifying, his wilder phantasies.

That this can happen, was dramatically illustrated in October 1972, when a barefoot American youth, clad in spotless white loincloth and homespun shirt, joined the huge throng of worshippers at the sacred Hindu fair at Pushkar, in Rajas'than. In spite of the ostentatious simplicity of his attire, this young man, who had been 'on the road' for many weeks, discoursing in fairly fluent Hindu with travelling holy men, and joining them nightly in smoking *ganja*, was far from being penniless. The heavy sandalwood chaplet which he carried had not been cheap; and in his pocket he had $1000 in travellers' cheques. To his dismay, he found that his pockets had been picked, leaving him with nothing. He appealed to the local police, who had already been taking an interest in him: they knew that at least one of the 'holy men' with whom he had been consorting was a bad character, so they pounced on him, and found the $1000 in his saffron robes.

All this took place within a matter of minutes. To the onlookers, the sum of money involved was enormous, and the speed of its recovery seemed miraculous. In no time, the rumour spread that this young Saddhu was possessed with supernatural powers. Crowds gathered round to venerate him, and the atmosphere of faith and devotion became so powerfully charged that the young man himself began to believe that he had indeed become supernormal. For days, he sat meditating, watched by an ever-growing multitude. Some villagers began to ask for his blessing, and for his divine guidance about sickness in their family, or the auspicious date for a wedding, or whether the rains would come in time to save them from the threat of famine caused by the failure of the monsoon. The young man blessed them, and prophesied, and for weeks thereafter remained firmly convinced that he possessed divine powers: it was in fact a good three months before he fully returned to earth.

From an objective, Western viewpoint, this could be viewed as an episode of psychogenic psychosis, induced by the highly charged emotional atmosphere of a Hindu religious festival. The young man's capacity for reality testing, already undermined by numerous trips on LSD, and by daily discourse with holy men for whom subjective experiences counted as much more significant than the phenomena of the material world, was temporarily overwhelmed by an omnipotent phantasy: and thousands of instant devotees were there to reinforce this phantasy, by day or night.

If we try to view the same incident from the viewpoint of the rustic Indian pilgrims, who had travelled to the sacred Pushkar lake from many miles around, it assumes a different form. These villagers, like the pilgrims of Lourdes, arrive expecting to see miracles. They display not merely a 'willing suspension of belief' but a positive eagerness to perceive manifestations of the supernatural: and such is their heightened level of suggestibility that they are seldom disappointed. It has to be remembered that they belong to a society in which from earliest childhood, they have been taught to share the common belief in the immanence of unseen spiritual forces – of gods, goddesses, demons, spirits of the dead, etc., etc. These unquestioned, universally held beliefs become social realities; moreover, they are frequently reinforced by episodes in which their village shamans, or their neighbours and friends enter a trance-like state of dissociation, and talk in strange accents. At such times they believe that an unseen spirit has taken possession of the subject's body, and is temporarily there in their midst, addressing them in their own local dialect. After having witnessed this phenomenon many times, they naturally assume that it may also happen to themselves, at a time of personal crisis when the spirit world becomes involved in their own affairs, and it does.

We have already discussed the Hippies' turning away from that emphasis on the cognitive intellect, on which modern science and its technological applications have been based, and their shift towards inward-looking, rather than towards mastery of the physical world; but we finish by confronting a remarkable paradox. The

same youthful generation which in the early 1960s found themselves emotionally liberated from the need to respect their parents,
and celebrated this emancipation in a long series of 'confrontations'
has now brought forward a succeeding wave of young – and again,
some not quite so young – 'seekers' who scour India and other
Eastern countries in search of a Guru. And having found their
Guru they seem willing to surrender themselves – and in particular, their critical, cognitive powers – in an ecstasy of devotion.

There seems to have been a distinct shift of emphasis, from
hedonism, sensual gratification and comradeship within the peer-
group, linked with a triumphant repudiation of their elders, to this
new quest for meaning, for significance in one's personal life.
Ambivalence towards the parents is still there, although they are
perhaps now seen as ignorant inheritors of 'bad karma' rather than
as wicked and perverse: but whereas, a few years ago, the mood of
the young was to reject all past knowledge because it seemed to
culminate in positivist reductionism, and in ever-increasing tech-
nocracy, the new Seekers have rediscovered the ancient texts of
mystical philosophy, and have come to realise that in this field at
least there are individuals who studied and practised for many
years, and who have something of real value to impart. Hence, the
gulf between the generations has been bridged, if only to a small
extent.

It has been a disconcerting experience, however, for many Hippies to find that they are often greeted with ridicule and even
hostility, particularly in the larger Indian cities. A stereotype has
rapidly developed of the Hippy as being the very antithesis of the
British sahib to whom generations of Indians paid (sometimes
grudging) respect. He is depicted as being dirty, probably vermin-
ous, addicted to drugs, sexually promiscuous and given to thiev-
ing. All this is usually untrue, but it justifies their being ill-treated,
cheated and robbed. This hostile stereotype can be seen as a form
of expression of some of the pent-up resentments against the
privileged offspring of the former Raj. It is only in the villages and
in remote ashrams that young Seekers are more likely to be taken
on trust, to be judged not in terms of a hostile stereotype, but on
their actual behaviour and to be offered simple but generous
hospitality: and yet even here they are liable to encounter sudden
accesses of doubt and suspicion as to their real motives.

These misunderstandings, perpetuated by the dynamics of conscious and unconscious emotions, for some Western seekers prove disillusioning, for others present a challenge to be overcome. They serve as a reminder of how doubly difficult it is to find the solution of one's personal emotional quest in a context of experience which is far removed not only from one's own family but also from one's cultural origins. Ordinarily, in the process of rebellion followed by reconciliation between the generations, both sides learn to modify their concepts and attitudes: young people find it easier to conform to a system of values which they themselves have been able to change, to however small an extent. It is a different matter when young people resolve their uncertainties by accepting the values of some quite other cultural tradition, because the 'outsider' gains admission as an initiate only by a total acceptance of the other culture's esoteric beliefs.

It remains to be seen whether this total self-surrender of young Westerners to Eastern modes of devotional worship and religious faith will result in a lasting stabilisation of their personality, or whether it will prove only to be a moratorium, to be succeeded by some form of reconciliation with the culture of their origin, as a result of which both they and that culture may experience change, and growth.

7

The Indian Guru and his Disciple

PETER BRENT

The institution of the Guru in Hinduism is based upon that religion's basic scriptures, the Vedas. It stems from the fact that for
centuries these were transmitted orally. Derived from the word
vid, to know, the Vedas are taken by Hindus to be a body of
knowledge which exists as natural law is thought to exist. Thus
they are supposed never to have been written down, nor even
received at some distinguishable moment as Moses is said to have
received the Tablets of the Law; rather, they were understood or
realized by wise men, the *rishis*, who had achieved a state of unity
with what was highest in the world and had in this way put
themselves in touch with the subtle vibrations of the Vedas. These
scriptures are therefore thought of as eternal facts of the universe
which have been, through good fortune and diligence, discovered
by Man.

It was always the function of the Brahmin caste to teach and
transmit the Vedas and in the *Rig-Veda* it tells us that the Brahmins
are God's mouth (a claim the antiquity of which is somewhat
undermined by the suggestions which have been made by Max
Müller and others that the hymn in which it occurs is a forgery, a
later interpolation). The Brahminical families which taught these
scriptures claimed descent from the various *rishis* who had first
become aware, so to speak, of this or that section of the Vedas. This
section then became their particular concern, and the Veda in
which they specialized was attached to their name, so that Brahmins who are Gurus in the old style still say that they are 'of the
Rig-Veda' or 'of the *Atharva-Veda*'.

Because of their importance and because of their method of
transmission, the Vedas form a part of *shruti* – 'that which is
remembered'. They were meant only for the higher three of the

four castes; *shudras*, those of the lowest caste, were threatened with
boiling oil poured into their ears if they so much as overheard one
of these hymns or ritual instructions. The transmission by word of
mouth of this literature must have gone on for many centuries
before writing became general in India; the Vedas are thought to be
anything from three thousand to six thousand years old. Yet the
oldest inscriptions that exist in India, those of King Ashoka, date
only from the third century BC and most manuscripts are considerably more recent than this.

It was the Guru, the Brahmin teacher, who ensured that these
basic 150,000 words or more would pass successfully and largely
unmutilated from one generation to the next. He was a married
man, a householder whose home became the home and the school
of his pupils. Students who were qualified by birth had to be
accepted and, once installed, they became the Guru's responsibility. They, in turn, undertook to serve him in every way, to
respect and honour him, and to beg for him. He was not, however,
allowed to charge for teaching, nor was the student allowed to pay
for being taught. (The way round this, at least for the wealthy, was
for the student to 'beg' from his parents; this still happens, and still
slightly unsettles the orthodox, even when they do it themselves.)

In the early days, the young men who came to the Guru would be
expected to do the household chores, the cooking and cleaning, to
bath, dress and anoint the Guru and, having begged for his food, to
eat only when he had finished and whatever he had left. On the
other hand, during the eight years which was the minimum period
of a young Brahmin's education – frequently he arrived at the
Guru's house as a child of eight or nine and did not leave until his
twenties – the Guru was expected to oversee his health, his sleep,
his diet, the company he kept and the places he visited.

This ancient Vedic tradition still continues and at various
centres in India, schools continue to teach these texts in the same
way as they have always been taught. One such centre is the small
town of Gokarn, on the coast of Mysore State, a place which legend
tells us is where the ten-headed hero-king Ravana put down the
atman-linga granted him by Shiva and saw it turn into a stone cow
and begin to sink by its own weight into the ground. Taking a firm
hold of the ears, he managed to prevent these at least from disappearing; ear-shaped rocks remain in sight there to this day and

have given the town its name which means 'cow's ears'. Here there are several families of Gurus who still own establishments where Brahmin children come to learn.

Not only must the texts be learned, but so must their right pronunciation. Vedic language has three levels, low (*anundatta*), high (*udatta*) and middle (*swarita*), which are usually spoken in that order, each syllable having its correct level. To get these wrong is to give a word a different meaning. The length of time each sound is to be held while chanting must also be learned; this metre is based on the *matra*, the time it takes to pronounce a short vowel, and is absolutely rigid. The boys learn by rote, twenty or more sentences a day, their voices rattling on a monotonous, apparently endless repetition only broken by the Guru's occasional corrections. When a boy has learned all the sentences of a *shukta*, or chapter, he then repeats the whole passage ten times. When he knows the whole of the Vedas word-perfectly, he is said to be *ghana-pathi* – and he then goes on to learn how to interpret what he now knows by heart. At the same time, he may display his proficiency at competitions of recitation; to do well at these is to ensure a useful flow of pupils when one begins to teach in one's own turn.

At the same time, since the Vedas are not only hymns but also instructions for rituals, Vedic Gurus perform priestly functions. Often they are the only people left who know how to organize and execute some of these complex ceremonies. Once rituals were the most important elements in Hinduism: the fourth century philosophy called Mimamsa taught that doing the rituals was enough by itself to ensure the rewards of *Karma* – since the Vedas were law, to do what they said brought automatic benefits.

Nowadays, however, when the emphasis has shifted to meditation and the merging of Self with the Absolute, fewer and fewer people are willing to spend time, effort and money on the more obscure rituals. Worship centres on the temple rather than the home, and is kept relatively simple.

In Gorkan, one Guru told me, 'All the ceremonies are becoming a problem to keep up. The chief Guru here has performed *soma-yagna*. That's very rare because it takes a week and costs a lot of money – about five thousand rupees (about £250, but in Indian terms of rather higher value). You have to hold the mouth of a sheep, so that it can't breathe. The sheep's stomach distends and you hit it and it dies. Then you bore a hole into its body and take out its liver and a portion of that is put on the holy fire. The part that's left is then eaten by those who have taken part in the ceremony. You have to kill a sheep a day for six days ... Ceremonies like that used to be paid for by the princely states, but of course they don't exist any more...'

He believed in the value of these ceremonies and thought that those who performed them did so for the whole world – the world needed them. He was sad, because he knew he was part of a collapsing tradition. More and more of the young people were being educated in schools of the Western type. Not only that – because there was so little money, a new rivalry had developed between Gurus and their pupils: 'They have to share out whatever Vedic ceremonies are arranged. It's naturally going to cost less to get a *chela* (disciple or student) to perform it than to get his teacher.' In the old days, he said, *chelas* would only do such a thing if they had their Guru's permission. Now, in their new need, Gurus refused such permission – so students if approached perform the rituals without asking their Guru first. This may sometimes be less profitable than it seems, since the man for whom the ceremony is performed can pay what he pleases, and if the student is less than proficient, or less than determined, he may not give much – certainly not as much as he would have given the Guru himself.

When one visits these places it becomes plain that even those most involved know themselves to be at the end of a tradition, among the last generations to keep it even half-heartedly alive. Nor is this strange; the Vedic Guru's function was obviously altered in a fundamental way, once writing became general and manuscripts easily available. It is as if in Britain the great bardic schools of Ireland and Wales have struggled on through the millennia, trying to keep alive skills and methods made redundant by the alphabet and, later, by printing. A rear-guard action has of course been fought over the centuries – the *Mahabharata* condems to hell those who write down the Vedas; and when I was in India I heard the story of an American who, refused by one teacher, learned the Vedas under another, then returned to the first in order to show off his skill in recitation. But the old man shook his head – the matter was not so simple, because as he said, 'When I recite them they are the Vedas – when you recite them, they are not!'

In this way, then, a vestige of the pure strain has been preserved. At the same time the teaching of the Vedas led to the teaching of secular subjects like grammar, logic, rhetoric and mathematics. Beyond all this, however, there seems always to have been another strain of teacher, philosophic, solitary, ascetic. Asceticism has a history which goes back at least as far as the period of the *Rig-Veda*, in which *munis* are referred to (a name still used for holy men, particularly among the Jains). They seemed to have worn soiled, yellow robes and their hair long – thus presenting an appearance very like that of today's wandering *sadhus*; they were said to be *vatarashana*, which has been translated as 'one who has only the air for his girdle'. It seems likely that these holy men, as they grew older in experience and perhaps reputation, gathered one or two congenial disciples, who accompanied them either on their wanderings or to the hermitages where they spent their time. And of course for this relationship there existed the model of the perhaps more orthodox Vedic Guru, by whom many of these people will themselves have been taught throughout their childhood.

As writing altered the importance of that mechanical tuition which is what the Guru had had to offer hitherto, so a change came over the basic philosophy of Hinduism. Between the Vedas and the Upanishads,* the earliest of which may date from around the sixth century BC, there is a shift in emphasis from, put loosely, man to God. Where the Vedas assured those following their precepts a rich, comfortable and successful life and define those terms in a completely mundane way, the Upanishads tell us (and I quote the *Chandogya Upanishad*, one of the earliest), 'Verily, this whole world is Brahman, from which he comes forth, without which he will be dissolved, and in which he breathes. Tranquil, one should meditate on it.' The *Mundaka Upanishad* says, 'He, verily, who knows the Supreme Brahman becomes Brahman himself.'

Thus there appears a new monism. Where the Vedas offer a multitude of gods, and favour one or another in different hymns and section, the Upanishads offer the idea that everything is One

---

* Properly speaking, they are all Vedas. Nevertheless, there is a fundamental difference – the *Rig-Veda* and others, as we have seen, are not considered human in origin, the Upanishads are recognised to have been written down. But all the scriptures of course interconnect, Vedas, Brahmanas, Upanishads, the later Puranas and so on.

and the One is Brahman. Attached to this is the idea of *Karma*, often translated as 'fate' but more properly the law of cause and effect – what we do now has repercussions later, and that 'later' means not, as in the Vedas, later in this life, in which we will be punished by sickness or an absence of cattle but in the later reincarnated lives which our souls shall live. The *Chandogya Upanishad* assures us that if we behave well we shall be reborn into one of the three higher castes, 'but those whose conduct has been evil will quickly attain an evil birth, the birth of a hog or the birth of a Candala' (the lowest of low, one whose mother was a Brahmin and whose father a Shudra).

All this formed the basis for the philosophy promulgated by Shankara in the eighth century and called *advaita vedanta*, the philosophy of 'non-dualism' which remains perhaps the most important strain in Hindu thought. Buddhism had for centuries before been India's dominant religion and Shankara was the leader of the Hindu revival which eventually drove it out. His ideas bear a clear Buddhist tinge, and even at the time he was occasionally accused of being a fellow-traveller.

The most important element in his thinking was perhaps his concept of *maya*, which he said was the condition of illusion in which humans live, and in which they see differentiation when there is none. Everything is Brahman; therefore to make distinctions between one individual or another, or one thing and another, or an individual or a thing, must be mistaken. If we could only perceive reality as it should be perceived, we would realize that it was illusory; because we do not, we react to it in the wrong way. His analogy, used again and again since, was that of the rope lying beside the road at evening which the passing traveller perceives as a snake. His response is absurd, because he has not understood what was in front of him. If we understood what was in front of us, we would be spared absurdity. What is in front of us is Brahman, the Absolute – not a personified God, but Being, the ultimate It of the universe – and our duty is to realize this. The result of such a realization will be that we and Brahman will appear to merge – 'appear', because we and Brahman always have been merged, but we have not understood this and acted upon the assumption of a separation. Once we learn, by meditation, by going into ourselves, that the spiritual part of ourselves and

Brahman are actually indivisible, that 'I' is a meaningless word –
once we have learned this, realized it utterly, then we will be able to
break the death-birth-death cycle and merge with the Absolute.
We shall have attained *moksha*.

In other words, what separates us from liberation, from break-
ing the bonds of this illusion, is our ignorance. Knowledge, or
jnāna, is the way we can achieve self-realization and the final union
with Brahman. The implication in this, of course, is that we need a
teacher. The Guru has as his prime function the guidance of his
disciple in the *jnana yoga*, the way of knowledge. However, truth is
discrimination between real and unreal and this can only be
achieved in the state of ecstasy in which it becomes directly realized. Because of this, the Guru teaches not merely that right
discrimination by which the ultimate truth might be determined,
but also those states of the mind in which it can be experienced at
first hand.

A later strain in Hindu practice, which although it seems to
conflict with *jnana yoga* is often practised in conjunction with it
(Asia is not hung up on 'either–or' configurations in the way the
West is; opposites are reconciled without any great problem), is the
way of devotion, *bhakti yoga*. In this, love of God reaches an
absolute pitch, an intensity at which all imperfections are burned
away. The philosophy which sustains this attitude is not usually
like *advaita vedanta* monistic, arguing instead that when the soul
achieves its highest state, it joins with God, but does not become
one with Him. The chief *bhakti* philosopher was, perhaps, Rama-
nuja, who with his *vishisht-advaita* or qualified non-dualism tried
to show how the soul was separate from, yet totally dependent on,
Brahman. The world, he said, was not illusion but real, spun out of
the very fabric of God as a spider spins a web out of its body. Souls
were of the substance of Brahman too, yet separate, as sparks are a
part of fire yet not the fire itself. In liberation, the soul achieves
Brahman rather in the same way as the Christian soul achieves God
in the doctrine of the mystic marriage. But, as one *bhakti* Guru said
to me, 'When you reach the intoxication level of love, you are God.'
In the end, the distinction between monism and this form of
dualism becomes so fine as to be almost invisible to any but
theologians. In any case, such divisions suggest a doctrinal rigidity
not actually met with in Hinduism.

There was a great *bhakti* revival in the fifteenth and sixteenth centuries, led by such holy men as Chaitanya, Kabir, Madhva and Vallabha, and certainly since then this has been perhaps the most important of the elements which go to make up the Guru–disciple relationship. By focussing his emotions on the God-realized figure of the Guru, the disciple is able to 'merge' with him. In this, since the Guru is consciously a part of Brahman – that is, has realized the Brahman within himself – the disciple is merging himself too with that great Absolute. The Guru in this way becomes the visible part of God, that which gives both reality and limit to the concept of divinity. At the same time, he remains a teacher, setting out the tasks which the disciple has to do in order to achieve spiritual perfection. And he is an example proving that these tasks, this devotion, lead to a successful end, since he himself has passed along this way in order to reach his present high condition.

The discipline by which the disciple is expected to achieve self-realization is called his *sadhana* (hence those following such a path are called *sadhakas*) and this is usually prescribed by the Guru. It normally includes *hatha yoga*, the *asanas* or positions of which are familiar to the West, where they are taught simply as 'Yoga'; *japas*, which is the repetition of a name of God, or of a *mantra*, sometimes for hours or even days on end; the reading of sacred texts; meditation. It goes without saying that the full-time disciple is expected to eat frugally and a vegetarian diet, sleep with the minimum of comfort and for the shortest time possible, eschew money and all wordly connections, and remain totally celibate. The disciple follows this routine because he trusts, he loves, his Guru, and as a result surrenders to him. Indeed, in this surrender lies the kernel of the relationship. Once you have given yourself up, God fills the resultant emptiness. How do you give yourself up? By surrender to the Guru. Once you have achieved this, everything else becomes possible to you. It is for this reason that potential disciples may spend years in searching for the Guru right for them, the one man at whose feet they may unload the staggering burden of the Self.

What are the rewards this strenuous and difficult process offers? First, the trance states it induces, the condition of *samadhi*, in which that unity of all phenomena of which the texts speak may be directly experienced. There are varieties of this state,

distinguished mainly by the route used to reach them, partly by the
depth and length of time of the experience. *Jnana yoga* leads to
nirvikalpa samadhi, and this, if it is sustained, becomes *sahaja
samadhi*, believed by some to be the highest state. Others may
achieve *samprajnata samadhi*, a state in which by concentrating on
an object, all else ceases, it seems, to exist; in this way the distinction between deity and devotee may be maintained. There is,
however, a further stage, *asamprajnata samadhi*, in which even that
object ceases to exist for the person in meditation; according to
Patanjali and others, it is this which is the highest state of trance.

Atreya, Chatterji and Danielou[1] describe *samadhi* as 'a unique
experience of objectless, thoughtless and differentless blissful existence' and quote a *yogi* who speaks of the 'immeasurably delightful and cool effulgence of millions of suns in which there is no
longing for anything.' This kind of experience, which many aspi-
rants begin to have quite early on in their *sadhana*, naturally not
only confirms them in their beliefs, but also reinforces their determination to continue.

Beyond that, of course, lies self-realization itself, the bursting
out into the mystic uplands after the appalling and exhausting
climb those steep slopes demand. Shri Nisargadatte Maharaj – a
Guru who sits unpretentiously in his small hall at the top of a metal
stair in a Bombay back-street – has written: 'I am no more an
individual. There is nothing to limit my being now . . . My present
experience of the world as the divine expression is not for any profit
nor any loss, but is the pure, simple, natural flow of beatific
consciousness . . . It is the unique, blissful experience of the primal
unity . . . He that once meditated on bliss and peace is himself the
ocean of bliss and peace.'[2]

All this explains what the Guru brings one – it does not explain
who he is or how one finds him. Kabir, in the fifteenth century,
told us why he was needed: 'In the midst of the highest heaven
there is a shining light; he who has no Guru cannot reach the
palace; he only will reach it who is under the guidance of a true
Guru.' But who is 'a true Guru'? In some ways, the picture
becomes very confused when one looks at it closely. Some people,
for example, say that anything that helps one in one's spiritual
progress is a Guru. And this is true, if one thinks that 'Guru' has
been translated as 'one who enlightens'. Then there are hereditary

Gurus. In some cases, for instance among the Vallahbacharyas, all the male members of a family are Gurus the moment they are born; in others the old Guru appoints a successor who may be his son, or perhaps his cousin or brother, but who is never anyone from outside the family. And of course such groups are only following the tradition of the ancient, Vedic Guru, who inherited his *shishya varga*, his group of students and disciples, from his Guru father, just as they inherited him from their fathers. Then there are sect-Gurus, men who are leaders of a defined group and who often claim spiritual descent from a founding deity, known then as the *adi*-Guru. Then there are *mahants*, the heads of monasteries, who perform the functions of a Guru. And it must not be forgotten that these categories are not mutually exclusive; at the same time, any holy man, once approached, may accept someone who comes to him as his disciple.

These last may indeed be among that highest level of Teachers, the *sad*-Guru – the 'teachers of reality', as that term has been translated. These are the Masters whom we in the West think of as 'real' Gurus. Often they come from poor families, they manifest their holiness early, they refuse to marry – it may be because they refuse that their sanctity first becomes apparent, they take to the roads of India, making their way in a pilgrimage sometimes decades long from one holy man or holy place to another. Or they may settle early, at the feet of a great teacher, taking over from him when he dies. Or they may decide to remain in one place, from which, little by little, the fame of their holiness and, perhaps, their miraculous powers, begins to spread about the land. In this way, they draw their disciples to them, they bring to their feet great crowds, some of whom will accept them as their Guru, others of whom have come only for the *darshan* of the great man – that view of him which the Hindu feels will enable him to draw up into himself some particle of a saint's or leader's virtue.

Particular followers of a Guru may decide that they should renounce the world and serve this saint and God. Most, however, will remain week-end devotees, travelling as often as possible to the *ashram* of the Guru, drawing on his wealth of spiritual power, staying perhaps in the guest-house the *ashram* provides, then returning to the city to continue their normal, secular lives. They will be no less a devotee of their Guru than those who, in ochre robes, stay at his side and minister to his needs twenty-four hours a day. As one secular devotee of a Guru put it to me, 'There are two categories, that of the householder and that of the renounced. The ultimate goal is the same for both – but the latter are in a better position to attain it.'

In choosing one's Guru, there often comes a moment of recognition, or of something perhaps a little sharper, a moment as emotional as that of 'falling in love at first sight' might be for us. Once one has had such an experience, there is rarely any going back on it; one has found the Teacher one has, consciously or not, been looking for. One *chela*, whose Guru was an ascetic who had not lain down or spoken for a dozen years, described their first meeting for me. 'I was staying in a small cave near here, and so I came to know that there was a holy man living here. I came to see him, and the first time I saw him it was as though I had been thirsty all that time and now the thirst had left me. I felt very peaceful. That is how I knew I had met my Guru.' Or the devotee of a female Guru, Godavari Mata, herself a woman: 'Somebody said, "*Mataji* has come." I turned round just to see – and at that very moment something in me . . . I don't know, I can't explain that experience. Something sort of . . . I just surrendered. She was at that time very beautiful, even physically . . . Really I can't explain what had happened to me. I am like one in a dream.'

Sometimes the recognition is in the other direction – it is the Guru who picks out the disciple. One devotee was being introduced to the Guru by his brother, when the Guru said, 'I know him, I have known him since long.' And when the astonished newcomer asked how that was possible, the Guru said, 'I have known you since your birth, during many births. I have always been with you.' At this time the Guru may give proofs of heightened powers – he may give advice on some problem about which the devotee is worrying but which he has not yet discussed with his new Master. In one case the Guru came to his prospective follower on the first day, after a period of silent meditation had been passed by the aspirant with as little result as always, and told him that the *mantra* he was using to concentrate on was too long. Impressed in this way – 'How did he know what my *mantra* was?' – the man became a life-long follower.

In this and other ways, both Guru and disciple are tested. The

Guru has the right at any time to send away a would-be disciple; conversely, although it may be frowned upon, it is understood that the disciple who makes no progress under a particular Guru may strike out to find himself another. In making these decisions, of course, the Guru as the enlightened man has certain advantages. As one Guru told me, 'As soon as a *shishya* comes and sits before a Guru, he sees the vibrations that emit from that *shishya*, and because he is more powerful, he knows what type of a *shishya* he is.'

Nevertheless, it is the disciple who, in a curious way, has the whip-hand; if he does not make an approach to the Guru, if he does not decide that the Guru is the man who can lead him to self-realization, then whatever the Guru may think of himself and his spiritual ability, he will be left without a follower. Only when the would-be disciple has made his decision can the Guru exercise what is his prerogative, the acceptance or rejection of the newcomer. Acceptance may then be formalised by *diksha*, initiation. Within a sect or a monastic order, this is naturally done with ceremony and ritual. On the *ashram*, however, initiation may be very informal, may involve no spoken word at all. Indeed, this kind of initiation is often considered the highest of all: distinction is made between the *diksha* which is *bahya*, external, and *abhyantari*, which is internal and most subtly effected. There are in this subtle initiation three further categories: *sparshi*, where the Guru simply touches the disciple; *caksush*, which is by a glance; and *manasi*, which is by thought alone. Another classification is similar: *sbakti*, in which the Guru's spiritual power enters the disciple directly, even when they may be physically separated; *sambhavi*, in which there is some contact, a touch perhaps, an exchange of words; and *anavi*, in which there is a ritual of some kind and the devotee is given a *mantra*.

What initiation proves is the mutual acceptance, one of the other, by Guru and disciple. What it does is to pass the divine power of the Guru into the disciple. It has been said that the Guru-disciple relationship is not a teaching, it is a transmission, and with initiation of whatever sort, but particularly perhaps of the silent, subtle kind, such a transmission is given a channel it can use. From then on, the process of self-realization can continue. For, as one Guru put it to me, 'The Guru and the *shishya*, they are like two kernels in one jack-fruit, one raw, the other ripe. The raw one wants to be ripe; the ripe one is ripe and wants nothing more. While the raw one feels different it will continue to demand, to want something. But there is no difference – it is all jack-fruit, all the same stuff. The difference is only felt by the unripe.' Once the disciple has been accepted and initiated, that ripening process can begin. The intensity of the subsequent relationship cannot be exaggerated. For the disciple, the Guru is divine. He is, he must be, believed to be self-realized and thus essentially indivisible from Brahman, not only in the general way in which this is true of everyone, but in the particular, direct way which follows upon the destruction of all the barriers of illusion. Not only that, he is visible, manifestly there, the Guide on the path. Again and again the devotees of one Guru or another – *sad*-Guru, sectarian Guru, hereditary Guru – said to me, 'Guru is greater than God, because he leads me to God.'

To illustrate the depth of the relationship, here are the words of a Swaminaryana monk: 'The invisible presence of the Guru is like a shelter that continues. He is the real liberator. Everything depends on him, when or whether he wants to raise us up . . . The ultimate stage will come when we realize his presence all the time . . .' And a secular follower of the same Guru told me, 'If he tells me to stay with him, then I have to. If he tells me to renounce the world, then I have to. It is his orders which mould our lives.' Or another devotee, an engineering student, speaking of his quite different Guru, 'There is no comparison between this and any relationship I have known. I feel that he is perfect. Disagreement can never be possible, you see, because the situation as Swamiji analyses it can never be wrong.' It is by way of such an intensity of feeling that the teachings of the Guru, or the power of the Guru, are transferred to the disciple. And for this reason much of what passes between Guru and *shishya* does so in silence. The Guru sits, often on the *gadi*, the padded throne, while before him, men and women separate, his followers, face him. They greet him by prostrating themselves, they offer a gift – fruit, a little money – then take their places in the assembly. If they have a question, they will ask it; otherwise, they simply watch him, or close their eyes and go into meditation. For long stretches, the hall in which these people are meeting their Teacher is absolutely silent – as one American disciple put it, 'He's got like great teats all over him and we just suck and suck that heavy goodness out of him.'

It is, because of the essential privacy of this relationship, because it is always unique, tailored for and by the personalities of one Guru, one disciple, very difficult to define in very strict and formal terms exactly what a Guru is and does. I have evolved a partial definition of the Guru; that is, I have isolated four conditions any two of which must be met by anyone claiming to be a spiritual Guru (obviously those teaching dance and music come into a different category). These conditions are: (a) the Guru must be able to achieve the state of *samadhi*; (b) he must be able to teach or transfer to others the ability to achieve *samadhi* (this as the visible sign of a high level of self-realization); (c) he is the established successor of his own Guru before him; (d) he has the right and the power to give initiation. The great *sad*-Guru on his own *ashram* will meet all four of these conditions; the hereditary Guru of a *bhakti* cult might only meet the last two. But two at least must be met for someone to be considered a Guru. A fifth condition, that of deep learning in the Hindu scriptures, will be almost universally met by Gurus, yet may not be by some who seem to have achieved a very high spiritual plane without experiencing a conventional education. Such proficiency, however, will generally be expected by would-be disciples.

It is plain that explanations for some of the intensity with which this relationship is entered into must be looked for outside it, in Indian society as a whole. When one does so, one sees that a highly-repressive puritanism is very wide-spread in India, which holds down not merely sexuality, but all emotion. Public tenderness between husband and wife is, for example, considered indecent, and any acknowledged feelings of affection between, say, an engaged couple are unthinkable. The vast majority of marriages are, in any case, arranged. Most people's lives are, therefore, emotionally very restricted. They are weighed down by the demands of duty towards their often widely-ramified families; their circle of friends is limited by class, caste and wealth; their opportunities in life restricted by the general poverty of the country and the commands of their parents. To these last they remain entirely subservient for the whole of their lives, living into middle-age with restrictions the Westerner has thrown off before he is into his twenties. In this situation, the relationship with the Guru is one of the very few in which the Indian may be respectably swept off his feet by his emotions. In many of these cases it seems to me that what has happened is a redirection of love, a love rebuffed hitherto by the many barriers convention puts in its way, either by prohibiting its expression or by demanding it as a duty.

Nevertheless, it is clear that for perhaps thousands of years men and women have been led to some kind of realization, some kind of spiritual development, by the personality and techniques of successive generations of Gurus. The institution is not, of course, unique; in many parts of Asia, both further West and further East, similar Masters teach their disciples the details of similar routes. (Zen and Sufi both, as a matter of fact, seem more interesting to me, since they are more aware that man is also partly intellect, that he must be taught to think in new ways, that his expectations, even of the Master-aspirant relationship, should be broken down before something useful can emerge; much of what passes between *shishya* and Guru seems to me to do so by rote.) If now the West is showing a greater and greater interest in these institutions, it seems to me to be because we have reached the end of an era in the history of ideas. Scientific materialism seems to be at its last gasp. We are watching with despair the world it has created, or tried to show us, a world of insane weaponry, of irrelevant endeavour, of pointless experimentation. We go to the Moon because we can, not because we must. Scientists work impartially on cancer cures or the virus of bubonic plague. Sociologists and psychologists settle with the same objectivity to the causes of poverty as they do to the methods of selling detergents. Behaviourists maim a million animals in order to prove what their very determination disproves of itself, that living is a matter of learned muscle-response. Land, sea and air become polluted. The world's natural resources drain away. Ideologues confront each other, those sad, threatening push-buttons under their fingers. From such a world, we are beginning to recoil; even scientists are asking whether an undifferentiated curiosity is really man's highest and most hallowed attribute. Heisenberg's Uncertainty Principle showed that even in physics the observer cannot exclude himself from his observations. Man is having to rediscover his inevitable presence, is having to reckon with himself in the particular; generalizations will no longer entirely do. If a new era of subjectivity is thus being ushered in, it may be that somewhere in the Guru-*shishya* relationships there are elements which will prove useful to us, that from this intense and alien institution we may yet have much to learn.

REFERENCES

1 *Indian Culture* by Atreya, Chatterji and Danielou; Universal Book and Stationery Co., New Delhi.
2 Quoted from *Self-Knowledge and Self-Realisation*, a pamphlet issued by the ashram of Shri Nisargadatte Maharaj, Bombay.

III

ENCOUNTERS IN THE MODERN WORLD

8

China Between Two Worlds

RICHARD HARRIS*

In the nineteenth century two things happened to China; the first was the decline and eventual fall early in this century of the ruling dynasty. The second was the intrusion into China of foreign powers, led actually by Britain, of a kind that the Chinese had not previously experienced.

Now the first of these events was not at all strange to the Chinese. They had had dynasties rising and falling before, so much so that they had formulated their own idea of how a dynasty worked. It is interesting that the Chinese sense of time was not like ours, pro-gressive, linear, but cyclical; they divided dynasties into five periods. The first was the energetic creative period of the dynasty; the second was the flowering, the Golden Age. Then there followed the beginning of the decline, the third period. The fourth period was an attempt by the dynasty, when conscious of its decline, to restore its competence and to re-establish itself, to pull itself together. But this, historians had noted, was not possible; one could not arrest decline, so the fifth period was the final decline; the dynasty finished and gave way, after an interregnum possibly, to a new dynasty.

That was happening in nineteenth century China, but what disturbed China equally was the intrusion of Western power which changed China in a way in which it had never changed before. I would like to remind you, to begin with, what the Chinese world had been and still was in the early 19th century. The China of the Han Dynasty, let us say, of the two hundred years before and after the birth of Christ, ruled more or less the area of present China. China was richer, bigger, more developed, more cultivated,

* The author has revised his 1976 text and substantially rewritten the latter part of it.

intellectually far more advanced than any of its neighbours and consequently there grew up in the Chinese mind a view of the world they lived in in which China represented not the biggest country but civilization itself. The smaller powers, however far distant they were, who came within Chinese cognizance were looked upon as barbarians, as lesser people. I should add that the term for barbarian which the Chinese used varied according to the kind of people they were dealing with. They did distinguish, for example, the people to the north of their country who were frequently invaders but whose characteristics as far as the Chinese were concerned were that they were nomads and rode horses, from other people who were agricultural, to the South of China.

This was a world system which the Chinese ran and it operated on and off for well over a thousand years. Missions came from these countries which were referred to as tribute missions; they came to the Chinese capital, they were required to kneel three times and at each kneeling to bow their heads on the ground as a sign of recognition of the authority of the Chinese emperor. There was a working world system of tribute missions; it does not follow, of course, that all the powers which sent these tribute missions took the same view of their function as the Chinese did. Nevertheless this was the world in which China lived and it was a world still functioning at a time when Britain, in the first Anglo-Chinese war of 1840, delivered the first blow which was to destroy the old Chinese world.

I would like you to think of China in a way that is quite easy because everyone knows about the Great Wall of China. If you can imagine a wall round the whole country from which Chinese have issued forth at various times and into which others have been admitted in exceptional circumstances, when they came as tribute missions or as honoured guests for some reason, this will, I think, give you the psychological condition about which I want to talk. And I would like to illustrate, right at the beginning, two cases of what I would call the movement in and out of this wall; movement inwards and the result of Chinese behaviour. If one takes the Tai Ping rebellion of 1851 to 1864, one of the major rebellions in the whole of world history in the number of lives lost, it was started by a man, who was subsequently found to be deranged, but who got hold of a Christian tract and saw himself as saving China in

Christian terms. Many missionaries at the time were fascinated by this prospect of the Christian faith being spread throughout China through the agency of this man and the very successful rebellion he was creating. But it was soon discovered by one of the missionaries that in fact Hung Hsiu-chuan, the leader, did not represent Christianity in a way that the West could recognize. He declared himself to be the younger brother of Jesus; now by calling himself the younger brother of Jesus, he immediately translated the Christian setting into a Confucian context; it was part of a Confucian family; he admitted the superiority of Jesus but he came next because he was the younger brother and the younger brother, in the Confucian system, came next to the elder brother in authority. I often think that the parallel between Stalin and Mao Zedong is not far different. But that was a case of China importing something for Chinese needs and translating it into Chinese terms.

If you were a visitor, what effect did China have on you as a foreigner? What did it gradually impose upon you? I would like to start with a quotation. The founder of the China Inland Mission, Hudson Taylor, who went to China from this country in the late fifties or early sixties of the last century, found that when he tried to preach to the Chinese, they looked upon him as a comical figure, because he was a foreigner; his daughter's biography tells us: 'Attention was continually distracted from his message by his appearance, which to his hearers was as undignified as it was comical. And after all, surely it mattered more to be suitably attired from the Chinese point of view when it was the Chinese he wanted to win. That night he took the step which was to have so great an influence on the evangelization of Inland China; when the barber had done his best, the young missionary darkened his remaining hair to match the long black braid. Then in the morning he put on as best he might the loose unaccustomed garments and appeared for the first time in the gown and satin shoes of the teacher or man of the scholarly class.' Certainly in the days of my own childhood in the nineteen twenties, whenever he went out on evangelical missions, my father always wore Chinese clothes.

I mention that because the whole Chinese attitude has, in the past, been one of 'if we bring them into our country, if we treat them in the right way, they will recognize, they will acknowledge the virtues of our civilization and they will become sinicized as a result of it.' Indeed, when Messrs Jardine and Matheson and suchlike were given room in Canton to become merchants there, it was the confident Chinese belief that in due course these stout Scottish merchants would become good Confucian followers of the Emperor. I am afraid the Chinese mistook Scottish capacities.

As a result of events during the nineteenth century, the Chinese realized that these foreigners could not be domesticated as they had tried to domesticate people in the past and they began a movement which was called a self-strengthening movement. The assumption was that the Chinese world need not be disturbed so long as the Chinese got the weapons which would be necessary to drive these foreigners out. It was apparent that the Chinese had been defeated in 1840 and again in 1856 because the foreigners had faster ships and better guns. In that case the Chinese must get better guns and faster ships and once they were equipped militarily and navally, they would drive the foreigners out and the Chinese world would remain undisturbed.

I would like to illustrate this assumption that China lived in its own world and that those who came, could only come if they came in the right spirit and behaved properly. The missionary Timothy Richard, in 1875, was in Shantung Province near a town called Chingchoufu and he was stopped in the street by a Chinese. The Chinese said to him, 'Where do you come from?' and he said from Chingchou; the Chinese said, 'But you're not Chinese! Where do you come from, what country do you come from?' so Timothy Richard said, 'I come from England.' 'England,' exclaimed the Chinese, 'that is the country which recently rebelled against us.' Timothy Richard said, 'But England couldn't have rebelled against China because it doesn't belong to China.' 'But she did,' he retorted, 'before that time she was one of the nations that paid tribute to China; when England revolted it was the greatest rebellion since the world began.' There was an ordinary Chinese in the street in 1875 and that was his view of the English and what had happened as a result of the two wars fought: the Anglo-Chinese wars of 1840 and 1856. Nevertheless, as time was passing there were other Chinese, of course, who understood that things were much more complex than they had imagined. And a new attitude developed: 'All right, if the Chinese world is being invaded, almost broken up, how can we preserve everything that matters and what are we going to do about this Western invasion?'. They adopted a slogan which took concepts common in Chinese history: 'Chinese learning for the base, Western learning for use.' These Chinese words *Ti* and *Yung* had been used by many Chinese philosophers, and can be translated by various words; sometimes they are translated as 'substance' and 'function', sometimes as 'principle' and 'manifestation', sometimes as 'foundation' and 'use'. But I think in the minds of the Chinese who used them, this being about the eighties and nineties of the last century, was the idea that Chinese philosophy, Chinese beliefs, Chinese values, Chinese society need not be changed, but what was evidently necessary was the process of industrialization; the scientific and technological achievements of the West must be imported into China so that China's strength would be equal to the West and China could hold the West at bay, keeping its values but simply adding, as it were, the top storey to the civilization in the form of the Western technology.

One gets a phrase here or there which reminds one of the Chinese attitude at that time and also, I may say, reminds one that the Chinese possessed a logical cosmology a great deal earlier than Europe ever did. Here is one Mandarin of 1879: 'According to the way of heaven, there is a small change once every several hundred years and a great change once every several thousand years. Now the European nations suddenly arise overseas by means of their knowledge of machinery and mathematics. They go everywhere in search of trade and diplomatic relations; it is not possible to close the doors and rule the empire in isolation. Therefore the empire has to be changed from a divided world, in which the Chinese are segregated from the barbarians, to an integrated world in which China and foreign countries are in close connection.' That was in 1879 and that was an admission of what China would have to do.

Nevertheless, in a country the size of China you have all sorts of attitudes and you have people clinging to their own ways, their own values. As late as 1898, when Chinese had begun travelling abroad (having sent their first ambassador to London in 1877), a Chinese mandarin who visited Britain had a simple view: 'As to human affairs,' he wrote, 'China emphasizes human relationships and honours benevolence and righteousness; in the West, on the contrary, a son does not take care of his father, a minister cheats his emperor, a wife is more honoured than a husband, thus the bond of the three relationships is broken. Because the proper relationship between husband and wife is not cultivated, the marriage ceremony is neglected; as soon as a girl is twenty-one, she is permitted to find a husband whom she likes; there are those who make many selections and trials before they make a match, they do not consider sexual relations preceding marriage as a shame. Beautiful young girls are seeking for males everywhere, the hoary-headed and the widows can invite male companions as they like; these customs are bad to such a degree.' There is your Confucian talking; he went on to complain about the different utensils the English use for feeding. 'This must cause the servants a good deal of work,' he said. 'And,' he went on, 'the English follow their unorthodox religion and allow the clergy to overrun the country, exhausting all the people's money in building churches, thus spending useful funds for a useless purpose.' I have heard as many silly things said about China in Britain, in the belief that they are perfectly right, by people who interpret China entirely in terms of their own culture and by its values, without considering that there might be any others.

So, by the beginning of this century China really was at a loss. What could it do? Was it going to have to give up its own world completely? There were a few Chinese at that time who began to think that complete Westernization was the only answer for China. But against that another basic view gained ground: it was that if China could not be at the centre of the old world they had always thought about, at least they would learn from the West the ideas of nationalism; they would learn the nature of a nation state as it had been shaped in the West and China could become an independent nation state. Thus nationalism grew up in the early years of this century.

I am not now going to go on tracing the history of China, working my way through this century. What I want to do is to come to 1949, not skipping over completely the early years of this century, but only saying that the nationalist government of Jiang Kaishek, for reasons I will not go into in detail, failed China; it failed to meet the needs of Chinese nationhood, it failed to produce the kind of economic development and the degree of independence that China wanted. Obviously, of course, the Japanese intrusion into China, their invasion and war against China, very much contributed to this failure, but in my view there were other reasons for that failure too, reasons of doctrine, reasons of social and political attitudes. When the Communists came in in 1949, I think their prime motives were exactly the same as Jiang Kaishek's motives had been; Mao Zedong was of the same generation and he had grown up in this China which looked absolutely for an independent China, a China which could be the equal of the West in every possible way.

I have called this lecture 'China Between Two Worlds' and I have described the old Chinese world; all the time I am trying to put the question: how far has China moved into a new world, or how far is China still tethered to its old world? Let us have the voice of Chairman Mao; in September 1949, three weeks before he proclaimed the new government, he made a speech to a gathering of the Central People's Consultative Council: 'Henceforth, our nation will enter the large family of peace-loving and freedom-loving nations of the world. It will work bravely and industriously to create its own civilization and happiness and will at the same time promote world peace and freedom. Our nation will never again be an insulted nation; we have stood up, the era in which the Chinese were regarded as uncivilized is now over, we will emerge in the world as a nation with a high culture.' I think if you analysed those sentences you would find a degree of ambiguity about them; he sees China coming into the world and he sees China as one nation amongst others, yet on the other hand he is clinging to a concept of what seems to me a slightly separate Chinese civilization, 'we will emerge as a nation with a high culture'. And it is not surprising that a man like Mao Zedong, who had shown no particular desire to leave China and had never left Chinese soil until 1949, should have been a representative of what one might call the self-reliant, China-based attitude.

For most Europeans looking today at China's past there exists a revolution which for them has vaguely the same impact as France in 1789 or more particularly Russia in 1917. However different Russia may be from China at least both revolutions were fought under the same banner of Marxism. And the attraction of that creed sprang from a belief in Marxism as an international doctrine; not merely applicable to all countries but likely to conquer all of them in time. When Chinese intellectuals were drawn to Marxism in the twenties these characteristics may have seemed relevant. If equality with the West was then their overriding aim, what better than a doctrine that stressed this international hope, a doctrine that proposed to sweep away the outdated ways of capitalism; might not China even get ahead of the capitalist West driven by this all-conquering force?

Such views of the communist success in 1949 are misleading in many comments on China in the past forty years. Certainly 1949 marked an important moment in China's 20th century revolution, but in retrospect its importance has been overrated – thanks to Mao Zedong, the lawgiver and charismatic leader. Only by seeing the revolution in terms of China's history – and no country has so long a continuously recorded history, or has reflected so often (as China has) upon the rise and fall of dynasties in that history – can we understand the distinctively national character and historical framework of what has been happening in these last forty years.

A necessary starting point is the 1911 revolution simply because the last dynasty then collapsed and Chinese opinion was by then united in thinking this was the end of a mode of government that had lasted for so many centuries. No one knew what the political future held. Sun Yat Sen's 'virginal naiveté', as Lenin tartly described it, dreamed of a China covered in railways and China would then be on the road to equality. Nevertheless, after 1911 the ingredients of a national consensus had taken shape.

A China that looked back over a century of humiliation by Western power was determined to restore its full sovereignty and to make its way as soon as possible to equality with the West in both the economic and military strength in which China had been found wanting. A city like Shanghai represented modernity and progress, and thinking Chinese flocked there rather than to a decaying Peking; how could they not react to the Sikh policemen directing the traffic as a reminder that this was a largely British-dominated 'international settlement'?

Eight years of fumbling led to a demonstration of protest by university students in Peking at China's treatment in the Versailles Treaty. The date, May 4, 1919, burst out into what has ever since been regarded as the real start of Chinese revolution. The national consensus thereby won a foothold of confidence. 'We are all children of the May 4 movement,' Mao once remarked, and undoubtedly all China's politically conscious leaders were launched by this new tide. Yet even in its earliest years the division between a China doing its own thing in its own way, or a China relying on the West as a source of knowledge and ideas, began to divide the thinkers. If China's identity as a nation was founded not on a religion – China's agnostic culture is still hard for the West to comprehend – then the Chineseness that was the lifeblood of the civilization had to keep its health and devotion: it must not be diluted or undermined. Moreover the case for close cooperation with Western industrial powers was hard to make while China's sovereignty was visibly trampled upon by those very powers. In all major cities foreign 'concessions' were flags that marked China's weakness. Nevertheless, it was still a curious chance of time and place that offered an answer to China's problem. If Confucianism was rejected as a political doctrine that had stultified China for too long, what else was on offer? 'Jane Austen doesn't mean much to us,' a Chinese once said to me, 'but all those Russians, writing about landlords and peasants, we felt at home in that world.'

So the first import was the idea of revolution, violent revolution – had change in China ever come about by other means? And was not China's history spattered with a succession of peasant revolts? It was easy to read China's political differences, as they had displayed themselves by the end of the 'twenties, as those between one party sharing the national consensus, but supported by landlords and another party founded on peasant struggle and guerrilla warfare on the grandest scale. Thus the way forward, founded on the idea of revolution and soon to be fortified by Marxist doctrine, was soon found to be the answer for a civilization whose whole history for two millennia had been enveloped in argument about the nature of government and the cohesion of society. The few advocates of Western liberalism were soon isolated and powerless.

Of course, this Chinese consensus was that of a tiny minority – the educated classes. It could feel that it represented the nation as it always had done. So first among the national aims was China's full independence: Western intrusions expelled, territorial losses restored to Chinese rule. Second was China's modernization, which was then and has ever since remained focussed on the Western powers – and on Japan which had succeeded in the previous half century in getting where China now looked for its own advance.

Third, though scarcely a problem that could be even defined in the 'twenties and 'thirties, was how China, a country which had lived in its own world, believing in its own superiority not as a civilization, but *tout court* as civilization itself, could adjust itself to the full 20th century reality of a world China had not before inhabited and what that might involve.

In one limited but not unimportant way China did join that world on October 1, 1949 when Chairman Mao Zedong proclaimed the new government: the country had turned its back on the cyclical record of dynastic rule by which the dethroned Guomindang had numbered its days from 1911. China would henceforth adopt this dating. All other links between a 'new' China and the world awaited completion of the first priority, an independent China, master of all the territories lost to Western control.

Certainly, after forty years, China has reached a new plateau of stability. The country is in no mood for any more revolutionary chaos of the kind Mao Zedong inflicted upon it. To look back and chart the shifts of mood and power one might say that the first seven years (1949–1956) was a time when the national aims were a priority, while Mao the revolutionary took a back seat. It was Zhou Enlai's happiest period, bruised by the Korean War (to which China had not been a party in its origin) and by virulent American hostility. Mao's zest for imposing his ideas came to the fore in 1957 with the 'hundred flowers', after which thousands of intellectuals suffered from exercising the freedom of speech promised them and an uncounted number disappeared to rural hardship or worse. Mao had never liked intellectuals and was satisfied that the flowers were stinking ones; China could expel these ingrates from any positions of influence.

At the same time Mao scented an external threat to his ideological throne. Khrushchev's secret speech telling the truth about Stalin (over which China was not consulted) was seen as risky revisionism in 1956, and the wires between China and the Soviet Union, always humming with suspicion from the start, broke into open ideological warfare in 1960. Meanwhile on the home front, Mao's simple view of a solution for the Chinese economy was pressed on his colleagues. Where was China's strength? In its vast manpower. The 'great leap forward' would mobilize this manpower to build dams, carve railways out of hillsides, make steel in backyards. Immense battalions were set to work. The output was valueless or worse. His colleagues turned on him – a very bad harvest also caused a famine whose extent was concealed for twenty years, but was appalling – and Mao, disgruntled, retired again from the front line. But the internal peace restored by 1962 did not last long. The advancing 'revisionism' of the Russians was infecting his own party. Mao's indomitable revolutionary spirit girded itself for yet another upheaval. In 1966 the 'cultural revolution' was an outright attack on all his old colleagues, conducted all over the country by teenage gangs of red guards.

It went on for three years, throwing the country deeper and deeper into anarchy. The total of deaths, suffering and distraught people everywhere has never been counted. Most of Mao's old colleagues were cruelly dealt with, millions upon millions were driven from their jobs. Even when these fires were banked by the ailing Zhou Enlai, a new crisis had built up. The Russians had reinforced their frontier. Relations reached an acute point in 1969 when diplomacy behind the scenes averted worse. A China that had superficially allied itself with the world communist movement was soon prepared to turn its back completely on any further doctrinal association. An isolated China – thirsting almost for a war in Mao's case – was lucky in 1971 to encounter an America ready to revise its view of China; Dr Kissinger's secret trip was followed by President Nixon's in February, 1972. This brought the promise of good relations with the major Western power, one that had seen China in the first half of the century as in need of sponsorship and uplift in becoming a modern power. Shattered by the events of 1949 the Americans had taken over two decades to see China without eyes blurred by virulent anti-communism.

This was one turning point. Another would be the internal settlement for which 1976 provided the drama. In January Zhou Enlai died. In April a vast demonstration in Peking – and other cities – ostensibly in memory of Zhou, was plainly anti-Maoist. Four outright supporters of Mao's cultural revolution who had been in advance of the party politburo were up against widespread sentiment against the disasters brought about by Maoism. In September, Mao himself died, and a temporary leader, Hua Guofeng, took over, arrested the 'gang of four', and set China back on course for its national aims. But the real change only came with Deng

Xiaoping's return to authority in December, 1978. He alone, among all the old guard, carried civilian military experience enough to quell or dilute the cultural revolutionists who had clambered into power. At heart a pragmatist, Deng began to correct the errors of the past and to turn China away from stupidity.

It is now ten years since China's national aims have been the sole object of government policy, undiverted by any supposed communist influence as such. The opening to the West and the logic of economic construction are both fixed policies. Japan is, of course, a counterpart of the same opening, though always an asset to China's economic needs. Yet if China's independence territorially and her national aims of equality are in progress, what of the 'two worlds' of my title? Here is a vast country that has lived for centuries within the walled security of its own Chineseness. The China that has ventured out from those walls in the early decades of this century is still as much absorbed by its problem of relations with the West, in the sense of being one civilization confronting another. Pride and the belief in an ancient identity has not been jettisoned; not in the least; what are the thousands of Western tourists hoping to see but evidence of this cultivated past? More than once in the last ten years, Deng's China has reverted to the censorious banishment of those who seemed to press Western freedoms to the exclusion of ancient Chinese consensual ideas of government. May Western materialist capitalism not undermine the country's progress? How can social cohesion, torn apart by the cultural revolution and now harried by the utter disbelief of a younger generation, be regained?

A balanced view of where China now stands must look back and ask how successful has been the attainment of the original national aims, no longer affected by the cloak of Marxism so lightly worn by China after 1949. At the end of the world war a start had been made in restoring national integrity. A country more than half under Japanese control, including all the old treaty ports such as Shanghai and Tientsin, had these out-dated colonial enclaves cancelled in 1943 by the Western powers that had held them. The exclusive diplomatic quarter in Peking followed in 1947.

For the rest, it must be remembered that China's geographical view of its weakness, dimly, but in the end firmly, brought home, was one of Western imperialism nudging against, or overriding, all China's borders. The Russians in Manchuria, the British in their

Indian Empire loosening Tibet from Chinese sovereignty, the British again in Burma, the French in Vietnam, not to mention the Americans in the Philippines, were followed by the crowning humiliation of a militaristic Japan defeating China in a small war in 1894, intruding on Chinese rights in 1915, detaching Manchuria in 1931, and sliding into open warfare in 1937.

What remained to be done when Mao looked out from the imperial seat of Peking in 1949? Tibet, for one, and China marched to restore rights that were indubitable in the Chinese view. Alas! for the tragic outcome of that beginning after forty years. The Mongolian People's Republic that had emerged under Soviet sponsorship, had been signed away by Jiang Kaishek, as agreed at Yalta at Roosevelt's bidding, and Mao had resentfully to follow suit when he visited Stalin in December, 1949. Taiwan, snatched out of China's expectations in the last months of the civil war in 1950 by the unforeseen outbreak of war in Korea, has remained a sore issue, but may now after forty years with the slow but steady dissolution of barriers find its way back to some kind of association with mainland China. Those who think Taiwan's independence a possibility must realize that as a national state this would mean an absolute rejection of the island's Chineseness – something that has no parallel in the whole of Chinese history. That leaves Hong Kong and Macao, both now subject to an agreed return to China, since no other conceivable outcome could follow the emergence of a strong government in a unified China. Thus all the events and the emotions of territorial recovery that moved the leaders in Peking so strongly have now ebbed nearly to vanishing point. With the passage of forty years, China has reached a new plateau of pride and independence in relation to the two major powers that threatened her during that period. The Americans have relinquished the virulent anti-communism which made them eager – had it been possible – to overthrow Mao's rule; the United States can now remain as a useful friend. So, too, the Soviet Union, always suspect as an ally and becoming for a time a dangerous enemy, as well as an ideological heretic in Mao's purist creed, is no less ready to accept an independent China going its own way. Ideology has been drained from the three points of the Washington–Moscow–Peking triangle and its stability is in the interests of all three governments.

The 'eighties have seen China's international conflicts settling down. Relations with Russia should soon return to normal – without any self-conscious communist partnership, which never really existed in the past anyway. This improvement should ease the difficulties China has had with Vietnam and Cambodia, both arising from the Sino-Soviet conflict and Vietnam's readiness to exploit these to its own advantage. Even the long-lasting break with Indonesia and the difficulties with India over the border date from the 'sixties, at a time when both these countries were only too ready to accept American cold war views of China or, as in India's case, to assume wrongly that British encroachment over India's northern border in imperial days could be upheld without reference to China. Such hard-line attitudes are softening.

It is less easy to forecast Japan–China relations. Economic advantage to both parties and a superficial readiness for friendship rests on no firm base if one looks back over what happened in the 19th century and after. In any case, the rivalry that erupted then presupposes some mutual acceptance of balance, the inevitable senior or junior attitude inherent in Confucian hierarchical thinking. Both countries share the same character of East Asian civilization; both are defending the survival of their own culture against Western influence, Japan no less than China, for all the effect that Japanese exports and the constant rise of the Japanese economy has created throughout the world. Both countries share the same sense of enclosure behind their own walls.

In the 'fifties and 'sixties Chinese intentions world-wide were read in terms of the Western world's entrenched views of Leninist and Stalinist Russia. Thus Zhou Enlai's description of Africa (1964) as 'ripe for revolution' surely confirmed China's promotion of revolution outside her own borders. In fact, Zhou was applying to Africa a process that the Chinese had deduced from Asian anti-imperialism. First, imperialism is overthrown by a nationalist movement. Its leaders are corrupted by power and eventually shifts to the left will bring to power a communist party founded on firm doctrine. In those days this was seen – hopefully – as an inexorable tide. Had they not backed the world-winning doctrine of Marxism . . . ? Such hopes have long been abandoned. China may still be a 'communist' country in the eyes of the octogenarians who grew up in the early era of the party and whose experience of the outside world was confined to Russia in the 'thirties. The response of this group, in the face of excessive student demonstrations as a threat of 'bourgeois liberalism' in June, 1989, must be seen as the last gasp of those founding fathers. The difficulty that will remain is that the party is still the organ of power, the top ranks of the civil hierarchy, the peaks of political ambition. It will take time and much juggling if China is to move away from this doctrinal anchor to something that ideologically allows the Confucian past to make itself felt, in the same way that it still does at all lower levels of society.

Suggestions that China may become a world power in the 20th century miss the point that China is still as much involved with its confrontation with the West, as one civilization measured against another, as it was when the division first became fully apparent to the Chinese a century ago. The drama remains the same; the stage the same; and the outcome, while far more distant than any Chinese imagined in 1911 or 1919, still provides the context of China's 20th century revolution. China's entry into the world does not imply an identity defined in any global sense, nor any association outside the Western developed world. For all the current tourism or the younger generation of Chinese going in thousands to universities and scientific institutes in the Western world and Japan, China's sense of its own enclosure, its own distinct identity, is undiminished and will remain so as long as the old priorities survive.

Obviously China's economic progress will take far longer than could have been thought in 1949. Another half century at least will barely be enough to bring China into real modernization. The progress made with the nuclear programme in the 'sixties and 'seventies was enough to give China confidence in her capacity to defend herself against nuclear threats and in naval, military and air power – essentially defensive in purpose, as experts agree, and China is content with this.

After forty years it should be possible to set some markers for China's political development over the next forty. Here is a country where the younger generation has absolutely no faith in communist doctrine and cries out constantly for greater freedom from a government that even in Deng's new era has disappointed them. Against this must be set the disillusionment of a great part of the population in China from the unstaunched wounds of the cultural revolution. And the reverse of that uneasiness is a feeling that 'we knew where we were with Mao; now we don't.'

As ever, the clues to China's future development will be found in China's past. The unquestioned power of authoritarian government has to be questioned – and has been through all this century. The idea that any institutions should exist other than those under government sponsorship was unthinkable in China's past. It was interesting to see how an agnostic civilization would handle religion in the 'new' China of 1949. It was simple to 'nationalize' the Christian missionary enterprise as the foreign missionaries disappeared early in the 'fifties. The answer then was to set up 'patriotic' Buddhist, Roman Catholic, Protestant and other bodies responsive to government leadership.

Can this habit of rejecting any independence – of the press or any other bodies of opinion – make its way in this changing China? By now there is enough opinion that is ready to urge such changes. But it would be a mistake if the Western world were to think that democracy is the simple answer. Adversarial government of the kind that is common throughout the Western world is wholly unthinkable in Confucian terms. Individualism is a European invention, foreign to Chinese thinking. Nothing will convince Mr Deng – nor anyone who is likely to succeed him – that China's progress needs organized political parties. What it does need in almost every aspect of society is greater freedom from government control. If that can slowly be achieved, and in the process the dominance of the Chinese Communist Party can be subtly reshaped into a new political hierarchy, then the 21st century will scarcely be long enough to see its fruition. Chinese civilization's strongest thread running through a millennium is the political one: it will not be altered radically except at a slow pace.

9

Black Culture and Social Inequality in Colombia

PETER WADE*

My interest in the subject of blacks in Colombia began in 1981 when I was living as a tourist, English teacher and part-time barman in the city of Cartagena on the Caribbean – or as the Colombians often say, the Atlantic coast. I had arrived there after extensive travels along the Caribbean coast of Central America, and everywhere along that littoral, the presence of the New World African diaspora was unmistakable and vibrant: perhaps also a surprise for many Europeans who are ignorant of the important black populations of many Central and South American countries. As a white, one was often automatically cast into a series of roles which had clear roots in the colonial past: whatever freedoms had been gained and economic progress made, the blacks still mostly performed manual and service tasks and a white person was regarded in the first instance as a wealthy individual. Cartagena was no exception. Under Spanish rule it had been a principal slave port for the empire and still in 1912, when the last racially classified census for that region was performed, its population was 40% black. Although black heritage was obvious in much of the city's population, it was equally clear that the working class neighbourhoods and the slums were inhabited principally by black people. In the elite neighbourhoods and on the tourist beaches, blacks were almost always performing some kind of service: domestic chores, mending cars, selling fruit and beer to thirsty sunseekers, cleaning windows, preparing food and so forth.

When I returned to England and gained a more bookish perspective, I found that official attitudes to race in Colombia, or at least towards the black population, were complacent. The

* The author has made minor additions and revisions to his original 1989 text of the same title.

135

CARIBBEAN SEA

PANAMA

PACIFIC OCEAN

SANTA MARTA
BARRANQUILLA
CARTAGENA
MOMPOS

VENEZUELA

UNGUÍA
RIVER CAUCA
RIVER ATRATO
RIVER MAGDALENA
MEDELLÍN
QUIBDO
BOGOTÁ
ORINOCO BASIN
BUENAVENTURA

COLOMBIA

AMAZON BASIN

ECUADOR

BRAZIL

PERU

CHOCÓ
ANTIOQUIA
BOGOTÁ
COLOMBIA

COLOMBIA

COLOMBIA
showing places
mentioned in the text
APPROXIMATE SCALE 1cm=120km

COLOMBIA showing places mentioned in the text

taken-for-granted social divisions between blacks and whites I had encountered, the easy stereotypes of blacks as culturally inferior did not, it seemed, constitute a 'problem'. The sociological literature had, in the past, and even sometimes in the present, supported this view, by painting optimistic pictures of the position of the black population.*

A year later, I flew back to Colombia with the aim of investigating the nature of racial discrimination and racism in Colombia. On the plane to Bogotá, I met up with a voluble Colombian medic who enquired after my business there. 'Race relations,' he exclaimed with a good-natured laugh, 'Why, there aren't any: we're all brothers in Colombia.' *Todos somos mestizos*, he said, a well-worn Colombian adage which translates roughly as 'We've all got a touch of the tar-brush.'† Some, however, have more of the tar-brush than others . . .

To grasp the question of race in Colombia, one needs to understand something of the geographical structure of the country and the distribution of its people (see map). From the south of Colombia, the Andes splits into three mountain ranges which run north, separated by the two giant valleys of the River Cauca and the River Magdalena. To the west of this central Andean interior lies the Pacific coastal littoral, a densely-forested, humid and selvatic region. To the east lie the Amazon and Orinoco basins – vast, flat extensions of plains and jungles – this region will scarcely concern us here. To the north, where the Cauca and Magdalena join and debouch into the Caribbean Sea lies the Atlantic coastal region, stretching from the Panamanian border to the top of the peninsula beyond Santa Marta and backed by an extensive hinterland of savannahs, low-lying plains and swampy backwoods. The Spanish

---

* Gilberto Freyre's works on Brazil have been criticized as creating too rosy a vision of black–white relations (see, for example, Freyre 1946). Donald Pierson's *Negroes in Brazil* (1942) has also met with such objections. For Colombia, Solaún and Kronus's more recent study of Cartagena (1973), while it admits the existence of racial discrimination, is generally optimistic about the amelioration of racism and sees integration as a more powerful force. More recently important work has counteracted this tendency. See for example Friedemann (1984) and Friedemann and Arocha (1986), and Whitten (1974). See also Whitten and Friedemann (1974) and Stutzman (1981).

† *Mestizo* literally means mixed-blood of any kind, but is generally used to refer to mixtures between indians and whites, the word mulatto being used for black–white mixtures.

landed first on the Atlantic coast and with its ports of entry this region continued to play a fundamental role. But the real centre of colonial settlement, wealth, culture and power became, and still is, the Andean highlands of the interior, especially around Bogotá, but also centring on the other highland cities as well. The Atlantic coast remained sparsely populated and under-developed, while the Pacific coastal region was hardly settled at all and exploited only for its gold deposits, using large, well-regimented slave gangs.

This regional distribution of wealth and power had corresponding racial configurations. Indian labour was relatively plentiful in the highlands, whereas in the coastal regions, black slaves were more common. They were especially used in the gold-mining areas, since indians proved to be less resistant to the rigours of mine labour. Together, these factors concentrated blacks in the coastal areas – also the least wealthy areas – although they also congregated in some lowland mining areas in the Cauca valley. In the Atlantic coastal region, race mixture with both whites and indians was extensive and blacks are a small minority there; in the Pacific coastal region, however, blacks are still almost 90% of the population.* My fieldwork concentrated on black people from a region called the Chocó, on the Pacific coast: these people are known as *Chocoanos*. My first study was in Unguía, a rural village near the Panamanian border in a zone of agricultural and cattle-raising colonization, where Chocoanos, *Antioqueños* from the highland region of Antioquia (a wealthy white/mestizo area) and *Costeños* from the Atlantic coast region all participated differently in the local economy. My second study was in the highland city of Medellín, the capital of Antioquia, where blacks from the Chocó migrated to seek work.† In both these places, I found that racial discrimination and black disadvantage were tangible aspects of everyday life, recognized by blacks and non-blacks alike, although predictably they had different attitudes to these realities. In Unguía, blacks held hardly any land or cattle, and participated only marginally in commerce – the three

* See Wade (1986) for a discussion of these patterns.
† My first trip was financed by a grant from the Social Science Research Council of Great Britain. The second trip was made possible by grants from the Social Science Research Council of the United States of America, and the British Academy, and by a Research Fellowship from Queens' College, Cambridge.

mainstays of the local economy. In Medellín, they were mainly domestic servants, construction workers and sellers of cooked food on the streets – all badly paid, unstable occupations. How, then, could the idea exist that Colombia was an example of a Latin American 'racial democracy'? Essentially, five claims are made in support of such an idea. First, the majority of Colombians are of mixed blood. Thus, apparently, there can be no specific group of blacks: there is only an infinitely variegated continuum from white to black with no definite breaks. Then, as Marvin Harris says, since the '*sine qua non* of any thorough-going minority system is a foolproof method for separating a population into superordinate and subordinate groups' (1974:54), there can be no such system in Colombia, because there are no 'sharply defined racial groups' (1974:54). Second, and as a corollary of the first, intermarriage between people of different coloured skin exists and is relatively frequent compared to places like the USA or South Africa: this, surely, is a sign of racial democracy? Third, some coloured individuals have succeeded economically and made it into the middle classes: here they are accepted socially as, so to speak, honorary whites. Fourth, and again as a corollary to the third, the position of blacks is said to be due to class inequality not race: blacks are simply poor and suffer as such, but not specifically as blacks. If a black person can succeed economically and be accepted, surely economics is more important than race? Fifth, there is very little overt violence directed against non-blacks by black people in protest at their position: therefore, perhaps, their position is not a bad one.

Let us look more closely at these points. To begin with, however, there are two ground-rules which have to be borne in mind. Firstly, there is no avoiding the fact that the situation is complex. We are not dealing with simple, straightforward black/white oppositions; we are not in South Africa, the USA or even Great Britain, where, whatever the complications of inter-marriage, group boundaries and particular modes of racial classification,* such oppositions are held to exist. Race mixture in Colombia has created a situation in which, at the last national

---

* See Watson (1970) for anomalies in the South African system (see also Dudgard 1978:59–63). See Myrdal (1944) for variations in USA classifications, and Benson (1981) for ambiguity in Britain.

census to include racial classifications (1918), 54% of the population was classed as mixed. After 1918, many departments stopped making racial classifications on the grounds that they were too difficult and arbitrary. The result of this is that there is no real *group* of blacks on a national level. One can talk of 'the blacks' as a general category, but as a coherent social group it is more or less impossible to locate them in any specific way.

The second ground-rule, and one which it is important to bear in mind against the idea that a black Colombian is the same as any other Colombian, is that in *certain regional and local contexts* blacks *do* form groups that are relatively unambiguously bounded and that have specific cultural and structural attributes. The Chocó itself is one example, and the specific context of Unguía and Medellín are others. In addition, at an individual level, black people may find themselves discriminated against in a way not designed to repress black people as a clearly defined minority, but which pressures individual blacks to redefine their own identity in the eyes of others against a background of pervasive and prejudicial images of blacks, a redefinition which ultimately involves the taking-on of a culture which is typically non-black and a disavowal of black culture and blackness itself, even if in the short term a certain amount of judicious role-switching will do the trick.

Bearing in mind these two basic rules is essential in appreciating the complex operation of racial discrimination in Colombia.

Race mixture and whitening

As previously stated, the majority of Colombians are mixed. Everyone has 'a touch of the tar brush'. There are many cracks in this veneer: the obvious predominance of darker people in the lower classes, the aversion of light-skinned middle and upper class people to having blacks or indians as spouses – although not necessarily as unofficial mates (Banton 1967; Bastide 1961). My own reaction is to invoke the second ground-rule set out above. Look at the elite neighbourhoods of Cartagena on the Atlantic coast where the blacks clearly form a servant class for middle and upper class people who are white or light-skinned. Look at the rural stretches along the Atlantic coast where black fishing households line the beaches and the non-blacks are immigrant entrepreneurs or tourists. Look at the Pacific coastal region where the direct descendents of black slave mining-gangs predominate over a small intrusive nucleus of white and mestizo merchants and capitalists. Look at Unguía where the Chocoanos are juxtaposed to an immigrant white/mestizo group of Antioqueño colonists and entrepreneurs and another group of mixed-blood Costeño immigrant farmers and landless labourers from the Atlantic coast region. Or look at Medellín where black migrants from the Pacific coast form a clearly identifiable racial minority. As Norman Whitten found in his study of Ecuador and Colombia, 'Blackness is the opposite of whiteness and national concepts of "mixed" in Colombia and Ecuador stand opposed to "black" just as white is the opposite of black' (1974:199).

In all these contexts, there are elements of an opposition between a group identified by themselves and by others as clearly black and another identified as non-black. There may be complex interactions between these groups, but even though some blurring of their boundaries results, in Unguía I found that statistically they maintain a distinct endogamy which is not based on class differences alone (see Wade 1984). Because of this and other patterns of intra-ethnic relationships, and the quite definite folk concepts of ethnic and racial identities that people hold, it is generally easy to delimit distinct groups.

This kind of data not only belies the image of the Latin American melting-pot which issues forth an undifferentiated light-brown population, it also undermines more scholarly accounts of the 'maximization of ambiguity' (Harris 1970) in Latin American racial classification, caused by race mixture, which supposedly makes it impossible to delineate a black group. Harris shows that a multiplicity of racial terms exists for classifying people racially and he concludes that this creates an ambiguity which irremediably blurs the boundaries of racial groups. However, in certain contexts, it is clear that *negro* is a relatively unambiguous category.*

So, black groups exist; but here it is necessary to remember the first ground-rule. They are not rigorously defined minorities. For example in my fieldwork in the Colombian town of Unguía, I found that intermarriage rates for blacks were of the same order of

---

* See also Sanjek (1971) who shows that the multiplicity of racial terms in fact concentrates around certain core images.

magnitude as Detroit Protestant–Catholic or Israeli European–
Oriental Jew intermarriage rates, and much higher than USA or
South African black–white rates. The situation in Unguía is complicated by the presence of the Costeños, a third, intermediate
group of mostly mixed people who diluted the opposition between
the entirely black group and the entirely non-black group: a great
deal of the intermarriage observed occurred between the Costeños
and the Chocoanos. Whatever the particularities of this case,
however, the point is that across the boundaries of the black groups
– even in these regional and local contexts where they form social
units – there exists a process of osmosis by race mixture. I also
found that in Medellín, black Chocoano migrants often married or
lived with non-black partners.

The irony here lies in the fact that it is precisely this process that
acts as a mechanism in the perpetuation of racial inequality. Race
mixture is not a morally neutral ratio of expected over observed
frequencies of intermarriage, it is a social process heavily loaded
with cultural meanings: it is conceived of as *blanqueamiento*, i.e.
'whitening'. It is seen as a distancing of oneself, via one's offspring,
from blackness – negatively valued – towards whiteness – posi-
tively valued. Blackness (and indianness) are seen by the
white/mestizo majority as culturally inferior, an aspect of, as it
were, the past of the country which can be superseded by progress
and development. In this ideology, 'primitive' elements of the
Colombian national image will be absorbed and erased, in short
whitened, constituting thereby a step upwards in the progress
towards civilisation and development (see Stutzman 1981, Whitten
1985). As a motive *blanqueamiento* may be stated openly by the
parties concerned in intermarriage, or inferred in gossip by others.
As a process it may consist of dark-skinned women giving sexual
favours to lighter-skinned men in the hope of lighter-coloured
offspring, of vertically mobile darker-skinned men exchanging
their economic success for the kudos of a lighter-skinned wife, or of
straightforward 'love matches' between people of distinct racial
types. Whatever the process, the meanings attributed to these
actions always acknowledge the superior value of whiteness and the
explicit or implicit slur cast on blackness. I came across black
women in Unguía and Medellín who said openly that they preferred a non-black husband or boyfriend. Other black women saw

this admission as 'grinding your own face in the dirt'. Even if such a motive is not admitted, others may well attribute it to the parties concerned. One Chocoano mother in Medellín whose daughters had married or had children by white men told me that she had been accused of being a 'racist' by other blacks, because, to them, condoning her daughters' behaviour indicated that she scorned blackness. In short, then, the very chance of escaping blackness publicizes the low value placed on it by society and by the blacks themselves.*

There are certain objective consequences too. If black people who achieve some measure of success 'marry up' racially then blackness is gradually bleached out of the middle strata into which these people ascend. Hence the maintenance of an overall correlation between race and class. Not only images of black and white, but the structural position of blackness are perpetuated.

Of course, *blanqueamiento* is predicated on the fact that only a few people can do it: if everyone could do it the system would collapse. Its nature is individualistic.

Individual mobility

It has always been the case in Colombia and Latin America generally that just as a handful of blacks whiten their offspring, another handful (not surprisingly, two overlapping samples) succeed in advancing their economic fortunes. Concrete examples appeared in my fieldwork. When I first copied out the records of the local government anti-hoof-and-mouth disease agency which censused the cattle on all the farms in the region, I found that, although the blacks as a group had been largely pushed out of landholding and hardly participated in cattle-farming, there was a handful of blacks (10% of the farmers) who owned about 880 cattle between them (6% of the total).† When I copied out the records in July

---

* Jackson (1976) gives a good account of the real meaning behind *blanqueamiento* or, as he calls it, 'ethnic lynching'. See also Banton (1967:280), Whitten (1985) and Stutzman (1981).
† The agency's censuses did not include the racial type of the farmers, nor their regional origin (in this case, the latter was an accurate guide to the former). However, the enumerators were able to identify all the farmers according to their colour and origin.

1985, three years later, that handful had almost doubled their holdings, registering a rise to 9% of the total cattle stock, an increase much greater than that achieved by the two other groups.*

Now, the cattle that farmers have on their ranches are usually not all their own property. They may rent out excess pasture and, more particularly, they may enter into profit-sharing arrangements with others. Here another person, with or without land, buys young cattle and puts them in the care of the farmer who raises them on his/her farm, bearing the costs of several years of fattening. These costs include maintenance of pastures by weeding and fumigating, vaccinating the cattle and purging them of parasites, branding, castrating, milking, providing salt-licks, etc. When the cattle are sold, the profits (less transportation costs) are split. Thus, for example, one black farmer had 150 cattle on his farm in July 1985 of which 60 were *a utilidades* ('at profits') with 4 different partners. Almost by definition, since the blacks here, as elsewhere, have the least access to capital, these partners are not fellow blacks. In this case, one partner was another black who had a small number of cattle *a utilidades*. Thus the lack of capital among the blacks means that economic success depends on forming links with non-blacks. The black farmer of this example employed blacks on his farm and associated mostly with them in his social life; to get capital investment however he had to look outside his own group.

This is the essence of the structure of black upward mobility. Only a handful make it (for reasons I will discuss later, but which centre on a combination of inexperience plus cumulative and direct racial discrimination), and those who do almost inevitably become involved in various economic relationships with non-blacks. Another example is the case of Chocoanos in Medellín. Although they often occupy the lowest social strata of the city, they are also often better off than they were in the Chocó. Leaving their poor and under-developed homeland and entering the non-black world of the highland interior where, although poverty abounds, there are the greater opportunities attendant upon a centre of power and wealth, gives the Chocoanos a chance of upward mobility, albeit

* This return visit was made possible by grants from several bodies, including the British Academy, the Durham Fund of King's College, Cambridge and Queens' College, Cambridge.

minor. For those with higher aspirations, exit from the Chocó is almost inevitable, since educational opportunities are so limited there. Again, then, the chance of a good education or better work opportunities is predicated on forming links with non-blacks.

Now this process in itself, in principle, presents no real problem; like race mixture, it may present, in abstract form, a benign façade. In reality, as before, this form of mobility itself becomes a subtle means by which racial inequality remains uncorrected. To begin with, it is too easily forgotten that black mobility is a minority process – the majority remain poor. There are also more hidden processes at work. While some of these economic links with non-blacks may remain at a purely business level, as in the case of the black farmer, very often they involve much more extensive social links, as is often the case with Chocoanos in Medellín. Two different, but related processes operate here. In the first place, the individuals themselves may begin to take on the cultural mores and values of their new territory and social environment – a well-known phenomenon in social mobility. This may involve accepting, at some level, current images of black culture and thus deprecating their own cultural origins; the culmination of this is often finding a lighter-coloured spouse. Clearly the ground is laid here for complex personal conflicts about identity, particularly because of the indelibility of race as a social marker. The actual rejection of one's own origins, and thus implicitly of self, is not inevitable: some blacks in Medellín, for example, form ethnic enclaves in which to protect their identity to some extent. But many others, and especially their children, adapt their ways to those of the Antioqueños.

The second process is that other, non-mobile blacks resent the association of mobile blacks with non-blacks and feel they have been betrayed. This resentment and accusations of betrayal can occur even when links are almost solely economic. One successful black farmer in Unguía was thus accused for certain commercial links he maintained with whites, despite the fact that he had a black wife, employed a black farm administrator and associated mainly with other blacks. Blacks living in Medellín often experience accusations of behaving as if they felt superior to other blacks because they have lost some of their Chocoano ways. In short, resentment arises and it may fuel itself from any evidence, however partial. I found that blacks constantly complained that 'we blacks discriminate against each other', that is, that some blacks, especially when they begin to rise socially, feel themselves superior to, and begin to look down on, other blacks. As one woman said, 'It's something we blacks have: you could say it was instinctive.'

The net result of these processes is a chronic lack of solidarity among the blacks which has two sources: one, the structural nature of black mobility which, especially when allied with race mixture, allows certain individuals to advance and transmute their identity; and two, the feeling, born of this and subject to stereotypic over-generalization, that blacks are constantly being betrayed by their own kind. The black category as a whole cannot be solidary; this is the obvious corollary of centuries of race mixture which have created a colour continuum. But even where black groups do form in local or regional contexts, the same types of mechanism operate which have undermined the creation of a national black group. That is, individualistic mobility, often combined with *blanqueamiento*, destroys the solidarity of the black group, both structurally (since certain people make the group's boundaries ambiguous in the act of penetrating them) and in terms of blacks' perceptions (since they accuse of betrayal both blacks who are trying to escape the black group and those who are still basically within it).

Now, it may be maintained that lack of racial solidarity is, at bottom, not a bad thing: individual competition is to be promoted precisely because it permeates group boundaries and, ultimately, destroys their significance, leaving everyone competing as individuals. This is clearly a notion which, while it may represent a viable strategy to be pursued for some groups in some situations – what Banton calls a 'low-profile strategy' (1983:406) – is unrealistic for a group suffering from subtle and deeply-embedded forms of exclusion. The possibility of the democratization of individual competition is, for them, a distant one. Here some kind of 'high-profile strategy' (ibid.) is better which draws attention to group membership, group disadvantage and needs group solidarity.

For example, in Brazil racial discrimination was only made illegal in 1950 when the black North American dancer, Katherine Dunham, was refused entry to the Hotel Esplanada in São Paulo. Her protests sparked a row and Gilberto Freyre (a member of the Chamber of Deputies and author of *Masters and Slaves* which portrayed a benevolent picture of Brazilian race relations) together with Afonso Arinos had a bill passed outlawing racial discrimination (Fernandes 1969:406–8; Degler 1973:138). Prior to this, Brazilian blacks had either not bothered to attempt entry to these hotels and other places implicitly reserved for non-blacks, or had not protested effectively at being refused, i.e. they had adopted a low-profile strategy when a high-profile one was much more effective in getting results.

In Colombia a handful of blacks achieve some kind of advancement. The majority remain below, with few opportunities for advancement. They form black communities which elaborate their own cultural forms and identity in symbolic and concrete resistance to the dominance of the non-black world. However, alongside positive feelings about Chocoano identity and pride in being black, I also found some blacks accepting in a piecemeal and ambivalent fashion negative images of black people (Wade 1984:124). As a group it was also clear that their solidarity and corresponding possibilities of political mobilization were undermined by the escape of some of their more successful members (and potential leaders). The blacks were riven by internal jealousies and lacking in the necessary confidence, solidarity and leadership to adopt a high-profile strategy.

Race and class

The question that has arisen more than once is: why do the majority of blacks not make it? What are the mechanisms that keep them in the lower strata?

Here we come upon a knotty set of problems. A typical answer is: 'class rather than race', i.e. it is because the blacks are poor, not because they are black. One has to remember here that 'the very idea of a "racial problem" . . . is an obstacle to clear thinking . . . problems which have loosely been called racial are economic, social, psychological and political problems' (Banton 1983:405). At the same time, one has to remember that certain economic and other problems may affect blacks more than others, or be specific to them as a group. The rather slippery formula 'class rather than race' thus becomes the more precise statement that blacks are in the same position as other Colombians, given the overall class structure of the country; or at least that the differences are insignificant.

Attempts to sustain this idea have used different kinds of evidence. One idea is that 'money whitens', i.e. economic success leads to a racial reclassification in the eyes of others. People use a different colour term to describe a person who looks well-off from that used for the same person looking poor (see e.g. Solaún and Kronus 1973). More generally, this refers again to the whole ideology of *blanqueamiento* which opens for black people the possibility of distancing themselves from the category 'black', this time by economic improvement rather than simply by 'marrying up'. This needs to be seen in perspective: in my experience, a person classed unequivocally as black – i.e. who has all the phenotypical attributes of a black – will never be classed as anything else no matter how rich he or she is. This possibility is only open to those whose racial identity is already ambiguous. An interesting contrary case emerged when I showed people a picture of a friend of my family sitting in my parents' drawing room in London. His dress and surroundings were unmistakably not poor, even to the foreign, inexperienced eye. His father is West Indian and his mother white. His skin is white, but his hair, although light brown, is observably negroid and his facial features show some traces of the same ancestry. When black Colombians saw this they unfailingly remarked upon it. Far from according him the status of an honorary white or 'not noticing' his racial heritage because he looked well-off, black Colombians were very acute in their perception of racial ancestry. Money may turn some blacks into social non-blacks, but their origins are never forgotten.

More systematic evidence than this has been brought to bear. Harris (1952) and Solaún and Kronus (1973) show that status groups are more homogeneous with respect to economic indices than they are with respect to racial types. In other words, the groups one sees 'on the ground' have a variety of racial types who are all more or less economically equal. A major problem here is that, since race and class largely coincide, the difference in degrees of homogeneity is rather small and not very meaningful. That is, the groups on the ground are *de facto* made up of people who are racially similar: a status group made up of poor people is also made up mostly of blacks with just a sprinkling of non-blacks. This picture is also extremely static. No indication is given of whether the coincidence of race and class is due partly or wholly to historical factors of racial inequality which are being currently overcome, or to contemporary and persistent processes of racial discrimination. Another problem is that 'status group', if not defined in an obviously tautological fashion by the economic indices themselves, is defined by some rather vague and implicit notion of 'the groups on the ground' and often these are defined by an equally vague criterion of 'best friends', i.e. who socializes intimately with whom. In effect the idea is that blacks are in the same position as everyone else because they have the same kind of best friends as others, at a given class level. However, both Harris and Solaún and Kronus demonstrate that it is precisely the blacks who achieve upward mobility into the higher classes who are subjected to exclusionary practices by non-black social institutions, such as elite clubs and social circles. Non-blacks and blacks may be 'best friends' in the lower and perhaps the middle classes – although this is by no means necessarily the case – but as one ascends the class ladder, blackness can become a serious barrier to social interaction with economic equals.

My own research indicated that the idea that blacks are undifferentiated from others is manifestly untrue; and the differences are substantial. I did find, as did Harris, that intimate friendships and marriages occurred more frequently across racial and ethnic boundaries than across class ones, but I also found that, on average, poor blacks had less economic opportunity than poor non-blacks due to patterns of patronage between the latter and richer non-blacks, patronage that is not extended to the blacks and was not as available to them from the small nucleus of richer blacks. Both in Unguía and in Medellín, a poor Antioqueño had a better chance of upward mobility than a black because he or she was able to benefit materially from connections with richer Antioqueños who tended to distrust the blacks and discriminate against them outside certain occupational spheres like domestic service and manual labour. In my case, race and class did *not* largely coincide, making an assessment of the differential patterns of mobility possible. I also found in Unguía that blacks as a group had been largely expelled from landholding, stock-raising and commerce, the three big money-earners of the region. They had experienced an absolute improvement, but a relative decline in their economic situation. In short, they occupied a very different economic niche from the other two groups, in which their opportunities were also different. In Medellín, too, statistical analysis showed that while Chocoano immigrants shared many features with other poor immigrants, they had certain characteristics which militated against equal opportunities for upward mobility. For example, they were much more heavily concentrated in domestic service (40% of their workers, compared to only 9% of immigrant Antioqueño workers) which is a notoriously underpaid occupation.* These differences are clearly due in part to ground-rule two, i.e. that blacks formed a distinguishable group with a distinct culture and history.

It is also worth bearing in mind more general considerations. While at some abstract level class and race have to be separated as factors, it is also true that 'race is the modality in which class relations are experienced . . . The two are inseparable' (Hall et al. 1978:394). One has to be careful of theoretically analysing the 'opus operatum' – i.e. the objective structures of racial and class stratification – to the detriment of the 'modus operandi' – i.e. how people are created by and themselves recreate those structures through their actions and experience (Bourdieu 1977). Thus it is regrettably theoreticist and ahistorical to ignore that a poor black *cannot*, in Colombia, be seen by another Colombian simply as a poor person, but is inevitably perceived as a poor *black*, the bearer of a specific, negatively-valued sub-culture and phenotype.

Again it is necessary to restate something quite obvious: 'class systems no longer function in the same way once class has phenotypical associations . . . processes of selection come into operation that cannot exist in a [racially] homogeneous population' (Pitt-Rivers 1967). This is to do with the special role race has as an indelible marker which creates a fixity of ascribed, and also subjective, identity (see Wade 1985 for a detailed discussion). It is also connected to the fact that racial, like gender, ideologies 'discover what other ideologies have to construct', i.e. differences (Gilroy 1982).

We can return then to the original question: why do the majority of blacks not make it?

* The material on Medellín is contained partly in Wade (1987) and in more detail in a forthcoming book.

Discrimination and adaptation

There is no question that blacks who form groups in the kinds of contexts I have briefly described suffer from direct racial discrimination at the hands of non-blacks who control substantial amounts of wealth and resources. A series of images and stereotypes exist which characterize blacks as irresponsible, lazy, spendthrift, good for only physical labour, disorganized in family and general lifestyle and so forth. While few people treat the blacks as if they firmly held these images to be the literal truth about every black, there is a gradual and usually covert exclusion of blacks from certain opportunities of employment and certain types of cooperative relations. In Unguía, some Antioqueños said frankly that they discriminated against blacks, affirming that it made logical sense to do so, in view of what they saw as their previous unfavourable experiences with them as, say, employees. In Medellín, to cite just one example, an experiment involving a black and a non-black group trying to rent rooms advertised in the local press showed that blacks were more frequently refused than non-blacks.

More significant in my view are the much more deeply-embedded structures of inequality. In Medellín, blacks take lowly occupations mostly because they are in the majority poor and badly educated migrants. In the region around Unguía, the blacks now hardly hold any land and one reason for their selling up lies in their particular attitude to land, agriculture and stock-raising; a further cause is that a handful of the Antioqueño white/mestizo colonists had ready capital to offer in return for land. Or again, commerce is dominated by the Antioqueños: the principal reason is a history of dynamic, adaptable entrepreneurship in their region of origin. In another example, blacks find it hard to get a position of trusted employment with these immigrants who discriminate against them; but then many immigrants have been robbed by their black employees. Why are most Chocoanos poor and badly educated? Why do the blacks have this attitude to land? Why do the Antioqueños have entrepreneurial talents (or vice versa, why are the entrepreneurs white and mestizo)? And why have they had bad experiences with black employees?

The answers to these questions are historical in form and also quite complex (see Wade 1984: chs. 2 and 6). Here I shall be brief.

The blacks are descendents of slaves used by the Spanish to mine gold on the Pacific coast. Settlement never got beyond the stage of impermanent and rudimentary frontier colonization. The blacks that were freed (mostly through self-purchase) were not integrated into colonial society but were rejected and retreated into the jungle. Later, wars of independence impoverished the mine-owners and in 1851 the slaves were freed. The whole area was then more or less abandoned, despite the continued presence of great wealth in gold deposits: there was very little infrastructure and the isolated and inaccessible life-style of the blacks, who maintained a fairly independent existence gold-panning in the jungle, posed great problems for the availability of labour (see Sharp 1976).

The region was thus deemed a poor prospect by the whites who maintained only a small dominant nucleus in the main town there, while the rest was relegated to the blacks. The blacks remained there because the possibilities of integration into colonial and post-colonial society had been and remained very restricted. A *de facto* racial segregation set in, stemming from processes of racial discrimination and based on economic and ecological specializations. The blacks became adapted to a specific niche in which agricultural land was limited and very poor; they depended on shifting cultivation, gold-panning, fishing and hunting. Thus attitudes which valued land highly, and entrepreneurial or commercial experience and aspirations were developed to a restricted degree. In short, their present disadvantage in the competition with the Antioqueño immigrants to Unguía or Medellín is due to a history shaped by cumulative forces of racial discrimination.

The opposite applies to the white/mestizo highlanders: they were not discriminated against in the same way and could participate in the currents of development that centred on the highlands. In reality, the facts are much more subtle and complex than this, but this is not the place to enter into the history of Antioquia, their region of origin (see Parsons 1968, Twinam 1982, Brew 1977; see also Wade 1984: chs. 2 and 6; and 1986). Suffice it to say that in this area, although slaves and mining were an important part of the economy, neither occupied a dominant role. Slave-gangs were not an economic form of labour and slaves were distributed singly and in small groups: they integrated both socially and racially and, in the highlands, a group of blacks did not really exist, although many people had black ancestry. At the same time, the indian population declined drastically and rapidly. The elite was forced to diversify and adapt and this formed a basis for their later entrepreneurial success. They relied neither on a stable subservient indian labour force, nor solely on large slave mining-gangs. Thus the eclectic investment portfolio of the elite and the absence of a large mass of blacks (and indians) are two sides of the same coin.

What this adds up to is that the relative non-blackness (and non-indianness) of these highlanders cannot be separated from their overall socio-economic position, just as the blackness of the blacks and the discrimination it entailed is intimately linked to their socio-economic position. Each group has adaptations that entail differential advantage in a competitive confrontation; and it is not by chance that the disadvantages have accrued to the blacks.

Thus the fact that some white merchants have had bad experiences with black employees stealing from them is due to a rather large income gap between them and the different opportunities that face each group, and these facts are in turn deeply embedded in a complex of social and economic structures rooted in the past. It is ironic that the blacks also often attribute the highlanders' success to unscrupulousness and sharp dealing, such that both groups have mutual images of suspicion and distrust that underlie everyday friendliness.

Violence and conflict

Solaún and Kronus (1973) call their study of Cartagena *Discrimination without Violence* and the task they set themselves is to explain how there can be racial discrimination of which blacks and whites are both aware, without there being a violent black reaction. The answer they come up with is that there are significant channels of mobility for blacks to move into the middle classes where they will probably mix racially and have lighter-coloured children who will join the ranks of the mixed-blood population which they find to be relatively complacent about racial discrimination, compared to the poorest black groups and the richest white groups. These channels of mobility represent a 'principle of integration' which outweighs the 'principle of discrimination' and effectively defuses conflict. They also argue that as economic development creates more opportunities, black integration will increase even further, creating even more racial equality. I have already commented on the drawbacks of individualistic upward mobility and its effects on group solidarity; it is also very pertinent to observe that a host of studies of economic development have shown that when change opens up a series of new opportunities, those who are better placed to take advantage of them usually do so to the detriment of the worse off, thus increasing overall inequality (see Long 1977 for some examples). Several studies of blacks in Latin America, including my own, show that in situations where blacks compete with non-blacks in a situation of expanding opportunities, they often lose out, relatively speaking, even if there is some absolute improvement in their position. Part of the reason for this is their inadequate preparation for competition with other groups, given their respective histories. But part of the reason is also that the more advantaged groups tend to discriminate against them in order to keep potential benefits for themselves, and the evidence shows that the more the blacks try and compete, the more discrimination they encounter: their mobility is allowed *on condition* that it takes place on a small scale.* The optimistic view of Solaún and Kronus is therefore not well supported by the evidence. The future may be one of *increasing* conflict as blacks demand fuller rights and benefits in society as blacks and on a group scale rather than as individuals and honorary whites.

In any case, Solaún and Kronus's description of the situation as being *without* violence may itself be rather blinkered. True, Colombia has not witnessed systematic lynching nor urban race riots like those of the USA, nor the violence of South Africa, but neither has it been without conflict in which race played a significant role. In colonial times, many was the time whites in Cartagena quaked in their beds as rumours abounded of murderous uprisings by the blacks, slave and free (Borrego Pla 1973). The backwoods sheltered many *palenques* or maroon communities where runaway slaves had formed their own settlements from which they made excursions to harass local farms and even towns (Arrázola 1970).

* See Whitten (1965 and 1974:198), Ashton (1970), Harris (1952:80), Van den Berghe (1967:74) and Friedemann (1976). All these authors describe situations in which blacks lose out in economic competition, or in which discrimination increases in the face of competition.

One author even goes so far as to state that in Colombia conflicts with the black population 'often took on the aspect of a civil war' (Jaramillo Uribe 1968:59). Even after emancipation in 1851, political configurations sometimes had racial undertones. Delpar (1981:22–24) describes how in the Cauca region of Colombia in the late nineteenth century violent conflict developed between a white Conservative elite and the negroid Liberal masses in which the latter attacked haciendas and individuals on the streets: in this case, race, class and political alignments coincided. Sharp (1969:177) also notes that 'it is very probable that among the many reasons that separated the Liberals from the Conservatives there has been the problem of race.'

On a contemporary level, I came across individual incidents of violent conflict that clearly had racial antagonism as a principal motive. In Unguía in the fifties and sixties, when the Antioqueños first arrived and began to impose themselves on the local area and its inhabitants, there were apparently some fights and even though these appeared under the guise of drunken outbursts, it is clear that they were part of an overall confrontation between the Chocoanos and the Antioqueños. In Medellín as well, in two neighbourhoods where the blacks formed a significant percentage and where they had established their own dance halls which attracted more blacks from other areas of the city, the local Antioqueños reacted violently, throwing stones at the dance halls and harassing the blacks. In both Unguía and Medellín, violence has decreased, but in both cases this is because the Chocoanos have submitted to the Antioqueños' dominion: in Unguía, the latter clearly now control the whole area; in Medellín, in those neighbourhoods where conflict had occurred, the Chocoanos have closed down their dance halls, or moved them away to peripheral areas where the Antioqueños let them be.

A more overtly violent case was recounted to me by a black friend in Buenaventura, a large port town on the Pacific coast, just south of the Chocó. Here the local black population participates unequally in the main sectors of the local economy which are run by white and mestizo outsiders. One small scale business that some of the locals used to operate was that of buying a case or two of whisky and other such goods direct from the ships in port and selling them in town. The customs agents, mostly whites and

mestizos from the interior, would allow themselves to be bribed or
turn a blind eye. Then, for reasons which are unclear, there was a
change in policy and resistance to petty contrabanding increased.
One manifestation of this was a spate of killings in which customs
agents shot down local blacks who were infringing the law. Finally
in May 1971, they killed a young student and this proved too much
for the local populace. There was a demonstration outside the local
customs office which quickly turned into an attack on the building.
Following this, the crowd rampaged through the town, locating
the places where the agents lived and burning their possessions.

Isolated incidents they may be, but discrimination *without* violence is undoubtedly an over-optimistic interpretation. From early
colonial times, blacks have experienced violent repression and
have reacted in ways that have also included violent resistance.

Conclusion

When I was in Unguía, a black friend of mine said to me, 'I
sometimes think the system they have in the United States is
better: where the blacks and the whites have their separate things.
That way everyone knows where they are.' My own impression, as
a white, was that in Colombia it is a good deal easier to get to know
and befriend blacks of any class than it would be in the USA. At
that level, at least, the Colombian system, with its relative absence
of conflict and outright hostility, is a good one. Perhaps as a
corollary, the blacks' chances of changing their position in society
and of reaffirming their culture without destroying its integrity are,
at present, rather less than in the USA.

REFERENCES

Ashton, Guido. 1970. Barrio Piloto: Variables económicos y culturales de
    una erradicación de tugurios en Cali, Colombia. In *Revista Colombiana
    de Antropología* 15:216–248.
Arrázola, Roberto. 1970. *Palenque, primer pueblo libre de América*. Carta-
    gena: Ediciones Hernández.
Banton, Michael. 1967. *Race relations*. London: Tavistock.
    1983. *Racial and ethnic competition*. Cambridge: University Press.

Bastide, Roger. 1961. Dusky Venus, black Apollo. In *Race* 3:10–19.

Benson, Sue. 1981. *Ambiguous ethnicity: interracial families in London.* Cambridge: University Press.

Borrego Pla, María del Carmen. 1973. *Palenques de negros en Cartagena de Indias a fines del siglo 17.* Sevilla: Escuela de Estudios Hispanoamericanos.

Brew, Roger. 1977. *El desarrollo económico de Antioquia desde la Independencia hasta 1920.* Bogotá: Publicaciones del Banco de la República.

Bourdieu, Pierre. 1977. *Outline of a theory of practice.* Cambridge: University Press.

Degler, Carl. 1971. *Neither black nor white.* New York: Macmillan.

Dudgard, John. 1978. *Human rights and the South African legal order.* Princeton, N.J.: University Press.

Fernandes, Florestan. 1969. *The negro in Brazilian society.* New York: Columbia University Press.

Freyre, Gilberto. 1946. *The masters and the slaves.* New York: Knopf.

Friedemann, Nina de. 1976. Negros, monopolio de la tierra, agricultores y desarrollo de plantaciones de azúcar en el valle del río Cauca. In *Tierra, tradición y poder en Colombia: Enfoques antropológicos.* Edited by Nina de Friedemann. Bogotá: Colcultura.

——— 1984. Estudios de negros en la antropología colombiana. In *Un siglo de investigación social: Antropología en Colombia.* Edited by Jaime Arocha and Nina de Friedemann. Bogotá: Etno.

Friedemann, Nina de and Jaime Arocha. 1986. *De sol a sol: Génesis, transformación y presencia de los negros en Colombia.* Bogotá: Planeta.

Gilroy, Paul. 1982. Steppin' out of Babylon: race, class and autonomy. In *The empire strikes back.* Edited by the Centre for Contemporary Cultural Studies. London: Hutchinson and CCCS (Birmingham University).

Hall, Stuart, et al. 1978. *Policing the crisis.* New York: Macmillan.

Harris, Marvin. 1952. Race and class in Minas Velhas. In *Race and class in rural Brazil.* Edited by Charles Wagley. Paris: UNESCO.

——— 1970. Referential ambiguity in the calculus of Brazilian racial terms. In *Southwestern Journal of Anthropology* 27:1–14.

——— 1974. *Patterns of race in the Americas.* New York: Norton Library.

Jackson, Richard. 1976. *The black image in Latin American literature.* Albuquerque: University of New Mexico Press.

Jaramillo Uribe, Jaime. 1968. *Ensayos sobre la historia social colombiana.* Bogotá: Universidad Nacional.

Long, Norman. 1977. *An introduction to the sociology of rural development.* London: Tavistock.

Myrdal, Gunner. 1944. *The American dilemma.* New York: Harper Row.

Parsons, James. 1968 [1949]. *Antioqueño colonization in western Colombia*. Rev. ed. Berkeley: University of California Press.

Pierson, Donald. 1942. *Negroes in Brazil: A study of race contact in Bahía*. Chicago: University Press.

Pitt-Rivers, Julian. 1967. Race, class and colour in Central America and the Andes. *Daedalus* 96(2):542–560.

Sanjek, R. 1971. Brazilian racial terms: Some aspects of meaning and learning. In *American Anthropologist* 73:1126–1144.

Sharp, William. 1976. *Slavery on the Spanish frontier: The Colombian Chocó, 1680–1810*. Norman: University of Oklahoma Press.

Solaún, Mauricio and Stanley Kronus. 1973. *Discrimination without violence*. New York: John Wiley.

Stutzman, Ronald. 1981. El mestizaje: an all-inclusive ideology of exclusion. In *Cultural transformations and ethnicity in modern Ecuador*. Edited by Norman E. Whitten. Urbana: University of Illinois Press.

Twinam, Ann. 1982. *Miners, merchants and farmers in colonial Colombia*. Austin, Texas: University of Texas Press.

Van den Berghe. 1967. *Race and racism*. New York: John Wiley.

Wade, Peter. 1984. Blacks in Colombia: identity and racial discrimination. Unpublished PhD thesis. Cambridge University.

1985. Race and class: the South American blacks. In *Ethnic and Racial Studies* 8(2):233–249.

1986. Patterns of race in Colombia. In *Bulletin of Latin American Research* 5(2):1–19.

1987. Raza y ciudad: Los chocoanos en Medellín. In *Revista Antioqueña de Economía y Desarrollo* 27:35–46.

Watson, Graham. 1970. *Passing for white. A study of racial assimilation in a South African school*. London: Tavistock.

Whitten, Norman. 1965. *Class, kinship and power in an Ecuadorian town*. Stanford: University Press.

1974. *Black frontiersmen: A South American case*. New York: John Wiley.

Whitten, Norman and Nina de Friedemann. 1974. La cultura negra del litoral ecuatoriano y colombiano: Un modelo de adaptación étnica. In *Revista Colombiana de Antropología* 17:75–115.

10

A Clash of Cultures
The Malaysian Experience

DAVID WIDDICOMBE

Introduction

The subject of this lecture is a distant part of the world. There is an eight hour time-gap from here to Malaysia and it takes 16 hours to fly there on a scheduled airline – that is one third of the way round the world. It is a country close to the equator, a tropical land of great beauty. It is prosperous by third world standards, indeed it is really moving out of the third world into the category of 'emerging countries'. It is well-situated geographically on world communication routes and it lies in a growth area of the world, namely the eastern side of the Pacific rim. At the same time it has an acute, perhaps uniquely acute, racial and community problem. The Malays, who are Muslims, constitute about 53% of the population, the Chinese constitute about 35%, the Indians about 11% and there are some indigenous people and a handful of Europeans. The Malays, from their numbers, have political control but the Chinese and Indians have substantial control of the business economy and the country's wealth.

Before looking at those groups more closely, I would like to remind you of Professor Deikman's definition of culture. He said that culture is the 'customs, ideas and attitudes shared by a group, transmitted from generation to generation by learning processes rather than biological inheritance; adherence to these customs and attitudes is regulated by a system of rewards and punishments peculiar to each culture.'[1] You notice that he describes culture as transmitted by environment rather than heredity. As I shall tell you later this is a very live subject in South-East Asia where they discuss whether their problems are genetic or can be solved by environmental remedies. Professor Deikman's definition is simple

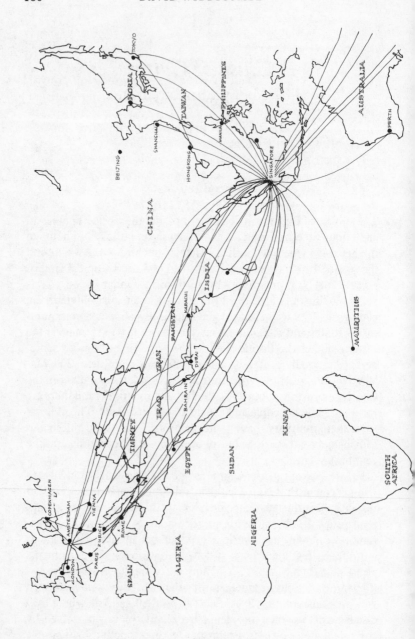

but its application can be complicated. There are many, many gradations of groups constituting a culture and many degrees of differentiation within what might be considered one cultural group. Are the Scots and the English one cultural group or two? But in the example we are going to look at, Malaysia, we shall find groups which are probably as firmly and clearly differentiated as can be found anywhere in the world. So it is a very good example of the problem of cultural groups in conflict elsewhere.

The map on page 160 is based on an ordinary airline map showing the Far East and South-East Asia, India, China, Japan and also Malaysia, with Singapore identified as a central point for airline communications. You can see what I said about the good location of the Malay Peninsula. It is on the route down to Australia and it is on the routes up the east side of the Pacific rim – Singapore, Hong Kong, Taiwan, South Korea, Japan – all important centres of growth. In South-East Asia you find about one sixth of the world's population, some 750 million people. The Malay race covers not only Malaysia but also Indonesia and the Philippines. So it is extensive apart from the Malay Peninsula. The Thais, however, are not Malays.

The map on page 162 is a political map. After the British left in 1957, a federation was formed of the Malay Peninsula, together with Singapore which is at its southern tip, and the old British colonies of Sarawak and North Borneo. The common element of the federation was that they had all been under British rule. Sarawak and Sabah, as North Borneo is now called, are very different indeed from Peninsular Malaysia; the racial mix is different and the economies are different. For that reason this lecture is confined to Peninsular Malaysia. Nor is it concerned very much with Singapore. Singapore is a city of two and a half million people at the tip of the Peninsula. It is 75% Chinese so it is different in racial composition from the rest of Malaysia. It was part of the federation at first, but separated in 1963 because the racial mix was so different. It is very much a Chinese city.

The Malay Peninsula (see map p. 164) is about 350 miles long, and 250 miles at its widest point. The seaward areas are flat land, and down the middle there is a ridge of highlands and some mountains. There is a lot of jungle, rain forest and magnificent beaches, some of which are being developed for tourism. It has in

Present-day Malaysia within South-East Asia

Kuala Lumpur, the capital, a modern city with the usual high rise offices, highways, traffic congestion, hotels and everything you associate with a busy city. The main industries in Malaysia produce 40% of the world's supply of tin, 13% of the world's hardwoods and a large amount of natural rubber, which is exported. Other agricultural products are rice, which is not exported but consumed at home, coconuts, palm oil, pineapples which are canned and exported, sugar cane, tea, coffee and pepper. There is also fishing along the coast.

Attitudes and Prejudices

I am going to look first at the history and origins of the present cultural mixture, and then give some account of the three races, their cultures and the conflict between them, as well as the policies which are being attempted to cope with the clash of the races. Finally I shall say a few inevitably inconclusive words about the lessons we might be able to draw from this. But before I embark on the descriptive part, there are two comments by way of warning which ought to be made in approaching this subject. First of all, it is necessary to be on guard against the attitudes and prejudices which we bring to this subject from our own culture. For instance, we have a certain attitude to the use of time and to work; I remember my own reaction the first time I went to Malaysia to do a case, how irritated I was that people did not seem to think it important to keep appointments on time. Here is something to test your own reactions. See if your prejudices are aroused by the description of a group of people given in this passage:

> Our neighbours were relaxed, they never appeared to fret or hurry, they never seemed anxious, they never ran for buses or got flustered. But then there was never any need to rush; not much was attempted beyond the basics of life; our neighbours never went cinemas, dances, exhibitions, they never had evening classes to attend and seldom gave parties beyond those dictated by the calendar of celebrations. They rarely travelled unnecessarily or read books. The men, in the evening, most often attended the mosque. For many the highlight of the evening was a Malay drama on TV. They had, in fact, a remarkable ability to do nothing; they were totally idle for hours, a state

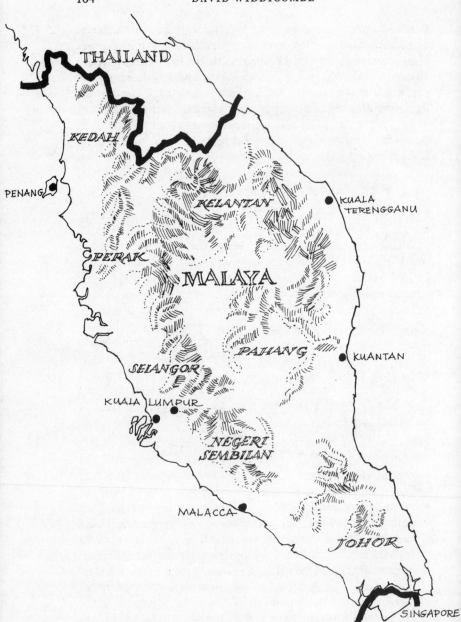

The Malay Peninsula

which would drive even the most easy-going Westerner to activity of some sort. Young men, waiting months or even years to be given a government job, knew nothing of the frustrations of unemployment, they simply waited patiently and unhurriedly for fate to play its next card. Their lives by Western standards were horrifically dull, their demeanour enviably relaxed.[2]

That is an account of life in a Malay kampong by two English school teachers who worked there for three or four years. As you see, it is very easy to call Malays lazy. You may have had that reaction, as I do. But to somebody who can sit and do nothing for hours we seem to be frenetic workaholics and the life we lead looks like a rat race, so which stand-point do you take? It is easy too for Westerners to sympathise with the Chinese and Indian elements of the population. The Chinese, like us, are basically a nation of traders and shopkeepers; they are pragmatic, materialistic, hardworking. The Indians are astute business men and very verbal. We are familiar with both races in the U.K. The Malays are much harder to relate to. There are none of them here and when we make contact with them abroad, as you can see, we bring a lot of prejudices to a life which seems perfectly normal to them.

So the first thing is to watch what we bring from our own culture to a study of theirs and the second comment, by way of warning, is to take care of the way in which history is used. History is to the group or the nation what memory is to the individual. Sometimes, indeed, if you know the history of a region it enables you to predict what is likely to be the future there. But history can be used and abused and this is particularly so in Malaysia. Arguments can be derived from history which sidetrack and divert from an objective consideration of the present. For example, in Malaysia, who was there first? The Malays, who call themselves Bumiputras, i.e. 'sons of the land', claim that they are the original people of Malaysia. But if you want to use history like this, you can show that they are not. There is an aboriginal population, not very many of them, it's true, but they were there before the Malays. It is also a fact that a great part of the present Malay population in Malaysia came there in the 19th century at the same time as the Chinese and Indians.

The pros and cons of British rule are another example of how you

can misuse history. The British brought the Chinese and Indians to
Malaysia in the 19th century and so it can be said that they created
the present problems; but if you want to argue this way about
history, you can say that the British unified the country and, if they
did bring the Chinese and Indians in, it is they who have developed
Malaysia's industry and business, which the Malays could never
have done by themselves. To use history like that is very unprofit-
able. What history does show is that there have been constant
waves of population coming down into South-East Asia from the
North which, over historical periods of time, have been settled and
absorbed into the economy of the area. In the long term, over
hundreds of years, that is a hopeful aspect of the situation in
Malaysia and other parts of South-East Asia.

Now before I look at the history of the area I must pay tribute to
two books. One of them, *The Malay Dilemma*, is by Dr Mahathir
Mohamad. He published it in 1970 in the period immediately after
some serious communal riots in Malaysia and it is about the racial
conflict there. Dr Mahathir Mohamad is now, and has been for
some years, the Prime Minister of Malaysia. It is a courageous,
realistic and illuminating book which nobody interested in this
subject can do without. The other book that I have found interesting is called *In Malaysia* and I have already quoted from it. Published last year by two British school teachers, who lived and
taught in a Malay kampong or village for several years, it is a
detailed, sympathetic and unprejudiced account of what they
experienced.

History

First one has to choose one's calendar. I am going to choose the
Christian calendar, but the Moslems of course start their calendar
from about AD 600 and the Chinese, if they were going to talk about
this, would do it with reference to dynasties. In the thousand years
before the birth of Christ, South-East Asia was subject to waves of
immigration coming from the North, mainly from the area which is
now South China. The earliest people living in the Malay Peninsula
probably arrived at that period. All these people were by way of
'religion' animist in their practices.

Then in the first thousand years of the Christian era the main

influence in this area came from India. There were a number of
Hindu and Buddhist kingdoms set up and physical remains of
them exist in Cambodia and in Java – for example, Angkor Wat in
Cambodia and Borobudur in Java. The island of Bali in Indonesia
(which is not quite what you expect from 'South Pacific'; it is in fact
a large agricultural, tropical island with tourism in only one section
of it) is Hindu, a relic from the time when the whole of this area was
Hindu and Buddhist.

From about AD 1000 onwards for about three or four hundred
years the influence shifted; instead of coming from India it came
from China. China has fluctuated from periods when it looked
outwards to periods when it looked inwards and kept foreigners
out. This was an outward-looking period when the Chinese sailed
the whole of the South China seas. They reached India, and they
settled especially in Malacca in the Malay Peninsula where the
ships that traded from Europe also came. You can see from the
maps on pages 162 and 164 how well placed it was. The Chinese
word 'junk' comes from the Malay word for ship (jong).

Islam was very late in coming to this part of the world. It did not
arrive until the 13th century, not by conquest as was the case in
other parts, but as a peaceful adjunct of trading. There were a lot of
travelling teachers of the Moslem religion who came to this area.
Then dynastic alliances were formed based on the establishment of
the Moslem religion. Effectively, the Arab Empire came to an end
in the year 1258 when the Mongols sacked Baghdad; that cut the
land routes across Asia and forced trade onto the sea. In particular
it forced Europeans to look to the west and the sea rather than to
the east and the land. Venice lost its predominant position, being
overtaken by the Atlantic countries, Portugal and Spain and later
by France, Holland and England. The Arabs themselves took to
the sea; in the 15th century they dominated trade throughout
South-East Asia.

In the 16th century the Portuguese arrived. Their first visit to
Malaysia was in 1509 and in 1511 they seized and held Malacca.
The Portuguese had a series of trading posts; they came round the
Cape of Good Hope to Goa in India. They possessed Malacca in
Malaysia, Macao at the mouth of Pearl River in South China and
Nagasaki in Japan which was the end of the voyage. They tried to
bring Christianity to the area but it made very little progress.

In 1641 the Dutch, who were now catching up on voyaging, seized Malacca from the Portuguese. They held it for 150 years until at the end of the 18th century the British arrived. Having established themselves firmly in India, they moved into this part of the world. In 1786 the British took Penang and in 1795 they seized Malacca from the Dutch. In 1819 they founded Singapore and in 1824 there was a treaty which defined spheres of influence. The British were to have Malaya and the northern part of Borneo while the Dutch were given what is Indonesia and that is the way it stayed from then on. Throughout the 19th century there was Chinese and Indian immigration into the Peninsula sponsored by British interests who needed them to work in the mines and on the rubber plantations; and it was in the 19th century that the present pattern of races in Malaysia was established. There was also, as I mentioned before, a good deal of Malay immigration in the 19th century, especially from Sumatra. There has always been a close connection between that island and the Malay Peninsula – the distance is very short. At night time, if you stand on the shore, you can see the lights of one from the other. Malaysia got its name from a kingdom in Sumatra during the period of Indian influence.

The Three Main Races

Throughout this period, although the racial mix was much as it is now, racial conflict was kept down by the strong external ruling force of the British. The conflict only came into the open when these races were, so to speak, left to themselves in the Peninsula. There are three main races. Before looking at them in turn, it must be remembered that each is in itself very diverse and there are many sub-cultures within each of them. The Malays have many diverse groups because quite a lot of Malay groups immigrated from Indonesia. The Chinese are all from the southern part of China, but they come from many different places and their dialects reflect that – they speak Cantonese, Hokien, Hainanese, and others. The Indians come mainly from South India, from the Madras area and from Sri Lanka. There are Indian Tamils, Sinhalese Tamils and then there are Sinhalese proper – so the Indians have a sub-cultural mix as well. More recently there are some Bangladeshis and Pakistanis who are distinguished from the others by being Moslem, not Hindu. Let us now look at each of these three main races in turn.

1) The Chinese

The *Chinese* account for about 35% of the population, that is 4.2 million out of a total population in the Peninsula of about 12 million. They mostly came in the 19th century, brought in to work the plantations and the mines; they mainly live in the towns although there are some in the countryside, they run shops and businesses, they are strong in the professions and – this is the important thing – they own 75% to 80% of the wealth of the country. In fact they control the economy. They speak various Chinese dialects but, although they are separated by their spoken language, they all use the same Chinese written language. They have a great respect for education.

Here is an example of how the Chinese have control of the economy – it is called 'The Tobacco Factory Case'. One of the most prosperous manufacturing firms in Malaysia produces cigarettes bearing the name of a well-known London firm. In order to demonstrate that it was in accord with government wishes, this foreign company appointed a Malay as Chairman of its board of directors and also took in a small number of Malays to work as gardeners, drivers and unskilled factory workers; the majority of the firm's employees, ranging from executive officers to clerks and skilled workers, were non-Malays. Suddenly a rumour was started that the factory had sacked Chinese employees and replaced them with Malays. Without waiting to confirm the truth of this rumour the local retailers of this brand of cigarettes, 95% of whom were Chinese shopkeepers, issued a boycott. Apparently no actual directive was given by any responsible organisation – by word of mouth the boycott spread throughout the length and breadth of Malaysia. Within a week this firm felt the pinch; before a month was out the situation had become so bad that the company was forced to seek the aid of the Chinese Chambers of Commerce. The company was forced to submit to an inspection by group after group of Chinese before it was admitted that there was no truth in the allegation and the boycott was called off. So the Chinese have a grip on the economy.

What of the religion of the Chinese? 'Religion' is a very difficult
concept for the Chinese to grasp. One reads that in the 18th
century, when Westerners first came in numbers to China, the
Chinese were nonplussed by being asked what their religion was.
In the end they said, 'We must do something to please these
people', so they called themselves Buddhists. In fact the Western
concept of 'religion' has no place for the Chinese. Here is an extract
from a very interesting book published in 1985 and written by an
English Chinese woman, born in China and brought up in
England. It is called *China's Sorrow* by Lynn Pan and here she
gives an account of a funeral in Xian, the ancient capital of China
and home of the famous 'terracotta army', which indicates the
attitude of the Chinese towards these matters:

This signalled the end of the rites and everybody trooped out.
Only the musicians remained and I asked them 'What happens
next?' 'Oh, this is the intermission,' one answered, 'the family
have adjourned upstairs and should be at their noodles now.'
'By the way,' I wanted to know, 'how could you know when to
go crescendo?' 'The service follows a formula,' I was told. What
formula? The rites I'd just witnessed, I was to understand, were
performed for the soul of the dead according to the Confucian –
Taoist – Buddhist mode. This, I must admit, was something of a
surprise. Not the fact that the creeds of the old society survived
after so much deliberate government suppression, for China is
notorious for its inability to shake off its past. Nor the fact that
Confucianism, Taoism and Buddhism were practised side by
side, for I know that the Chinese are little disturbed by the
scrambling of the forms of rival persuasions . . . What surprised
me was the easy way my informant said it, as though it should be
quite obvious. 'What could be more natural?' his tone implied
when his voice pronounced 'the Confucian – Taoist – Buddhist
mode' without a moment's hesitation or doubt. 'What, with all
those invocations to the Chinese Communist Party?' I ventured
to ask. 'Why not?', he answered, thinking it neither remarkable
nor inappropriate that the Party should be called upon in
prayers for the soul of the departed along with the deities of
Confucianism, Taoism and Buddhism. 'They can't all be right,
but one of them might be,' he said, utterly seriously. He

couldn't have expressed a more Chinese opinion, declining to be purist in the matter of belief systems.[3]

The Chinese are described by Dr Mahathir as materialistic, aggressive and with an appetite for work. All true. I have worked with Chinese on many occasions. They are unsentimental people, secretive and clannish. Their unbroken 3000 years of culture give them a deep self-confidence. They are also traditionally not active in politics which is interesting because that is why they have not, until recently, taken a very active part in politics in Malaysia. The Chinese have always been very respectful of authority, there is a lot in their education which induces that. They have not in any way challenged the Malays in their hold on the government of Malaysia.

The Chinese in Malaysia are just one element of what are called the 'overseas Chinese'. There are Chinese groups in many countries of the world, but they are particularly strong in South East Asia and the situation you find in Malaysia is repeated, though not on such an intense scale, in the Philippines, in Java, which is the most densely populated part of Indonesia, and in Thailand. There are 30 million overseas Chinese in the areas I have identified. They are enormously successful everywhere and, although they do not dominate the other places mentioned, that is only because their numbers are smaller. In Malaysia they have such a grip on the economy because they are so numerous. The only place the overseas Chinese are not successful is Japan; apparently they cannot compete with the Japanese in these business qualities we have been talking about. The overseas Chinese send money home to China and there are areas of China which, by all accounts, have paved their roads and built their schools and their hospitals all on money from their overseas relatives. In Malaysia this contact has, to some extent, weakened because after the Communist revolution in 1949 in mainland China, a lot of Chinese in Malaysia felt more detached from their homeland. This is in fact a hopeful development because for the first time the Malaysian Chinese are beginning to consider themselves as Malaysians as well as Chinese. So to sum up, the Chinese have got all the right attitudes for success in the modern world except perhaps interest in political power.

2) *The Indians*

The *Indians* are 11%, or thereabouts, of the population. They
mostly arrived in the 19th century. They are mainly Hindus and
have the caste system. They live partly in the towns and partly on
the big estates which they run. They speak Tamil and Sinhalese.
They are strong in the professions – a good many lawyers and
doctors are Indian – and they have something of a monopoly in
running the railways.

3) *The Malays*

Then we come to the 53% *Malays*. The Malays have a higher birth
rate than the others so that percentage may grow. They have been
there the longest. They are mainly rural in location; they work in
agriculture and on the land. They are very strong in the civil
service, administration, the police and the armed forces because
that is where they were employed by the British. They are not in
the professions; I have never met a Malay lawyer, and they are not
in business to speak of. Because of their majority in the population
the Malays have a majority in the government. It is a coalition
government but the Malay element is predominant. They speak
Malay and its various dialects. There is said to be no real demand
amongst Malays for education, in contrast to the Chinese. By
religion they are all Moslems but it is very noticeable that it is Islam
combined with, or superimposed on, a strong animist tradition.
They have medicine men who are widely consulted and a large part
of their life seems to revolve around animist practices as well as the
practice of the Moslem faith. Islamic fundamentalism is growing in
Malaysia and there is apparently a good deal of veiling for women,
just to take one aspect of it, spreading in Malay communities. The
Moslem religion, in its formal aspects, is very strong in Malaysia
and, if you go there, you feel it is all pervasive. It is the state religion
and it and its attitudes officially pervade almost everything. The
difference in this area of religion between the Chinese and Indians
on the one hand and Malays on the other is well demonstrated by a
test on the school children carried out by the two English school
teachers I mentioned earlier. They asked them to write essays
about the things that they were most afraid of. The Chinese and

Indians all wrote about snakes and tigers, the Malays all wrote about God.

Now what are the Malays like? Dr Mahathir says they are spiritually inclined, tolerant and easy going; here is a quotation from his book:

> The Malay is courteous and self-effacing, his world is full of nobility and he is never far from his Rajs and chiefs. He gives way and he shows them deference, it is good manners to do so. It is not degrading, it is in fact a mark of breeding. It is typical of a Malay to stand aside and let someone else pass . . .
>
> What is good [for the Malay] is not what is pleasant but what is proper. What is proper is laid out in the strict religious code of Islam and of adat (custom). To be well thought of is good for the community and it is also good for the individual; but generally the individual is regarded as secondary to the community.
>
> Formality and ritual rate very high in the Malay concept of values. What is formal is proper . . . Hedonism as such has no place in the Malay code of ethics. Pleasure, whether physical or mental, is considered base. Nothing is done for the sake of pleasure alone. To serve one's fellow man may give satisfaction and pleasure but that is not why a Malay should be of service to others. It is only duty and propriety which move him. The moving force is to appear right in the eyes of God and man. In other words a deed is done because it is proper not because it is pleasant or because it gives one the pleasure of achievement. Physical pleasure is regarded as lowly and must be suppressed or at least hidden. Eating good food in excess is frowned upon, and the drinking of intoxicating drinks is forbidden by religion and partly by public disapproval. There is no Malay equivalent to the Epicurean philosophy of 'Eat, drink and be merry' . . .
>
> There is a fatalism which characterises the Malay attitude to life . . .[4]

and the author expands on that.

Now these attitudes place a great strain on those that adhere to them and this is why, in Malay communities, people from time to time 'run amok'. They did so in 1969. The Chinese had done rather well, too well, in the elections that year and were holding ceremonial parades in Kuala Lumpur and other towns. The strain was too great for the Malays and they ran amok. Dr Mahathir describes it thus:

> Amok is a Malay word. It is a word now universally understood. There is no other single word which can quite describe 'amok'. And the reason is obvious for 'amok' describes yet another facet of the Malay character. 'Amok' represents the external physical expression of the conflict within the Malay which his perpetual observance of the rules and regulations of his life causes in him. It is a spilling over, an overflowing of his inner bitterness. It is a rupture of the bonds that bind him. It is a final and complete escape from reason and training. The strain and the restraint on him is lifted. Responsibility disappears. Nothing matters. He is free. The link with the past is severed, the future holds nothing more. Only the present matters. To use a hackneyed expression he sees red. In a trance, he lashes out indiscriminately. His timid, self-effacing self is displaced. He is now a Mr Hyde, cruel, callous and bent on destruction. But the transition from the self-effacing, courteous Malay to the Amok is always a slow process. It is so slow that it may never come about at all. He may go to his grave before the turmoil in him explodes . . .
>
> [Amongst Malays] the intemperate man is not admired. The impression given is one of continuous restraint which taxes the will. It seems to lead to an inner conflict, and at times the restraining bonds seem to burst and suddenly the polite formality disappears to be replaced by a violent outburst that is frightening in its intensity.[4]

So what conclusion do we reach about the Malays? It is the opposite to the Chinese. Unlike them, the Malays have all the wrong attitudes for life in the modern world and this is the essence of the problem in Malaysia.

Overall Picture

So the overall picture we get of these three races is of three uniquely different cultures with practically nothing in common. Let us run down the list: physiognomy – they look different; language – they all speak and write different languages; occupations are different; locations – they live in different places, the Chinese mainly in the towns, the Malays in the country; their religions are different; they eat different food; their clothes are different; they have different holidays and festivals (one of the advantages of a multi-racial community is that you get a lot of holidays – there are 13 national holidays in Malaysia and about the same again at the state level). The architecture of their buildings is different; their customs are different – for instance the Moslem Malays take off their shoes and expect visitors to do likewise when they enter the house, but you do not have to do that in a Chinese house; their superstitions are different – just to give an example, everybody knows that Chinese ghosts and demons travel in straight lines and do not like to see themselves in mirrors. This is why, if you go into a Chinese garden, the bridges and paths are all crooked, zig-zags and curves, never straight lines, and why you sometimes see in Chinese houses and flats a mirror placed outside the window facing outwards so that the demon sees itself as it approaches and goes away. But I never heard anything to suggest that Malay ghosts and demons, of which there are good collection, are in any way inhibited like this; as far as I know, they can go in any direction, in any curves or zig-zags just as they like; and I have seen no mirrors outside Malay houses. So they don't even share the same approach to such an important thing as ghosts and demons.

As I said food and drink are also different. The Malays, being Moslems, are not allowed alcohol or pork and all the meat they eat must be Halal, which is meat slaughtered with a prayer by someone facing Mecca. The Chinese, on the contrary, as one of my Chinese friends assured me, go by the rule that 'if it moves we eat it'. They are particularly fond of pork – you remember Charles Lamb's essay on the origin of roast pork, which he says was discovered in China by a peasant when his house burnt down. There is no prohibition on alcohol amongst the Chinese. They eat with chop sticks, the Malays and the Indians eat with their hands or with cutlery. So, to quote again the teachers who lived and taught in a Malay kampong, they say that the races remain largely ignorant of, and uninterested in, each other. There is no dialogue between them. For instance there are not many Malay filling stations, but such as there are the Chinese do not use, nor do they employ Malays, except perhaps as drivers or suchlike.

What have the races in Malaysia got in common? I can only think of one thing: they all share the same defined geographical area. What are their attitudes to this situation? Well, the Malays say that they are the original people, they point out that they have got no other country to go to, unlike the Chinese who can go back to China, and the Indians to India. They feel that they are the have-nots in their own land. They resent the Chinese and Indians, and envy their business success and wealth. Inevitably they harbour feelings of violence against them, which at times of social stress can break out openly. It seems that for the Malays, their problem is really to learn the attitudes and abilities required in the modern world. And it must be stated that the Moslem religion as it exists there is not exactly a help in their making that change.

As for the Chinese, they say that they have been in the country a long time, a hundred years or more, and the attitude is that they have got as much right to be there as the Malays. They say that they have developed the country by their business skills, and they resent the protection and privileges which are given to the Malays. They are contemptuous of the Malays, regarding them as dirty, lazy and generally useless. As far as they can, they treat the Malays as if they were not there.

The Indians, whose numbers are much smaller, and who have the same colour of skin as the Malays, prefer to keep a lower profile than the Chinese, but generally speaking share their attitudes. The problem for the Chinese and Indians is to share some of their wealth and success in order to live in harmony with the Malays, because if they do not there will be more violence. It calls for very great self-restraint on their part. In Malaysia, every community feels that it is being discriminated against and that the others are the ones in a more advantageous position.

Policies

What policies have been followed to deal with this potentially explosive situation? They are almost entirely ones to strengthen and bolster the Malay element of the racial mix and to try and enable it to achieve some sort of equality, as far as business is concerned, with the non-Malays. It is called 'constructive protection', but another term for it is 'positive discrimination'. Many of the measures that I am going to mention were started by the British but the policy has been developed further since independence. It is easy for the government to introduce these measures because, as I said, the Malays have the majority in Parliament. The national language is Malay and the national religion is Islam, the religion of the Malays. There are compulsory directorships for Malays in all the larger companies. You remember the tobacco factory had a Malay chairman: that is because the law says there must be at least one director who is a Malay. 70% of all university and college places go to the Malays and the Chinese have not been allowed to have a separate university. In the civil service the Malays have four places to every one for non-Malays. There are large areas of Malay land reserves, where only Malays can own land. That is a necessary protection because if there was a free market in land, the Malays would rapidly be bought out. They get priority in the grant of many government licences and for new business lettings in certain areas the first offer of a tenancy must be to a Malay. They get loans at a cheaper rate than anyone else. One measure which was proposed turned out to be too extreme: a few years ago there was a law passed saying that all cheques must be written in Malay. That was dropped because it was unworkable, there being a great many people in Malaysia who can only write cheques in Chinese characters.

The Malay share of the country's wealth has been increasing. In the early 1970s it was very low – a single figure percentage – but it's now about 18%. The aim by 1990, under the national plan, is to give the Malays 30% of the country's wealth or economy, though in practice it may turn out to be more like 22%. In fact that is quite a success story for this policy. The qualification that one has to make is that the Malay share of the economy is concentrated in the hands of a few urban Malays who have become good businessmen and who are the directors of the companies; there is no real spread of this wealth among the Malay population.

Conclusion

One looks at this situation and concludes that it is potentially explosive. If economic growth continues – and at the moment there is a recession because of the decline in world demand for rubber and tin – then all will probably be well, at least on the surface. But if the present economic problems continue, the prospects for racial harmony are not very encouraging. In the recent election there was an increase in support by the Chinese for the opposition parties so there are signs of tension growing up again. The main hope is that the events of 1969, when the Malays ran amok, have impressed themselves so deeply on everybody in Malaysia that they will not let it happen again.

I promised to touch on the interesting question of heredity and environment as a source of cultural characteristics. I would not dare touch on such a delicate and difficult subject if it were not that it is a live issue in this part of the world. Dr Mahathir considers at some length whether the subsidiary position of the Malays in this racial mix may be due to genetic factors. And he cites, for instance, marriage customs. The Malays in-breed a great deal and apparently it is obligatory in their community to get married even if you are mentally unfit or have some congenital handicap. The Chinese have got a different attitude. Their marriage customs specifically prevent in-breeding because the marriage must not be within the same clan.

In Singapore, the government is concerned because an increasing number of educated men and women seem reluctant to marry and have children. Most of the children are being born to the poorer sections of the community. To encourage the better educated and, one supposes, more intelligent sections of the community to marry and have children, the government has set up a marriage and dating service. It remains to be seen whether the genetic theory on which it is based turns out to be right or not.

On the other hand, environment is obviously a very important factor. The Philippinos are Malays, but two or three centuries of Spanish and American rule have produced a much more active personality there than in Peninsular Malaysia. The Chinese and Japanese have emigrated in large numbers to America and after they have been there, say, three generations it is practically impossible to tell them from other Americans except by their appearance. One wonders whether Malays exposed to these different influences might not also become more businesslike and aggressive.

Dr Mahathir points out one thing about the origins of these races which suggests an important effect of environment. As he says the Malays are the people of lowlands. They have had no problems of survival. They have lived on growing rice and other agricultural crops which gives a lot of time, since they get one, and now two, crops a year and in between they do not need to do much. They live in small villages and this has encouraged them to be the very peaceful people that they are. On the other hand, look at the Chinese. They come from South China. It is an area of disasters. There are epidemics, typhoons, floods, starvation. There have been many invaders, wars and rebellions. They have had to leave and make their lives elsewhere. There are plenty of cities in South China, they are familiar with urban life. The result, it is suggested, is that the Chinese have developed into a very hardy race. They have had to survive and the unfit have been weeded out. So it may be that the stimulus you get from your environment is an important factor. How to increase the amount of stimulus on the Malays is a difficult question but if there were the stimulus it seems likely that they would respond to it. However, the odds must not be too great – look what happened to the American Indians and the Australian Aborigines. They had stimulus, but it was too great and they were overwhelmed.

Generalising from all this, where does it take us? Well, Malaysia is no more than one perhaps rather extreme example of a problem found almost everywhere in the world. There are the blacks and whites in America, the Jews and the Arabs, Protestants and Catholics in Northern Ireland. Britain has its ethnic minorities. All these are examples of the clash of cultures. It is not easy to find a country without the problem of conflicting cultures.

It may be that cultural clash is a condition of the human race, at least at its present stage of development. If we are to get away from it we shall have to develop a better understanding of groups and living in groups.

REFERENCES

1 Quoted from *The Invisible Cult*, a lecture delivered to the Institute for Cultural Research, 6 March, 1987 by Arthur J. Deikman, M.D., Professor of Clinical Psychiatry, University of California, San Francisco.

DAVID WIDDICOMBE

From *In Malaysia* by Stella Martin and Denis Walls, Bradt Publications, 41 Nortoft Road, Chalfont St Peter, Bucks SL9 0LA, England (1986).
3 From *China's Sorrow* by Lynn Pann, Century Hutchinson, London (1985).
4 Excerpts taken from *The Malay Dilemma* by Dr Mahathir bin Mohamad, published by Times Books International, 1 New Industrial Road, Singapore 1953 (1970).

IV

GLOBAL
IMPERATIVES

11

Ecology and Development

MARTIN HOLDGATE

Introduction

'Man inhabits two worlds. One is the natural world of plants and animals, of soils and airs and waters, which preceded him by billions of years and of which he is part. The other is the world of social institutions and artefacts he builds for himself, using his tools and engines, his science and his dreams, to fashion an environment obedient to human purpose and direction.'

In this, the opening paragraph of their book *Only One Earth*, written as a global perspective for the Stockholm Conference of 1972, Ward and Dubos (1972) sum up the basic essential of the human situation. Man is an animal with over three thousand million years of evolution behind him. That pathway of organic development has been shaped by interactions with other components of the natural world. Today we still depend on that world for our survival – for breathable air, drinkable water, food, and behind all, for the sun's energy which drives the whole complex living system. Ecology is the scientific study of living creatures in relation to their environment. It is the study of the first world of man.

But the outstanding feature of the last ten thousand years has been the construction of the second human world: the emergence of an increasingly complex social system, and the development of increasingly advanced skills whereby people have escaped, in part and for part of the time, from the vagaries of the natural world. Through forest clearance, the creation of pasture, the expansion of intensive cultivation, the alteration of drainage systems and the creation of technology man has increasingly changed the pattern of productivity of the natural world. This is development. He has been able, as a consequence, to greatly increase his numbers. This lecture is about the interplay between Ward and Dubos' two worlds.

The ecological background

Everybody knows that, broadly speaking, there are two kinds of living organisms – plants and animals. The former are mostly static, spreading broad surfaces to the sunlight, and using the green pigment chlorophyll, able to employ the sun's energy to join water from the sea, rivers or the soil and carbon dioxide from the air to make carbohydrates which can then be 'burned' in the process of respiration to provide the energy that drives their physiological systems. We call living things that have this capacity to build up their own basic food from simple inorganic constituents *autotrophes* – or literally, 'self-feeders'.

There *are* green animals in the world, but they are rare, and anyway most of those that carry chlorophyll around with them do so by enclosing plant cells in special hairs or tissues where they probably don't help much in the energy balance. Most animals are mobile, unable to produce their own basic food from inorganic sources and dependent on plants: we call these *heterotrophes* or 'others-feeders'.

We should not forget that the whole ecology of the living world depends utterly on solar energy and its fixation by the process of photosynthesis. In the same process, the carbon dioxide released as a waste product of animal and plant respiration is reconverted into basic carbohydrate food, and oxygen is released back into the air. Man, however advanced his technological development, is still, like all other animals, totally dependent upon these basic processes of green plants.

There are evidently outer limits to photosynthesis, and hence to the production of plant carbohydrates on earth (and these outer limits also define the potential of the oxygen renewal system). The ultimate limits must be imposed by the amount of solar energy (about 1.3×10^{21} kilocalories) (Nobel, 1973) falling on the earth's surface (hence the potential variation in productivity with latitude and the potential effects of pollution through screening out some of the incoming radiation). About 5% of this energy is absorbed by green plants, but their ability to use it also depends on the availability of carbon dioxide and water (hence the barrenness of arid zones and the potential of irrigation). Other important environmental factors include temperature and the availability of nutrients – especially nitrogen, phosphorus, potassium, sulphur, calcium and magnesium – from the soil (hence the value of fertilisers). Many of these factors can be altered by man. But the input of solar energy seems destined always to be beyond human control: it sets an outer limit to potential agricultural development.

There are also biological variables. The amount of dry plant matter produced by photosynthesis on a unit area of land in a unit of time depends on both the size and the efficiency of the photosynthetic system and these are measured in terms of the leaf area and the net assimilation rate which is the balance of photosynthetic gain over respiratory loss. About 1% of the solar energy absorbed by plants is converted into carbohydrate (Nobel, 1973). The efficiency (in energy terms) of the conversion of sunlight into plant food *produce*, such as grain, is said to be considerably less: about 0.05% (Southwood, 1972). There is a vast amount of information about how this rate varies in response to environment (see, for example, Watson, 1958). Different plants vary in their photosynthetic efficiency – hence the possibility of improved production through cultivation and crop breeding. Clearly, if we could either increase the amount of radiation plants trap, or their conversion efficiency, we could greatly enhance food production. But these potentials for development can only improve the extent to which the world's plant cover utilises the incident solar radiation, and produces it in a form more suitable for our kind of animal to use.

Plants are spoken of as *primary producers*. They stand at the base of the 'food chains' or 'trophic levels' which ecologists define in living systems. Many animals (herbivores) feed directly on these primary producers: the process of conversion of plant matter to the living animal material in the bodies of herbivores is spoken of as *secondary production*. Carnivores stand 'higher' in the sequence of trophic levels. Each of these steps is far from efficient in the conversion of food matter to the body material of the feeder. Generally these 'conversion rates' range (in growing animals) from 10% to 25%: that is, it takes from 4 to 10 kilograms of plant to make 1 kilogram of herbivore, and this in turn would make one quarter

Table 1. *Land (in acres) needed to produce 20 kg of protein in one year under various crops*

Beans	0.1	Grass	0.1– 0.25
Cereals	0.23	Potatoes	0.27
Dairy Cows	0.44–1.1	Sheep	0.8– 1.9
Fowls	1.44	Beef cattle	1.0–25
Pigs	2.2		

(Source: 'World Population and Food Supplies', Sir John Russell, cited by Bender, 1963.)

to one tenth of a kilogram of carnivore. If the efficiency of conversion of solar energy to grain is 0.05%, the efficiency of conversion of solar energy to meat is around 0.015%. This is why in a natural ecological system the numbers of animals – and the total weight of living matter – in the different trophic levels decreases as one moves up the food chain, to give a kind of pyramid. This is also why one can produce much more protein, or much more gross weight of edible living matter, per acre from plant crops than from livestock (Table 1) (Bender, 1963) – and why lion farming would be an inefficient process even if the beasts were highly palatable.

Table 2. *Energetic input and dissipation through biological systems (after Nobel, 1973)*

1. Solar radiation reaching Earth	1.3×10^{21} kcal/yr	
2. Absorbed by green plants (5%)	6×10^{19} kcal/yr	
3. Converted to carbohydrates (1%)	6×10^{17} kcal/yr	
	or 150×10^{9} tonnes/yr.	
4. Dissipated in plant respiration (60%)	3.6×10^{17} kcal/yr	
5. Retained by herbivores and decomposers (say 10%)	6×10^{16} kcal/yr	
6. Dissipated in respiration or passed to other decomposers (90%)	5.4×10^{16} kcal/yr	
	or 13.5×10^{9} tonnes/yr.	
7. Retained by carnivores (say 10%)	6×10^{15} kcal/yr	
	or 15×10^{8} tonnes/yr.	
8. Total human food energy demand (1974) (at 2,400 kcal per head per day)	4.5×10^{15} kcal/yr	
	or 11×10^{8} tonnes/yr.	

Recent calculations suggest that total world primary productivity on land is around 100–120 billion (10^9) tonnes per year ($\pm 5\%$) while the primary production of the seas is around 50–60 billion tonnes per year. World herbivore production might therefore be around 18–45 billion tonnes and carnivore production around 2–10 billion tonnes. In energetic terms (Table 2), Nobel's estimates suggest that man's contemporary food demands are already around 1% of total world production of carbohydrate by photosynthesis. If we ate lions, we would be already near the limits of present production.

Ecological systems should not be thought of as linear. Energy may flow in a defined pathway from sun to plant to herbivore to carnivore. But this is only one pathway in a complex system. The 'food web' of interactions involves many species. It is not the fate of every plant to be grazed or every herbivore to be eaten. Some fall to parasites or pathogens. Many live through to senescence and die at the completion of the average life span for the species. Their dead remains, together with the inedible portions of prey and the undigested matter of the faeces of herbivores and carnivores, are returned to the cycle through the decomposers, the vast numbers of bacteria, fungi and small animals that inhabit the upper levels of the soil or disperse through the air from one such organic substrate to another. This recycling through the decomposers restores essential nutrients, including metals, nitrate and phosphate, to the soil. The proportion of the energy derived from incident solar radiation that passes through the system to decomposers, as against that going through to herbivores can be very large. Normally organic matter does not accumulate in oil or among the sediments of lake and sea bed. But there are exceptions. Like green plants, most decomposers are aerobic: that is they need oxygen for their respiration. In waterlogged swamps or stagnant lake and sea basins oxygen levels may become depleted to the point where many decomposers cannot operate. Under these conditions dead organic matter accumulates as peat, coal or oil – the 'fossil fuels' we are now bringing into the air and oxidising, thereby releasing the energy that was denied to the decomposers millennia or millions of years ago.

Evolution has been characterised by increasing complexity and by the development of physiological systems which have made the organisms possessing them increasingly independent of the environment. Such mechanisms include those whereby the balance of salts in a body fluid is kept constant even when a shrimp or a fish like a salmon swims from a concentrated to a dilute medium or back again: those which stop a cactus, an insect or reptile drying up in a hot desert, and those which allow the maintenance of a constant body temperature. Because of these systems animals have been able to colonise harsh environments too; we, for example, can remain active at the South Pole under conditions where a frog would freeze up. But there is an energy cost: a small mammal with a large amount of surface in proportion to its volume radiates a lot of heat and has to eat disproportionately heavily to keep going in the cold (which is why the extremities of animals, like ears and necks, tend to become more rounded and compact in cold regions, why very small warm-blooded animals do not colonise the poles, and why small mammals in cold temperate regions hibernate). The most efficient converters of plant food to meat, as Pirie (1958) put it 'have a lethargic temperament and a more or less spherical shape' – like the hippopotamus. Man is intermediate, big enough to be fairly efficient but too skinny and badly insulated by his naked hide. He is not pre-adapted to the poles, and got there only in borrowed pelage.

Ecological systems have two apparently contradictory properties. On the one hand, they show constant change. On the other, they display a degree of inertia or stability. The most evident changes are successional, classic examples of succession being those leading from bare ground through pioneer grass and herb vegetation to scrub and forest or from lake through reedswamp and fen to woodland. The stability is seen in the way a system remains the same despite variations in rainfall or temperature, or changes in grazing pressure. There is a good deal of argument about how far stability is related to diversity – to the richness of a system in species. Some of the confusion arises because there are several kinds of stability and of diversity. Within certain limits a very diverse system is stable because its species are co-adapted: their interactions have evolved over a long time and it is characterised by a high level of competition. If one component is reduced by disease there are others to take its place. It is unlikely that a single insect 'pest' will become very abundant because there are many parasites

and predators to keep it in check. But complex systems like tropical forests may include many species not adapted to physical
disturbance or the stress of pollution or grazing and such systems,
once disrupted, are unstable in the sense that they do not recover
easily. Desert systems, in apparent contrast, are adapted to great
variations in climate and are 'stable' at a low level of competition
(Grime, 1974) – but are not stable when man imposes new kinds of
stress. In both cases, the system may have 'resilience' within
certain outer limits of stress and disturbance, but change rapidly
when these limits are exceeded.

The important lesson is that to a certain degree plant and animal
associations have self-balancing properties like those of the human
body, within definable limits. Grazed at a certain level by herbivores, a vegetation type can sustain itself. Overgrazed, some of its
component species may be killed out. Often the most spectacular
changes of this kind are seen when vegetation types that have
developed without mammalian herbivores are exposed to this new
stress through human action: the destruction of large coastal tus-
sock-forming grasses on southern hemisphere oceanic islands by
sheep is a good example (see Holdgate, 1968). Similarly, an animal
population has a finite capacity to support predators: over-
cropped, it may decline to the detriment of the predator itself. This
capacity to withstand cropping is due to a fact basic to all evolution,
namely that all living species have a potential reproductive capacity
far beyond that needed to sustain a stable population. Natural
selection can operate because an excess of offspring is produced,
with varying genetic properties, and the most adapted are 'selected' by competition or environmental stress. Predators can subsist because of the crop of 'extra' young produced by prey, and they
generally take the weakest young or the weakest adults, thereby
opening up a place in the adult population for the strongest young-
sters and actually aiding the evolution of the prey species. The
amount of harvest that can be taken out of an ecological system
depends critically on the capacity of that system to make good the
loss through natural processes of reproduction or re-growth and
this available crop is called the *sustainable yield*.

In nature, populations of animals and plants are regulated.
Except for short periods when a species is able to invade a new
habitat – maybe because man has enabled it to cross an ocean

barrier or because of genetic mutation (Elton, 1959) – rapid and sustained population growth does not happen. Natural populations remain stable because the surplus young die. The mechanism of regulation varies. Sometimes it involves competition for breeding territories. Sometimes there is direct competition for food. Sometimes numbers remain more or less static, rising in good years and falling in bad. Sometimes fluctuations are cyclical, peaks when the population overshoots its food supply being followed by 'crashes' of high mortality and/or low reproduction. The point is that the regulation of animal numbers is a universal ecological fact. We are cushioned from this fact because man has, for the past century or two, evaded through technology, the processes that used to regulate his numbers. This does not mean that those processes have ceased to exist. One of the lessons the natural world has for the technological world is, I believe, that we cannot ignore forever the facts of ecological life, and the most fundamental of these is that the earth is finite in its dimensions, energy supply, capacity to produce living matter, and potential human population.

A quick and superficial ecological analysis thus demonstrates:
(1) that the basis of all living systems is the conversion of solar energy to potential food energy by green plants, and while this varies with controllable factors such as water, soil nutrients and genetic strain, it is ultimately limited by solar processes which are beyond our control;
(2) that this energy is passed, with relatively low efficiency from plant to herbivore and thence to carnivore;
(3) that ecological systems must however be looked on as complex networks rather than linear sequences, and the recycling of nutrients by the decomposers is of vital importance;
(4) that for any component species in the system there is a sustainable yield due to the fact that reproductive potential exceeds that needed to sustain a stable population: this surplus can be taken by a herbivore or predator, but if more is extracted then there is bound to be a decline in the species being cropped;
(5) That there are limits to the potential populations of all species, including man.

With these points in mind, let us look at man's impact on the natural world.

The impact of man

Our earliest ancestors were probably omnivores: that is they ate a wide range of plant foods including fruits, roots and the juicier and more nutrient packed stems, along with insects, worms, shellfish, eggs and any fish or small mammals they could catch. Our teeth are typical omnivore's teeth, like those of bears, which have a highly catholic diet. Our guts are provided with digestive juices that can tackle most kinds of food, but we are clearly not designed as herbivores for we lack the large stomachs and alkaline fermentation chamber systems that are needed if you are to consume a large bulk of plant material and retain it for long enough for bacteria or protozoa to break down the cellulose cell walls that mammalian digestions cannot tackle.

There are still people with this way of life today (Balicki, 1973; Holdgate, 1961). The Alacaluf canoe indians of the western Patagonian channels, for example, subsist largely on the abundant mussels of the intertidal zone, with variety added by small fish, caught in branch corrals on a falling tide, wild birds' eggs, berries, herbs and occasional birds, seals and deer. The mussels (*Mytilus edulis Chilensis*) have a high biomass and a high food value, and a substantial human population could survive as hunter-gatherers on this kind of shore and indeed cool-temperate coastlines generally. Where larger mammals can be caught, of course, they offer the attraction of a much greater food resource per unit of hunting effort, and there is evidence of the taking of medium sized mammals in Africa from mid-Pleistocene times onwards, probably as soon as bone clubs had been developed (Balicki, 1973).

The direct impact of hunter-gatherers on ecological systems were probably small at first. But as their impact grew, these early hunters undoubtedly altered the population structure of the prey species, and more intensive exploitation by man has at times had devastating impact. What happens is worth brief illustration. In an exploited population that is stable in numbers and in balance with the environment, deaths equal births, and the recruitment of new individuals into the breeding population balances the loss from that adult population through mortality. As exploitation begins, recruitment rates rise, deaths from natural causes fall, and the average age of the population and the age at which breeding begins both come down. The sustainable yield is the surplus of young produced over the total number removed by natural mortality. Surprisingly, the highest sustainable yield generally occurs when the population size is reduced to about half that in the unexploited population, for at this level, reproductive output is high, the bulk of the population is in the age groups that reproduce fastest, and there is less likelihood of food supply or breeding space being limiting. Cropping beyond this level, however, causes a decline in the production of young, and a fairly rapid population crash. The recent history of whaling has provided some dramatic examples of the consequences of over-exploitation. It has also, together with similar experience in fisheries, led to the development of advanced methods of calculating maximal sustainable yield of a population, and regulating cropping accordingly (see, e.g., Le Cren and Holdgate, 1962: Ovington, 1963).

There is dispute over how far early man caused the extinction of species by overcropping. Maybe, as new hunting methods were perfected, and people's numbers rose, man became able to kill large, slow-moving and slow-growing herbivores with low reproductive rates, and the result may have been fairly numerous extinctions (Martin, 1971). But in this same period, early man may have had a profound effect through altering the habitat, especially in the drier and hotter parts of the world. Fire was discovered while many peoples were still in the hunter-gatherer stage, and its use in order to stampede game towards traps, and as an agent in clearing hunting areas, may have also been an early discovery. Fire has the effect, like pollution, of changing vegetation towards the earlier successional stages in which short-lived herbaceous as against long-lived woody forms are most prominent. It could have led to re-placement of open forests by savanna over large areas of East Africa, with an accompanying increase in the populations of medium-sized 'plains game'.

But whether or not that was so, the advent of the pastoralist, with his flocks and herds, led to major vegetation changes of this kind. Open grazings were cleared from the forest, probably especially by fire. In southern Chile a decade ago this system could be seen in use. The first firing of the forest was aided by piling cut brushwood about the larger trees, so that they would be more readily killed. A second firing produced open glades amid standing dead trunks, which were left to fall when decay weakened them and a storm came up. Grasses expanded across the cleared areas. Axes were used to the minimum extent necessary to clear the most intractable patches and to cut useful timber for houses and palisades. We can imagine a similar activity over the chalk hills of southern Britain four thousand years ago.

This process of clearing by burning has dramatic ecological effects. It destroys at a stroke a large part of the organic matter that was locked up in the 'standing crop' of the forest, passing it back into the air as carbon dioxide, oxides of nitrogen and water vapour. It releases a large quantity of nutrients. It may also burn much of the leaf litter of the forest floor and the upper organic layers of the soil, with a further release of nutrients, and it opens these soils to wind and rain at a time when, devoid of their vegetation cover, they are especially prone to erosion. The result can be a significant nutrient loss that may require many centuries of soil maturation or a major input of fertilizers to put back. One experiment (Likens, Bormann, Johnson, Fisher and Pierce, 1970) demonstrated a net loss of 65–90 tonnes of 11 nutrients per km^2 year in cut forest as against 4.5 to 6 tonnes from uncut forest: the latter levels could readily be made good in rainfall. If domestic stock grazing is allowed to develop too fast, the grassland that succeeds the forest may never completely bind the soil, and erosion may persist.

Pastoralists convert forest, which is characterized by the domination of large, long-lived trees in which the net amount of new living matter produced each year is small in relation to the standing crop, and in which the nutrients in the system are mainly locked up in the standing crop, into herbaceous, and especially grassy, vegetation types where the annual production is large in relation to the standing crop and nutrients are cycled more swiftly. They also replace large wild herbivores, like bison and predators that took their surplus like wolves, by more manageable stock like cattle and sheep, with man as the sole predator (see Elton, 1958). Agriculturalists growing selected plants which usually have annual cycles, extend this process. In both, the principle of sustained yield is important. In both, if the crop rate exceeds the capacity of the soil to replenish essential nutrients, and man does not return nutrients – anciently by fertilising the ground with his own body wastes, the wastes of his livestock and the residues of the crop that he does not eat – fertility will decline. Most natural or undisturbed vegetation has a low and sometimes intermittent nutrient flow and overall balance: in woodland, some 90% of nutrients are cycled within the system. The whole point about agriculture is that nutrients are taken away, though in simple and primitive systems with light management, only to a limited distance.

Shifting (or 'slash and burn') cultivation is primitive man's answer to this problem of getting plant matter and nutrients out of a soil low in fertility, in areas with abundant land. Trees and shrubs are cut at the end of the dry season. After 10 days or so they are burned. This releases nutrients, especially potassium, calcium, magnesium and phosphorus, to the soil. The enriched soil is then cropped intensively for up to three or four years. In that period there is a rapid oxidation of humus and old roots, up to 5 tonnes or so per hectare per month. At the end of three or four years, crop yields on the depleted soil fall and weed control problems increase and the plot is abandoned, to be regenerated slowly, maybe over a century. Given plenty of land this process need not be inefficient. Conway (1973) quotes a situation in Thailand where an originally stable system, managed in this way, has been disrupted by more intensive use of the fragile and infertile soils, leading to erosion, falling yields and the abandonment of three or four million hectares of land.

If ecological systems are to be modified extensively for food production, management effort and especially the deliberate application of fertilisers to balance nutrient losses in the crop, must increase. This increasing application of fertilisers to land on which a single crop species is grown over large areas has been a dominant feature of agricultural history. The production of useful food per unit area has increased dramatically in consequence, as Table 3 shows. But as the intensity of management has risen so agriculture has been more and more dependent upon an urban technology, driven by fossil fuel energy, to supply the fertilisers and herbicides that make the intensive cultivation possible.

Table 4, based on Odum, 1967 (cited in Institute of Ecology Report, 1971) provides insight into what has happened. The tropical forest system, almost unaltered by man, supported a low density of human population with no management effort at all. The

Table 3. *Wheat yields in Britain since 1200 (from Cooke, 1970).*

Date	Event	Yield (cwt/acre)
1200	Open field system	4
1650	Enclosure, fallowing	5
1750	New seed drills	8
1850	4-course rotation	14
1900	Fertilisers. New varieties	17
1948	More fertilisers. Selective weed killers	20
1958	Short straw varieties	25
1962	Increased use of nitrogenous fertiliser	34

simple, lightly managed tribal grazing system in Uganda supports 25 times as many people, again with negligible management effort and moderate stability. Indian monsoon agriculture supports 10 times the population on the land and makes a significant contribution of food energy to the cities, and again this is not subsidised by fossil fuel energy. The most efficient system, in the USA, again sustains about 10 times more people, but is totally dependent upon fossil fuel energy and technological input.

The history of man's impact on the ecosystems of the world has not been one of simple improvement in food yields at the cost of more energy and effort devoted to cultivation, fertilisers and

Table 4. *Energy inputs and outputs from four types of ecological systems*

System	Energy Input ($kcal/m^2$ year)		Human Food ($kcal/m^2$ year)		People Supported (number on land per km^2)	City
	Solar	Fossil fuel	Plant	Animal		
Rain forest	1.5×10^6	0	0.4		1	0
Uganda grazing	1.5×10^6	0	19.5	0.2	25	0
Indian monsoon	1.5×10^6	0	250	27	230	50
US intensive arable farming	1.5×10^6	135	1000	0	61	2000

(Simplified, from Institute of Ecology Report, 1971)

pesticides. There have been failures and wastefulness. I have already mentioned how easy it is to lose nutrients accumulated over millennia of soil maturation in a few years of careless clearance. This wastage has not been confined to tropical forest zones. There is evidence that it happened in the wet west of Britain early in our history. In our own uplands, forest clearance, grazing and burning are often said to have depleted nutrients and lowered productivity (see, e.g., Pearsall, 1950; Cragg, 1958). Selective grazing by animals like sheep, which take the most palatable herbage and encourage the spread of less nutritious species, can lead to declining productivity. Trampling of soil by sheep and cattle can compact the land, and combined with grazing, promote gully erosion and aggravated nutrient loss. There is a parallel here with the savanna system where lack of water is a major problem and where overgrazing can open up soil and herbage, reduce the water holding capacity of the land, and lead on to scrub and bush encroachment which the pastoralist commonly combats by fire, leading to a short flush of palatable vegetation because of the release of nutrient, but a longer term of further depletion, often compounded by the development of fire-resistant vegetation which is also unpalatable to stock. Any lands with high seasonal or low rainfall, with problems of water retention, or conversely, very high rainfall with problems of the washing out of soil or nutrients, need development with great care, and have commonly been mismanaged in human history. We have a less fertile earth than we could have had.

Another effect of the conversion of forests to grasslands and cultivation is a reduction in ecological diversity, and this has been one of man's major impacts on the world's ecological systems. In a tropical forest there are several hundred species of trees to say nothing of the abundant climbing and straggling plants and the species of the shrub layers and the forest floor. Even in a British woodland there may be several hundred plant species and many thousand insects. This kind of system has a high level of competition but low physical disturbance and stress and is stable while these conditions prevail. In contrast, a crop monoculture is species-poor by design. Open ground is deliberately maintained by disturbance. This ground is readily colonised by quick-growing, aggressive ruderal species ('weeds'). Hence intensive cultivation and selective herbicides are needed. But the crop also offers great opportunities to herbivorous insects or parasites, specialising in the species grown, because there is so much of it in one place and because the habitat changes tend to remove from the system the predators that might control the potential 'pest'. Hence the need for more management, and pesticides. Some of these toxic substances can have side-effects on wild life, further reducing the natural enemies of the pest. The result is a reduction in the natural checks and balances and increased dependence on management, supported by technology and hence by non-solar energy, at a considerable cost.

The development of agriculture, quite obviously, cannot therefore be separated from the development of urbanisation. Indeed, it was the increasing efficiency of food production that freed an increasing proportion of the community for other activities including crafts. There is an analogy between the urbanisation process and the development by animals of physiological mechanisms which have freed them from the vicissitudes of the environment. Shelter, warmth, clothing, tools and medicine have greatly reduced natural mortality and prolonged life. Population growth has inevitably resulted. Initially, the growth in human population probably improved well-being because it allowed more land to be brought under cultivation and more people to be available for technological development, and in our global generalisations we should not forget that there are countries in the world where this is still probably true. But at greater population densities much of the enhanced production is swallowed up by population growth and by the increased complexity of society. At present, world food industries increase by 6% per annum while food production rises only by 3% (Institute of Ecology Report, 1971): the other 3% is due to the increasingly difficult task of getting the food to the people.

This separation in space of the food producers and food consumers has another consequence – a massive nutrient flow from land to city, which, owing to the curious features of our sewerage system, leads in turn to the discharge of massive amounts of nutrients to the sea. For example, about 14 million tonnes of phosphorus are lost each year in this way. Phosphorus is a vital nutrient, and moreover, of all key plant nutrients, one of the least replenished from the air, through rainfall. Probably only 0.1 million tonnes a year return in this way from sea to land: most natural replenishment comes from

Table 5. *The energetics of urban man in Britain*

	(1) 1970	*(2) 2000*
Population	54.1 million	62.3 (medium projection)
Food/yr	54.1 million kcal/yr	62.3 million kcal/yr
Food Weight	8.9 million tons/yr	10.23 million tons/yr
Energy equivalent	2.56 million megawatts/yr (7020 MW/day)	2.95 million megawatts/yr (8100 MW/day)
Total CEGB output capacity, 1974	68,500 MW★	
CEGB increase in generating capacity 1974–1999		90,000 MW (i.e. 90 × growth in food energy demand)★

★These figures are for continuous output capacity, not consumption, and are for generated electrical energy only. Total fuel consumption in Britain is approximately four times the CEGB usage rate.

rock weathering (Institute of Ecology Report, 1971). Man has probably doubled the global flow rate of this and other nutrients. But the massive drain to the ocean can only be made good by mining reserves of phosphatic rocks, which some calculate will run out in a century or so. Unless, of course, we stop wasting the nutrients in the sewage we discharge to the sea – and this is not as easy as it sounds.

The urbanisation process has led to our demand for food energy, sustaining our animal biological processes, to be rapidly outstripped by our use of non-food energy. Ward and Dubos' second world has certainly, in energetic terms, come to dominate the first. All the predictions of population growth even for a country like Britain, with a very modest rate of increase (Thompson, 1974), imply an accompanying and disproportionate increase in this dominance of non-food energy and Table 5 gives some figures. As I have already shown, we shall need some of this to sustain our intensive agriculture.

Urbanisation has two main ecological consequences. One is the removal of land from biological production. Ehrlich and Ehrlich

(1969) have illustrated this for California, pointing out that for each additional 1000 people some 238 acres of land has been built over or paved: over the period 1960–2020 the total non-agricultural land in the state is projected to increase from 3 million to 13 million acres, half of the state's arable land. In Britain, as Stamp (1958) and others have pointed out, medieval and earlier settlement was naturally concentrated on the most productive soils: town centres thus lie in rich agricultural areas and urban expansion has had a serious effect on productivity. In Stamp's terms, if a new town requires 5000 acres and is situated on the finest farmland it will rob the country of 10,000 units of potential production: if located on poor sandy land like that on which Bournemouth is built, then only 500 units would be lost.

The other urban impact is pollution. Man has always shed body wastes and food residues into the environment, and these organic materials returned nutrients to be recycled via the decomposers. Only when the scale of pollution becomes large, as when a mass of raw sewage is discharged into a small and stagnant lake or sluggish river, do problems arise. The decomposition of such wastes requires oxygen: its consumption by the decomposers depletes the water; other organisms such as fish may be unable to survive and in the worst situation the river may become lifeless and stinking.

But it is the development of urban technology that has produced the most serious pollution problems, even if it has also provided the technological remedies, through the growth of abatement methods. The products of fossil fuel combustion for energy generation include carbon dioxide and particulates which might affect the balance of radiation reaching the ground and hence alter climate and primary production (see Royal Commission Report, 1970). There is also an inevitable release of waste heat which is already on a scale sufficient to create islands of warmth over cities at night and areas of warming where circulated cooling water is released to rivers and seas, and these effects could be significant on a regional scale if capacity increases greatly. Sulphur dioxide and oxidants produced through interactions involving other products of fuel combustion can damage plants: the Programme Analysis Unit computed air pollution in Britain could be costing agriculture £40 million per annum and in the United States the figure has been put at $4.9 billion annually for damage to materials and vegetation

(C.E.Q., 1971). On the land, persistent pesticides can have ecological impacts far beyond their points of application and intended targets (Mellanby, 1967). Industrial wastes can sterilise rivers and contaminate the sea on a scale that, while not yet globally serious, has caused concern (Ward and Dubos, 1972) and action (see Command Paper 4984, 1972). Even if the processes of pollution are at present local rather than global, there is abundant evidence that badly-sited industry, allowed to discharge waste on an excessive scale, can do severe ecological damage and in Britain, when we discovered this in the aftermath of the unplanned development of the Industrial Revolution, there has been over a century of effort and expenditure to put things right.

Man's impact on ecological systems has thus been:

(a) to alter the age structure and balance of some populations by cropping up to or above maximal sustainable yield: in some cases this caused extinctions.

(b) to alter vegetation, substituting short-lived, disturbed and species-poor communities with a low level of competition for long-lived competitive and diverse ones.

(c) to selectively develop a small series of high-producing plants and animals and greatly expand the range of habitats these occupy, with concomitant demands on technology to sustain the associated intensive management with fertilisers and pesticides.

(d) to reduce productivity of many areas through urbanisation and associated pollution, and to greatly expand the demand for non-food energy, with the concomitant release to the environment of waste heat which can augment pollution and other urban by-products as disturbers of local ecological patterns.

Ecology as a guide in development

There are two overriding needs in the world today: to provide enough food for a world population now doubling every 30 years and likely to reach around 7 billion by AD 2000 and to raise the standard of living for the great majority of these people who fall far short of what a European or North American would call minimal living standards. There are real doubts about how far we can achieve both goals, and still more doubts about the wisdom of uncritically trusting science to sustain indefinite population and economic growth.

If one person needs 1 million kilocalories of food energy per year (which is about right), today we need about 4×10^{15} (or 4 thousand million million) kilocalories to feed the world: by AD 2000, we shall need 7×10^{15} or nearly twice as much. There are two basic ways of doing it: cropping more land or water, and improving the productivity of what we crop. Both inter-relate. In 1967 it was estimated that there were 7.86 billion acres of potentially farmable land on earth (Ehrlich and Ehrlich, 1969). This, though only 24% of the total ice-free land area, is three times the amount currently under crops. 88% of potentially cultivable land in Europe was being used and 83% per cent in in Asia. The big apparent reserves were in South America and Africa. But, as I have already shown, we should not look on this land as suitable for cultivation with the same ease that land in a temperate region with equable climate and steady rainfall can be opened up. Some could only be worked with irrigation, and irrigation properly managed so that it did not just promote good yields for a few years and then create further problems through salt accumulation in the soil. Some, in tropical areas, is under dense forest with most of the nutrients locked up in the trees, and the soils are of low fertilty. (The richness of tropical vegetation, developed over hundreds of thousands of years, is no guide to the potential production of the area, if cleared.) Much of the land needs to be developed much more carefully and expertly than our ancestors opened up the lands of Europe, yet the resources available to the people concerned are no better, and may be worse. There is a real risk of the Thailand situation described by Conway (1973) or the West Highland situation described by Fraser Darling (1955) repeating itself.

You cannot extrapolate one type of agriculture to a different region uncritically. McCulloch (1973) gives a good illustration; in India tea has been grown traditionally under the shade of larger trees, and in Kenya, when tea planting began, shade trees were established as a part of 'correct' management. But whereas in Assam, tea yields were greater under shade, the reverse proved true in Kenya. Why? Because in Assam intense sunlight was associated with high air temperatures and excessively high leaf temperatures in the tea plant: shading brought these down and improved the crop. In Kenya, at high altitude, the sunshine was just as bright, but the altitude kept the air temperature down; leaf temperature did not become limiting whereas the shade tree roots competed for water with those of the tea plants.

The first need, in considering new development, is to survey and describe the ecological systems that are already there. Careful studies of soil nutrients, rainfall, soil water relations and other ecological factors can allow prediction before new lands are developed of what crops will grow there and what yields may be expected. Such studies need to be long-term: the drought that comes every tenth year can destroy the efforts of the previous nine, and cereals and ground nuts failed in areas of Africa with an unpredictable and variable climate for this reason. To continue with this area, as an example, it is one where the annual rainfall is almost everywhere less than the potential loss of water from the land by evaporation and the native plants root deeply. To increase growth of shallow-rooting crops, irrigation is needed. To conserve the necessary water in the catchments it is essential to keep human pressures on the land down, for forest clearance and trampling of man and grazing animals compact the soil, accelerate erosion and flood run-off (McCulloch, 1973). Sound development thus demands man-management, and this may not always be socially acceptable to the community that lives there.

How much can we really expect to increase world food production by expanding the area of land we use? Faced with the demonstration that radical changes in land use have been, and remain liable to be, ecologically disastrous unless carefully managed – often at great cost – many authors have concluded that there is a limited potential for greatly expanding the area of cultivation on the earth's surface. Many believe that in our existing state of knowledge it is moreover desirable to maintain a mosaic of intensively managed, lightly managed and unmanaged land, and that the mosaic of soil, with widely varying fertility, will impose such a pattern on us anyway. Probably we would be unwise to expect more than a doubling of world food production through this means, and this would no more than keep up with population growth over the next 30 years.

What about the sea, covering most of the earth's surface and at present only used through the culling of wild populations? In 1970 the total world catch of aquatic organisms from the seas was about 60 million tonnes. Fish and crustacea have been the traditional crops, with a small contribution from molluscs. Moiseev (1970) cited Soviet estimates that these traditional sources might yield up to 80–90 million tonnes/year. Whaling, at its peak, yielded some 2 million tons/year from the Antarctic, and at that time accounted for maybe 10% of world marine food landings (Gulland, 1970). In recent years it has been computed that the whale's chief food, krill, a pelagic shrimp, in Antarctic waters might yield a sustainable crop of 50 million tonnes, thereby almost doubling world fishery landings and bringing the total harvest of the seas from all sources to maybe 150 million tonnes/year. This would seem to be the maximum obtainable crop on a sustained yield basis, without totally new oceanic management. It would, incidentally, be only 0.5% of the latest estimated world oceanic primary production, but since man takes only animal food from the sea, and much of it is in the form of fish which in turn eat small animals, this represents a much higher proportion of the actual input energy than might appear.

The most interesting prospects in developing the world to produce more food without disturbance to ecological balance lie, in my opinion, in ways of enhancing the efficiency of land and water use. Only 5% of the solar energy reaching the earth is caught by green plants, and only 1% of that converted to carbohydrate. Can we improve this, for example by breeding plants that are more efficient users of solar energy or grow more rapidly to allow multiple cropping in the year? We have some successes to record. New strains of wheat produced in the early stages of the 'Green Revolution' in 1962 doubled yields in Mexico and other countries (Conway, 1973). The rice strain IR 8 which matured in 120 days as against 150–180 in the preceding varieties dramatically enhanced yields in south-east Asia, for example making the Philippines self-sufficient for the first time. Multiple cropping is clearly more efficient as land use: as Stamp (1958) commented, if a diet of 2,460 kilocalories per day is based on meat and milk it takes 2 to 2.5 acres to support a person whereas rice, giving two or three crops per year, can sustain six or seven persons per acre. But these systems only work of course if nutrient and water supplies are maintained: as agriculture becomes more intensive, more energy has to be devoted to management. Monocultures of high-yielding plants

may, if derived from genetic stocks of limited diversity and cultivated without a break over large areas, provide an ideal habitat for
disease. The Irish potato famine of the mid-19th century was the
first massive example of this; more recently the new rice strain IR 8
proved vulnerable to leaf virus in Bangladesh and the Philippines
and brought the latter country once again, in 1971, below the level
of self-sufficiency. More recent crop breeding (e.g., rice strain IR
20) has aimed at producing a variety which may yield a little less
but is broadly resistant to pests and diseases and also fairly tolerant
of unfavourable conditions (Conway, 1973).

In theory we could augment plant production in three ways. We
could improve the efficiency of the basic biochemical process of
photosynthesis, getting more sugar per unit of sunlight, we could
expand the leaf area of the plant and get more sugar per unit area,
or we could extend the growing season or speed the maturation rate
of seeds and fruits, getting more sugar per unit of time. The new
rice strains use the third system. Watson (1958) concluded that this
was probably the most hopeful approach. Increasing leaf area has
the snag that a given region can only accommodate just so much
leaf before mutual shading starts interfering with the process.
Improved biochemical efficiency may be possible, though a degree
of biological scepticism is in order here since the photosynthetic
process has been, throughout evolutionary history, the energy
'trap' that has driven the world and one might have expected
natural selection to favour strongly any genetic factors that enhanced efficiency. A fourth approach, already well tested, is to try
to enhance yields by improving water supply and nutrient status
and by even more efficient pest and disease control. There is
evidence however that we are on a declining curve of efficiency so
far as fertilisers are concerned. To double food production in this
way and hence support the population we shall have in 30 years
time at today's nutritional level, we might need 6.5 times as much
fertiliser, six times as much pesticide and 2.8 times as much power.
We may have to do it, but we should not exclude other possibilities.

The 'green revolution' was essentially based on more efficient
use of existing agricultural techniques. An ecologist may suggest
that there are bolder visions before us. There are several surprising
things about today's agriculture. We use very few species – a
hundred or so plants out of a third of a million, and an even smaller

proportion of the world's animals. Our crops and livestock are restricted in the habitats they can live in. Most plants are short-lived, herbaceous species. They have been chosen, almost all long ago, because we can digest their nutrient packed seeds, roots or fleshy leaf stalks easily, without elaborate preparation. Our guts cannot cope with masses of cellulose, so we cannot eat the leaves and stems of grasses. We choose plants that accumulate packets of concentrated nutrition including sugars and starches, unprotected by thick cell walls. Where we use grass or straw we process it through a herbivore. But all this is no longer theoretically necess-ary. The biochemist can get protein out of a leaf more efficiently, that is, with a higher conversion ratio, than a cow (Pirie, 1958). The advantage of this is twofold. We might be able to get more food per acre, and incidently, without the saturated animal fats that some nutritionists dislike. But from the ecological standpoint, we might also be able to use plants which grow better than our crops because they are native to, and adapted to, the areas of the world where the environment is harsh. We might use herbage containing several species, not monocultures. Cropped mechanically, more-over, we can adjust the rate at which we mow the plants to the environmental circumstances and nutrient inputs: we are more likely to be able to ensure that we obtain maximum sustainable yield, without nutrient depletion or instability.

There is a parallel in the animal world. Many of our livestock come from the temperate zones. It is well-known that cattle are not always productive in semi-arid tropical areas like East Africa. There are disease problems (e.g., trypanosomiasis). The beasts need water and grassland. In contrast, the wild game includes a range of species all able to subsist on the unaltered natural veg-etation, which in turn maintains soil stability. They crop the vegetation at different levels; browsers on the bushes, grazers on the herbs. Pearsall (1962) pointed out that in East Africa in the wild there are up to 100 large and 90 small herbivores per square mile: this is not very different from the 80 cattle and 133 sheep and goats in Masai country although the latter are on the better land. Thus human management on altered habitat produces little or no more protein than wild animals on unaltered habitat, though in more valued form. Rather similarly, an area in Rhodesia studied by Dasmann and Mossmann (Matthews, 1962) seemed likely to yield a net profit of £3200 per annum under game and £2500 under cattle, after expensive habitat improvement. It is ecologically more sensible, and potentially equally sound nutritionally, to use the animals that are in balance with vegetation that has evolved in balance with the conditions of the area. Numerous studies (e.g. Bannikov, 1962) have shown that 'wild' species like saiga antelope and eland, or even Scottish red deer, can be domesticated and managed much more easily than one might expect.

Logically, since the 'decomposers' provide about 80–90% of secondary production in many areas, we might consider using them. The giant African snail, a large ground-living herbivore has been shown to have food potential (Orraca-Trench 1962). Nobody, so far, has cropped earthworms (though this was suggested in a jocular aside at the 1974 International Conference of Ecology). I do not suggest that you should send your daughter into the garden on a dewy morning to provide a human version of the early bird catching the worm, but the point is that we have not thought through the possibility of enhanced food production from areas that are ecologically difficult to manage when radically altered, through cropping new species that are native to, and stable in, such areas.

There are many other speculations into which I cannot go. I have only talked about food, but there are broad tracts of land which may be used best for timber production, at the same time providing soil stability and nutrient retention, and so aiding catchment management. Mosaics of woodland and pasture or crop can often provide the wisest pattern of land use. There are possibilities of using tree leaves as a protein source, thereby allowing a food and wood crop from land whose soil would be endangered by general clearance. There is fish-farming, especially in freshwaters where we might crop waterweeds in turn fertilised by some of the nutrients we now waste to the sea. Farming the sea may be technically impossible, but there are many inlets in which balanced ecological systems might be maintained, with enhanced crops.

Be all that as it may, what does ecology have to say about the need for development, and ways of development, in the world? First, I think we must accept that development must happen. We expect world population to double in 30 years, and although people may eventually be converted to the concept that it is better to limit human populations by deliberate choice rather than by famine, we must cater for at least another doubling in the first half of the next century. If we also aim, as we must, at improving the standard of living of those people that will then live in the world, we must expect a fourfold to sixfold increase in food requirements. This takes up to around 25–30 thousand million million kilocalories per year (or 6–7 billion tonnes), which is about 4% of world primary production. I have suggested that bringing new land into use might double our supplies: we might get twice as much as we now do from the sea, and improved strains and more efficient agriculture could give us another doubling of present levels. New and unconventional, and ecologically wiser, forms of land use backed by biochemical processes could also help. We may save food energy by shifting our kind of food, and this is especially likely in the developed western nations, eating more plant matter and less meat. With all these devices, we are going to have to put a lot of energy and effort into multiplying present world food production by four or even six. There will be considerable ecological challenges, for we cannot afford to secure short-term gains at the cost of long-term nutrient loss.

I said the first step in developing new lands, or planning more efficient use of existing ones, was survey and analysis of the environmental system. This is unlikely to come up with a single optimum way of improving land use. It will give us alternatives – alternatives expressed in terms of how much food of what kinds we might take from the area, how much energy we should have to put in, how much alteration to the ecological systems we would make, what risks of nutrient or soil loss we ran if we miscalculated, and what the landscape would look like under the various alternative options. Such comparative analyses of environmental options are a vital part of development planning. They are already a well-advanced art. The problems are of choice.

Here we cannot neglect social factors. Societies have strongly held views about the environment they are content to live in and the food they are prepared to eat. Experience has shown how hard it can be, even in times of famine, to give maize to rice eaters, to stop nomadic herdsmen overgrazing parched range with excessive numbers of dying cattle, and still more, to turn nomads into sedentary pastoralists. It is a principle of biology that in explaining animal evolution by deducing 'missing links' between a fossil ancestor and a modern descendent, each has to be biologically plausible and capable of having competed efficiently with its contemporary species. If you are trying to explain how a bird's wings evolved from reptilian forelimbs, you cannot postulate a creature that was for ever tripping over its feathers. It is the same with societies. A new form of land use that is ecologically wise and potentially productive has got to be arrived at by smooth and socially acceptable transitions from the present system.

This is why developed country ecologists have to be cautious about their suggestions for developing countries. Our efficient agriculture is a high-energy intensive system with much effort devoted to fertilisers and pesticides applied mechanically. It is not easy to export these to labour-intensive societies with very little energy generation capacity. The trouble in many such countries is that attempts are being made to go at one jump from unmanaged ecosystems like forests to a completely altered ecosystem like arable land, without the means to contain nutrient loss or replace the nutrients that wash out from the bared soil. We need schemes for smooth transition through slightly altered, but more productive systems (as shifting cultivation does provide) to the most productive forms. Commonly it is wise to plan for a spatial mosaic, with some unaltered, some slightly managed and some intensively managed areas in the same landscape. But the people of the region have to make the choice. The ecologist's task is to crystallise the options for them.

Let me end with an example near home. If we stare into our crystal ball and see a Britain 30 years hence with a population of 63 million, needing 10 million tonnes of food a year, under conditions where the developing countries are ceasing to have a food surplus to export to us, or where world food prices have been driven up disproportionately compared to the sales value of manufactured goods, then we may decide that we should intensify food production at home. How do we do it? There are several options, and we would need to choose the blend after a thorough survey of our ecological and agricultural potential. One facet in the evaluation might be a decision to constrain urban expansion into the fertile countryside still more, and make housing development still higher in density. We would need to consider how much land we set aside for recreation and amenity. Priorities for agriculture, forestry and wild life conservation would be reviewed. But we would then come down to how to expand production. Could we intensify land use on the uplands, which make up 25 to 30% of the surface of Britain but produce only 4% of our agricultural production (Cragg, 1958)? Almost certainly the answer is 'yes', for many upland areas were more productive in the past. We could reclaim some of the nutrients we waste in sewage and use them for intensive cultivation on land, freshwater or landlocked seas. We might not be able to become self-sufficient at the kind of standard of diet and type of diet we are now used to, but we could certainly, given the economic incentive, reduce our dependence on overseas supplies. But there would be social and environmental costs, because of the competition for a limited land area that must exist in any small, densely peopled country. The ecologist can help state the options. The ultimate decision on what to do is a political one that must take account of wider social issues, in this as in any other country.

The over-riding lesson the ecologist has to drive home in all this is a stark and simple one:

(1) The earth has a finite capacity to sustain life.
(2) All animal and plant species have a reproductive capacity that, if fully realised, produces a surplus of young.
(3) In nature, competition eliminates this surplus and drives evolution through natural selection.
(4) This permits man to crop ecological systems.
(5) The level of potential cropping is regulated by this surplus, expressed in terms of sustainable yield. It can be greatly increased by management. This however alters ecological systems and may reduce their stability.
(6) Cropping, and attendant ecological change, can deplete an area of soil nutrients that are only slowly replaced. Intensively managed ecosystems must have their nutrients replenished by management. Management is often also needed to control organisms we call pests, because we have given them more potential food and removed many of their natural enemies.
(7) Human land use history is full of examples where we have allowed fertility to decline through a failure to maintain nutrient levels or prevent irreversible ecological change.

(8) In development of new areas, we have to study the ecological
potential before we act, and choose an option that is both
ecologically sound and feasible for the social and technological circumstances.

(9) There may be outer limits to world production, but we can
greatly increase our own food supplies, both by conventional
and new means. Intensive agriculture is however inescapably
linked to energy inputs from technology.

(10) We can see, now, ways of sustaining the population in 2050 at
a reasonable standard, albeit at costs in terms of natural
beauty, and wilderness, and at ecological risk since we shall
be more and more dependent upon man as a manager in place
of natural checks and balances. But there are ultimate limits.
We would be well advised to bring our numbers into balance
with our environment while there remains some surplus capacity in the system: some room for miscalculation, partial
breakdowns in the complexities of society, and environmental vagaries like climatic change which we cannot guarantee to
bring under control.

Afterword, 1989

This paper was written in 1974. Fifteen years later, its main
conclusions are still valid. But during those 15 years pressures on
the world environment have escalated. The theory I was urging in
my lecture may be (more or less) right, but it has not been put into
practice. Too many development projects have failed to adopt
sustainability as their watchword. Losses of topsoil through
erosion far exceed the global replenishment of this vital resource.
Deforestation is converting large areas of the tropics to systems
with a lessened productivity. The deserts continue to spread. Food
production *per capita* in Africa has fallen by some 14% since 1974,
and there are disturbing signs of downturn in some other developing regions as well. The high-yielding new crop species of
which I spoke so optimistically have also proved to require sophisticated management, and the intensive agriculture of Europe and
North America is sustained by the injection of energy from fossil
fuels, used in the manufacture of fertilizers. Ground water tables
have been dropping as irrigation 'mines' them at rates far above

natural replenishment. The encroachment of humanity on the natural world, impelled by the population explosion which has slowed only slightly since 1974, is causing the loss of species (many of them still undescribed by science) at an uprecedented rate. And now, in the late 1980s, the likelihood of perturbation of the world climate system as a result of the accumulation of so-called 'greenhouse gases' in the atmosphere, is being taken increasingly seriously by world leaders and scientists alike.

There are, of course, good examples of environmentally sound development, to show that optimism is not totally absurd. And the need for such an approach is widely accepted by Governments. The World Conservation Strategy stated for the first time, in clear, simple, terms that conservation and development had to be viewed as components of a single process. The World Commission on Environment and Development has emphasised the imperative for development that is sustainable, meeting the needs of the present without jeopardising the capacity of future generations to meet their own needs. Summit Conferences on environment and speeches by Heads of Government on environment multiply. The World Bank and other lending and development aid agencies evaluate all projects in terms of environmental sustainability.

The problem and the potential have both been recognized. Yet the gap continues to widen and the environment on which tomorrow's billions will depend continues to deteriorate. I am less sure than I was in 1974 that we *can* sustain the population in 2050 at a reasonable standard. Certainly we will not do so unless wise words are translated into effective action during the next 15 years on a far greater scale, and with far greater wisdom and deftness of touch, than they have been in the past decade and a half. The next 15 years are likely to be critical for human relations with nature.

REFERENCES

Balicki, A. (1973). The hunter's ecology. In *Nature in the Round*, ed. N. Calder (Weidenfeld and Nicolson).

Bannikov, A. J. (1962). Exploitation of the Saiga Antelope in the USSR. In *The Better Use of the World's Fauna for Food*, ed. J. D. Ovington. *Institute of Biology Symposium No. 10.*

Bender, A. E. (1963). The relative merits of plant and animal proteins. In *The Better Use of the World's Fauna for Food*, ed. J. D. Ovington. *Institute of Biology Symposium No. 10.*

C.E.Q. (1971). *Environmental Quality: Second Annual Report of the Council on Environmental Quality* (Government printer, Washington).

Command 4984 (1972). *Convention for the Prevention of Marine Pollution by dumping from Ships and Aircraft* (London, HMSO).

Conway, G. R. (1973). Aftermath of the green revolution. In *Nature in the Round*, ed. N. Calder (Weidenfeld and Nicolson).

Cooke, G. W. (1970). The Carrying Capacity of the Land in the year 2000. In *The Optimum Population for Britain. Institute of Biology Symposium No. 19* (Academic Press).

Cragg, J. B. (1958). The Future of the British uplands. In *The Biological Productivity of Britain*, ed. W. B. Yapp and D. J. Watson, *Institute of Biology Symposium No. 7*

Ehrlich, P. R. and Ehrlich, A. H. (1969). *Population, Resources, Pollution* (San Francisco).

Elton, C. (1958). *The Ecology of Invasions by Animals and Plants* (London, Methuen).

Fraser Darling, F. (1955). *West Highland Survey* (Oxford University Press).

Grime, J. P. (1974). Vegetation Classification by Reference to Strategies. *Nature*, 250, 26–31.

Gulland, J. A. (1970). The development of the resources of the Antarctic seas. In *Antarctic Ecology*, ed. M. W. Holdgate (Academic Press).

Holdgate, M. W. (1968). The influence of introduced species on the ecosystems of temperate oceanic islands. *Proceedings, IUCN 10th Technical Meeting*. IUCN Publication, New Series, No. 9. pp. 151–76.

Holdgate, M. W. (1961). Man and Environment in the South Chilean Islands. *Geogr. Journ.*, 127, 401–416.

Institute of Ecology (1971). *Man in the Living Environment. Report of the Workshop on Global Ecological Problems.*

Le Cren, E. D. and Holdgate, M. W. (eds.) (1962). *The Exploitation of Natural Animal Populations. British Ecological Society Symposia, No. 2.*

Likens, G. F., Borman, F. H., Johnson, N. M., Fisher, D. W. and Pierce, R. S. (1970). Effect of forest cutting and herbicidal treatment on nutrient budgets in the Hubbard Brook Watershed Ecosystem. *Ecol. Monogr.*, 40, 23–47.

Martin, P. S. (1971). Prehistoric Overkill. In *Man's Impact on Environment*, ed. T. R. Detwyler (McGraw-Hill).

Matthews, L. H. (1962). A new development in the conservation of African animals. In *The Better Use of the World's Fauna for Food*, ed. J. D. Ovington. *Institute of Biology Symposium No. 10.*

McCulloch, J. S. G. (1973). The thirsty soil. In *Nature in the Round*, ed. N. Calder (Weidenfeld and Nicolson).

Mellanby, K. (1967). *Pesticides and Pollution* (Collins, London).

Moiseev, P. A. (1970). Some aspects of the Krill resources of the Antarctic seas. In *Antarctic Ecology*, ed. M. W. Holdgate (Academic Press).

Nobel, P. S. (1973). Free Energy: The Currency of Life. In *Nature in the Round*, ed. N. Calder (Weidenfeld and Nicolson).

Odum, H. T. (1967). Energetics of world food production. *The World Food Problem*, 3, 55–95.

Orraca-Trench, R. (1962). The Giant African snail as a source of food. In *The Better Use of the World's Fauna for Food*, ed. J. D. Ovington. *Institute of Biology Symposium No. 10.*

Ovington, N. D. (ed.) (1963). *The Better Use of the World's Fauna for Food. Institute of Biology Symposium No. 10.*

Pearsall, L. W. H. (1950). *Mountains and Moorlands* (Collins).

Pearsall, L. W. H. (1962). Food production by East African Ungulates. In *The Exploitation of Natural Animal Population*, ed. E. D. Le Cren and M. W. Holdgate.

Pirie, N. W. (1958). Unconventional production of foodstuffs. In *The Biological Productivity of Britain*, ed. W. B. Yapp and D. J. Watson. *Institute of Biology Symposium No. 7.*

Pirie, N. W. (1958). Contribution to discussion, p. 49 in *The Biological Productivity of Britain*, ed. W. B. Yapp and D. J. Watson. *Institute of Biology Symposium No. 7.*

Royal Commission on Environmental Pollution (1970). *First Report* (London, HMSO).

Southwood, T. R. E. (1972). The environmental complaint: its cause, prognosis and treatment. *Biologist*, 19, 85–94.

Stamp, L. D. (1958). The Land Use Pattern of Britain. In *The Biological Productivity of Britain*, ed. W. B. Yapp and D. J. Watson. *Institute of Biology Symposium No. 7.*

Thompson, J. (1974). Factors in population growth and possible paths for the future. In *Population and the Quality of Life in Britain* (Royal Society of Arts).

Ward, Barbara and Dubos, Rene (1972). *Only One Earth* (Deutsch).

Watson, D. J. (1958). Factors limiting production. In *The Biological Productivity of Britain*, ed. W. B. Yapp and D. J. Watson. *Institute of Biology Symposium No. 7.*

12

The Outlook for Population

EUGENE GREBENIK

In this lecture I shall discuss some of the factors which are likely to affect the future of world population. Any attempt to do this must consider the present situation and analyse the past movements in population growth which have led to the present state of affairs. I shall, therefore, begin by putting a few very simple facts before you.

In 1970, the United Nations estimated that the world's population amounted to 3,600 million persons, of whom 1,100 million lived in developed countries, and 2,500 million in less developed countries.[1] Rates of growth differed considerably between the developed and the less developed world: in 1970–74 the rate was estimated to be nine per 1000 per year in the developed world and 24 per 1000 per year in the less developed countries.[2] The implications of these rates can best be illustrated by considering the time that a population would take to double, if it grew at these rates. The growth rate of the developed world would lead to a doubling of the population in about 77 years, that of the less developed countries, on the other hand, would mean a doubling every 29 years. For the world as a whole, the annual rate of growth in 1970–74 was estimated to be 19 per 1000, equivalent to a doubling period of 37 years.

Demographically, therefore, we live not in one world but two. The less developed regions of the world are growing two and a half times as fast as are the richer, developed regions. Taken together, the world's population is at present probably growing at a faster rate than at any other time in the world's history. During the 15 years between 1960 and 1975 it is estimated to have increased by a quarter, from 3,000 to 4,000 million.

How has this state of affairs come about? For the world as a whole, population can only increase through births and decrease through deaths. These two components of population growth will, therefore, have to be looked at separately. When they are equal, population will be in equilibrium. This can happen, either when both birth and death rates are high or when both are low. The recent demographic history of the developed countries is one of transition from the former state to the latter: in the less developed countries the process of transition has begun but is not complete.

Consider the death rate in the first instance. Demographers measure mortality by means of a figure called the expectation of life at birth. This figure shows the mean length of life of a newly born child, who would, throughout its lifetime, be subjected to the risk of dying at each age which prevailed at the date of his birth. During the last 175 years this figure has risen in England and Wales from a value of about 30 years to one of about 70 years, and the latter figure is not unrepresentative of the position in most developed countries today.

In a population in which the expectation of life at birth is low, between 20 and 30 per cent of all babies born will die as infants before their first birthday and only about 54 per cent will survive to the age of 20 to begin reproducing in their turn. By contrast, a population with a life expectancy of 70 years will lose only about two per cent of its births as infants and some 95 per cent of all children born will survive to reproduce. Clearly, a change in mortality of this magnitude is likely to affect reproductive attitudes, and I shall return to this point later.

I have quoted the experience of England and Wales as typical of that of a developed country. But, in the less developed areas of the world the fall in mortality started much later. For instance, in British India life expectancy in the 1930s was probably less than 30 years. But, once the decline had started – and in some areas it did not begin until World War II – it normally proceeded much more quickly than it had done in the West. Though gaps in mortality continue to exist between the developed and the less developed areas of the world, they are narrowing. In their latest publication, the United Nations quote life expectancies at birth of 71 years for developed countries, ranging from 67 years in temperate South America to 73 years in Japan: the figures for less developed countries are 54, with a range of 41 years for West Africa to 64 years for

Polynesia.[3] The fall in mortality in less developed areas owed much more to advances in medical technology and therapeutics than was the case in the West, where there was also a much closer association between the fall in mortality and the rise in the standard of living. In the less developed countries falling mortality was not necessarily associated with rising living standards.

The pattern of mortality has also been changing. In areas with high expectations of life, cardio-vascular diseases and cancers are the principal causes of death, in the less developed countries infectious diseases and epidemics still remain important and infant mortality continues to be high. There is considerable scope for further reductions in death rates in the less developed areas: in the developed countries there is little likelihood of further reductions, except possibly for the elderly. Indeed, there are some indications that for certain age groups, mortality may have been increasing slightly.

Mortality declines are important, for historically they have in most countries been a pre-condition for a reduction in fertility. Given the near universal desire to have children surviving into one's old age, there is little incentive for men and women to limit their fertility, until the mortality of infancy and childhood has been reduced to reasonably low levels. In most developed countries, limitation of births only began to be widely practised after infant mortality had been reduced. In the less developed countries of today, there is no reason to expect a reduction in fertility whilst mortality levels remain high.

Turning next to fertility, the measure most widely used to measure this is the gross reproduction rate (GRR). Briefly, this figure indicates the number of live daughters that would be born to a woman, who throughout her reproductive life was subjected to the rates of giving birth at each age prevalent during the year for which the GRR is calculated, and assuming that there was no mortality before the end of the reproductive period. The UN estimate of the GRR for 1970–75 was 1.13 in developed countries and 2.60 in less developed countries,[4] indicating that fertility in the latter regions was more than double that of the former. To measure the combined effect of fertility and mortality on population growth, the so-called net reproduction rate (NRR) is frequently used. To explain its exact meaning would lead us into technicalities, but it may be interpreted as the number of live daughters that a newly born female would have given birth to, if throughout her reproductive life she was subjected to the rates of dying and of giving birth at each age, prevalent in the year of her birth. In 1970–75 the UN estimate of the NRR was 1.08 in developed countries, ranging between 1.00 in Western Europe and 1.39 in temperate South America; in less developed countries the estimate was 2.16, ranging between 1.65 for China and 2.71 for Middle America.[5] The difference between the NRR and the GRR is due to the influence of mortality before the end of a woman's reproductive life, and the greater gap for less developed countries indicates the higher level of mortality of the former.

What are the implications of these figures for future population development? Generally, a NRR of unity means that if fertility and mortality were to continue unchanged into the future, the population would *ultimately* become stationary, a NRR above unity implies *ultimate* growth, one below unity *ultimate* decline. But, I have stressed the word 'ultimate', for the value of the NRR does not tell us anything about the immediate future. This can best be illustrated from an example given by the United Nations.[6] In 1970–75 fertility and mortality were not very different in Western Europe and Japan. Life expectancies at birth were 71.8 and 73.3 years respectively, the GRRs 1.04 and 1.05, NRRs 1.00 and 1.02. (The Western European figure is always quoted first.) Yet, the population of Japan was growing at an annual rate of 12.6 per thousand during that period, against a growth rate of 3.5 per thousand in Western Europe. The reason for this apparent inconsistency can be found in the phenomenon normally called 'demographic momentum'. Fertility had been low for longer in Western Europe than in Japan, and although a continuation of present fertility and mortality conditions implied that women in both areas would have similar completed family sizes, the difference in their demographic history meant that 50 per cent of the Japanese population were in the reproductive age groups (15 to 44), as against only 41 per cent of the Western Europeans. By contrast 7 per cent of the Japanese, but 13 per cent of the Europeans were 65 years old or older. This excess of elderly and relative deficiency of people of reproductive age meant that the absolute numbers of deaths would be larger and the number of

births smaller in Western Europe, so that the immediate growth
rate would be smaller. A continuation of present mortality and
fertility rates in Japan would gradually modify the Japanese age
distribution until it had become similar to that of Western Europe
and then the growth rates of the two populations would converge.
By the time that this had happened, however, the Japanese population would have increased over its present level much more than
the Western European.

This example serves to demonstrate that there are certain ines-
capable consequences for future population growth which derive
from the present age structure of the population and which cannot
be avoided, even if family size were immediately to fall to a level
which was no more than adequate for long-term replacement.
Neither the difference between the birth rate and the death rate,
nor the calculation of the NRR can by itself show what is likely to
happen to populations in the immediate future.

The most exhaustive investigation of the implications of present
age structures of populations has recently been undertaken by
Tomas Frejka.[7] He has shown that if fertility were to be reduced to
a level consistent with long-term replacement during the present
quinquennium (1970–74), the world's population would ultimately become stationary at a level of 5,700 million people by the
year 2100. If this reduction in fertility were not to be accomplished
before the 1980–84 quinquennium the figure would be 6,400 million and if we had to wait until the quinquennium 2000–2004 for
stabilisation of fertility at replacement level, the ultimate stationary population would rise to 8,400 million. Clearly, even on the
most optimistic assumption we must expect that – in the absence of
unforeseen catastrophes – there will be at least half as many people
again living in the world as there were in 1970 before the population would become stationary.

At this stage, it is perhaps worth while to digress for a moment
on a phrase which has been much bandied about of late 'zero
population growth'. If this phrase were to be interpreted in the way
in which we have discussed it in the preceding paragraphs, i.e. a
stabilisation of fertility at replacement level followed by a period of
changing age structures in which births will adjust to deaths, then a
state of zero growth would not be brought about for some considerable time and at a level of total population much higher than

today's. But it is also possible to interpret this phrase more radically to mean an immediate limitation of births to a figure in which they would not exceed deaths. Leaving aside the problem of whether such a procedure is practical or realistic, Frejka has shown that if the population of Belgium, which was already growing at the very low rate of three per thousand per year were to be stabilised immediately in this sense, the average size of completed families would have to fall from a figure of 2.4 in 1965–70 to 1.7 in 1985–90, a reduction of some 30 per cent. Thereafter, it could be allowed to increase again to 1.9 in the quinquennium 1995–2000. In India, the achievement of cessation of growth by the end of the present century would require a fall in family size from 5.5 in 1965–70 to 1.1 in 2005–10, a decline of 80 per cent. After that period, however, fertility could be allowed to rise again to reach a figure of 3.0 children per family by 2045–50. These calculations serve to demonstrate that even in developed countries, immediate cessation of growth would imply changes in family size which would be very considerable and difficult to bring about, and that the situation in the less developed countries is such that even fairly remote achievement of stabilisation seems unlikely. It is therefore pretty certain that we shall have to accommodate much larger numbers than at present at the end of the century.

Clearly, this situation cannot continue for long. By some means or other population growth will have to be reduced. But, the demographer really cannot take matters much further in attempting to forecast what actually will happen to the world's population. Different skills are needed for this, those of the economist, sociologist, social psychologist or even the political scientist. But it would be wrong in a lecture with this title to leave matters at this stage and I shall therefore permit myself the luxury of speculating about what might actually happen.

Clearly, the crucial variable to consider is fertility. We may expect that attempts to reduce mortality in the less developed countries will continue and that there will be further advances in medical and therapeutic techniques. But the future of fertility is much more difficult to forecast, because human attitudes towards fertility are ambivalent. I have already mentioned the almost universal desire for human progeny. In less developed countries, in addition, children have a positive value for their parents as they can assist in production from a relatively early age and they provide a kind of social security during old age. On the other hand, pregnancy and lactation interfere with the mother's capacity for work and in developed countries particularly, the long period of dependency of the human infant competes with other claims on her time. Children produce psychic satisfactions for their parents and may contribute to household production, but they also compete for the time and resources of their parents and of other siblings.

In the past, children were the inevitable consequence of the sexual act and the strength of the sexual drive ensured reproduction. Whilst there are few, if any societies, in which some attempt has not been made to control reproduction through social means, it would not be far wrong to suggest that in the past the number of births depended mainly on the number of women of reproductive age in the population – it was a biological variable. Today, this is certainly no longer true in the developed countries. Contraception has made it possible to divorce reproduction and sex, and most couples try to adjust the production of their children to the social and economic conditions affecting them.

One of the results of this change is an increase in the year-to-year fluctuations in numbers of births. For married couples attempt to control not only the total number of children they produce, but also the time at which these are born. When, as is presently the case in developed countries, the average size of completed families is nearer two than three children, it is perfectly feasible for a woman to postpone the beginning of childbearing for as long as ten years after her marriage and yet to produce a family which is near the average. If, therefore, in periods of social and economic adversity couples react by postponing the births of children there may be very considerable fluctuations in the numbers of births consistent with the maintenance of a near-constant family size. This is the main reason why annual birth figures are difficult to interpret, because it is impossible to know to what extent the younger women of today will make up the births that they do not have at the moment. Thus, the present low birth rate in the UK may be a reaction to our present difficulties or an indication of a secular decline in family size, or a mixture of the two. We shall not know for certain until women at the peak childbearing ages of today reach the menopause in 20 years time.

Completed family size in the past has changed more smoothly and regularly than annual birth figures. The norms of family size are formed in childhood and adolescence and changed relatively slowly. I do not believe myself that attitudes towards children and the family have changed to such an extent in developed countries that completed family size will fall significantly below the level required for replacement, though there is also unlikely to be a further permanent rise. I would therefore expect that the population of developed countries will increase as a result of demographic momentum, that the rises will be small and that there may be year-to-year fluctuations which will mean that in some years deaths may exceed births. But, I must emphasise that this is no more than an informed guess on my part.

The situation is much more complex in the less developed countries. Contraception has not made nearly as much headway as in the developed world and completed family size remains high. There are those who believe that the transition which the developed countries have experienced during the last century will be reproduced in the less developed countries and that fertility will be brought under control. If they are right, demographic momentum alone would lead to a much higher population, but fertility control will come and there is light at the end of the tunnel.

It is, however, also possible to take a less optimistic view. The reduction in mortality in the less developed countries was not accompanied, as it was in the West, by rising standards of living or by industrialisation. In many areas, the population continues to be mainly agricultural and is only influenced by modernisation to a limited degree. The individual couple does not necessarily see limitation of fertility as advantageous to themselves, and would have to be persuaded of its value. This would imply governmental programmes of persuasion and the adoption of deliberate policies designed to reduce growth.

The prospects for such action in the immediate future do not appear propitious. It is true that a number of governments in South and South-East Asia have recognised that excessive population growth is a major obstacle in the way of economic development. But, there are also important currents of opinion which deny the importance of population as a factor in underdevelopment. At

the recent UN World Population Conference in Bucharest, for
instance, many delegates from African, Latin American and
Communist countries explicitly maintained that problems of
underdevelopment were due to a maldistribution of resources and
opposed attempts to include reference to family planning in the
World Population Plan of Action. Indeed, the Chinese delegate
went so far as to talk about the 'so-called population explosion'. In
addition, the attitude of the Holy See to population limitation
could only be described as unhelpful. As a result, only a very
watered down version of the World Population Plan of Action
was finally adopted after debates which were long, tedious and
marked by some acerbity. Moreover, population policies designed
to reduce growth are unlikely to be politically appealing and
may prove only doubtfully effective.[8] Given the opposition
shown at Bucharest there must be doubt about the willingness of
governments to apply such policies *in time*. For demographic
momentum means that it will take a long time before the benefits of
policies designed to reach a stationary population can become
evident. Less developed countries are in the position of the Red
Queen who had to keep running very fast in order to stay in the
same place.

On the other hand, the optimists could point to the fact that
governments, when faced with the pressure of events, do not
always practise what they preach. There is evidence which suggests
that in China, for instance, there is awareness of the disadvantages
of rapidly growing population, and that the government is taking
steps to try and alleviate excessive pressure. And the pace of social
change has quickened to such an extent that any transition from
high to low fertility may take place much more rapidly than the
pessimists expect.

It is perhaps worth mentioning that the contrast between policies designed to reduce growth and policies designed to modernise
developing countries, of which so much was made in Bucharest, is
entirely artificial. There are few students of population who believe
that it is possible to reduce population growth in the less developed
country, without economic development and modernisation. In
particular, a considerable extension of women's education and
a change in their status is essential before attitudes towards
reproduction can change. But, whilst development is a necessary

condition for reducing population growth, it is also true that a reduction in population growth is necessary for development. The two objectives must be achieved together and those who suggest that one may be attained without the other are unlikely to achieve either.

Clearly, it is impossible for population growth to continue at present rates for any length of time. The growth rate must be reduced, and the only question is whether it will be reduced by voluntary and relatively painless means or whether a reduction will be forced on us through the old Malthusian devils of famine, pestilence and war. I have tried to give some indications of factors which will influence the course of events one way or another. Demographers are not prophets and cannot forecast what will happen. Their views about the future are determined by their temperament as much as by their analysis, and it is for every one to judge whether the more optimistic or the more pessimistic scenario is the more likely. In Bucharest, the Chinese coined the slogan 'The future is infinitely bright'. If fertility is not reduced and population growth continues at present levels for much longer, they are unlikely to prove correct.

Afterword, 1989

It is a salutary experience to be asked to look over a lecture delivered some 15 years ago in order to assess whether the points that I made then are still valid. Statistics relating to an additional 15 years need to be digested in order to consider whether the new figures that have become available lead to a modification of the opinions that were originally expressed on the lecture.

In my original lecture I quoted a figure of 3600 million for the world's population in 1970: the UN later revised that figure upward, and the corrected value came to 3697 million. Fifteen years later, the figure quoted by the United Nations was 4837 million, an increase of some 30 per cent. This means an annual rate of increase of about 1.82 per cent, which in turn implies that the world's population would double within a period of approximately 38.5 years.

In the original lecture I said that 'demographically . . . we live

not in one world, but in two'. The difference between the demographic situation in the more developed and the less developed
countries of the world, to which I drew attention, has persisted.
The annual rate of population growth in the more developed
countries between 1970 and 1985 was 0.77 per cent; in the less
developed countries it was 2.19 per cent, with doubling periods of
90.8 and 32.0 years respectively. In other words, the population of
the less developed countries increased 2.85 times as fast as that of
the more developed countries; during the previous 20 years, the
increase in the less developed countries was only 1.97 times that in
the more developed. There were considerable differences between
the growth rates of different less developed regions of the world. If
the major regions of the world are taken, the population of Africa
increased by 2.91 per cent per year, that of Latin America by 2.42
per cent, that of Southern Asia by 2.28 per cent. By contrast the
figures for North America were 1.01 per cent and for Europe 0.46
per cent. The continuation of such rates would imply a doubling of
the African population every 24.2 years, and of the European
population every 149.8 years. The disparity between the growth
rates of developed and less developed countries has, therefore, if
anything increased since the original lecture was delivered.

On the other hand, the actual rate of increase of the world's
population which reached a maximum of 2.04 per cent during the
1960s fell to 1.88 per cent during the 1970s and to 1.68 per cent for
the quinquennium 1980–85. The figures for the more developed
countries were 1.03 per cent during the 1960s, 0.83 per cent during
the 1970s and 0.64 per cent between 1980 and 1985, and for the less
developed countries 2.47 per cent, 2.27 per cent and 2.03 per cent
respectively. The reduction in the rate of growth has, therefore,
been larger in the more developed countries in which fertility has
been falling fast. It has also had the effect of reducing interest in the
problems of population growth, because many people believe that
their urgency has considerably diminished. The medium variant of
the projections published by the United Nations assumes that the
rate of growth will continue to fall and that by 2025 it will amount
to 0.96 per cent each year for the world as a whole, to 0.29 per cent
for the more developed and 1.10 per cent for the less developed
countries respectively. It must be stressed, however, that these
variants are statistical extrapolations of past trends and are not

based on an analysis of the factors that determine rates of population increase. In particular, they assume that completed family size per woman in the less developed countries will fall from a figure of 4.1 children per woman in 1980–85 to 2.4 children per woman in 2020–25. There are some demographers who question whether falls of such magnitude are likely to be realized in practice.

These are global figures. Differences in life expectancy between the more and the less developed areas of the world continue; in 1980–85 they ranged from less than 50 years in Africa to 71.5 years in Northern America; and during the same period total fertility in the less developed countries was double that in the more developed (4.1 and 2.0 children per woman respectively). In Europe, maintenance of completed family size at levels experienced during the immediate past would result in numbers of births which would, in the long run, be insufficient to maintain the population at its present level, and ultimately lead to population decrease.

In my original lecture I concluded that 'clearly, this situation cannot continue for long'. It is obviously impossible for the population of the world to continue to increase indefinitely, and even if an annual rate of increase of 0.96 per cent per year were to be achieved in 2020–25, this would still mean that the world's population would double within a period of 72.5 years, i.e. in less than a century.

I devoted the last part of my lecture to speculation about the likelihood of achieving a reduction of population growth to a level which would be much nearer to zero. What has the experience of the last 15 years told us about this? Perhaps, one of the most significant developments during the last 15 years has been the success of the government of the People's Republic of China in reducing the rate of growth in that country much faster than most experts would have considered possible. However, this reduction has been brought about by a mixture of methods of mass persuasion and compulsion which many people outside China would regard as being unacceptable. Nor is it by any means clear whether the reductions that have been achieved can be maintained permanently, though it is unlikely that fertility will return to the high levels of the past. But the Chinese example has not been followed elsewhere. Fertility remains high in Africa, in Muslim Western Asia, and in other less developed countries. Moreover, internal policy considerations in the United States, connected with the objections to abortion by some sections of the American public, have resulted in a reduction of assistance given to some of the less developed countries in their efforts to curb population growth. Whereas the Chinese government now recognize (as they did not at the time of the Bucharest conference in 1974) that excessive population growth is an obstacle to economic development, some economists in the United States have moved in the opposite direction.

This very brief survey of the situation during the last 15 years leaves me in the fortunate position of not having to change my mind about the principal conclusion that I then reached. It remains true that 'the growth rate must be reduced, and the only question is whether it will be reduced by voluntary and relatively painless means, or whether a reduction will be forced on us through the old Malthusian devils of famine, pestilence and war'. I see no reason to alter this conclusion. The events of the last 15 years have not made me feel any more optimistic that the population growth rates will be reduced sufficiently quickly, or that policies designed to bring about this result will be easily compatible with the democratic process. The problems caused by excessive growth rates of population are likely to remain with us in the foreseeable future.

REFERENCES

1 United Nations: *Concise Report on the World Population Situation in 1970–1975 and its Long Range Implications* (New York, 1974). Table 1, p. 5.
2 *Ibid.*
3 *Ibid.* Table 7, p. 18.
4 *Ibid.* Table 6, p. 13.
5 *Ibid.* Note that I have given these figures as if they were accurate and exact. They are, of course, subject to considerable margins of error and are based on estimated data to some extent. Nonetheless, the order of magnitude of the figures and their differences are likely to be reasonably correct.
6 United Nations, *op. cit.* Table 19, p. 39.

7 T. Frejka, *The Future of Population Growth. Alternative Paths to Equilibrium* (John Wiley & Sons, New York, 1973).

8 I have discussed the difficulties of controlling population growth elsewhere. See E. Grebenik, 'On Controlling Population Growth' in J. W. S. Pringle, *Biology and the Human Sciences* (Clarendon Press, Oxford, 1972).

13

The Energy Imperative

ALEXANDER KING*

In the course of an earlier lecture to the Institute, I developed the idea of the 'world *problematique*', the concept that most of the contemporary problems of our planet are interrelated and interacting in a great complex tangle of issues and that to deal with each in isolation causes disturbances in the others, often unforeseen and only dimly understood. This was well illustrated by the petroleum crisis of the early 1970s when the sudden increase in the price of oil caused perturbations throughout the world and across a wide spectrum of human activity. Not only did high cost and sudden scarcity have a serious impact on industry and transportation, but the recycling of the huge Arab oil royalties created a new pattern of world investment. The consequent rise in the price of synthetic fertilizers became an increasing burden for the Third World countries and inhibited their development, while the crisis had a considerable influence on world politics, *inter alia* in shaping United States policy towards the Middle East.

In this brief paper I shall take a look at energy as one of the main strands in the tangle of the *problematique*. Energy is, of course, the fundamental element of material life and, through the Einstein equation, it can be taken to include matter – but we shall not speculate on the significance of this here. Agriculture and the food it produces is one of the most important parts of the world energy system. Thus we have to look far beyond the more obvious energy sources such as coal, oil, gas and wood, the last incidentally still being the unique form of energy available to the majority of the inhabitants of the planet.

The concept of the *problematique* has only recently been recog-

* The present text has been substantially modified and adapted by the author from his original of 1974 in the light of recent developments.

nized in practical terms. What it really says is that 'everything in the world is of a piece' and hence interconnected; it goes back to the holistic concept of the Hellenic philosophers and has always been realized by wise people. Today, however, with recognition of increasing interdependence of the nations and with new knowledge arising at the interfaces between disciplines, quite practical considerations make it necessary to take account of the interconnections which are often more significant than the individual forces. The structures of governments and also of academic and research institutions are normally based in the first case on vertical or sectoral ministries and, in the second case on vertical, unidisciplinary departments. In both instances this results in little or no horizontal contact. There is thus considerable need to introduce innovations in the structure of governments and other institutions, if the problems of contemporary world society are to be faced realistically.

These considerations are particularly pertinent when one takes account of a number of world trends and especially those of scale and of rapidity of change.

The world is at present in the early stages of a transition towards an entirely new type of society, which will be as different from that of today as was that ushered in by the Industrial Revolution from the agrarian society which preceded it. Many factors are active in shaping this transition; some of them are inherent in the present evolution of geopolitics, others flow from the arising of the new, advanced technologies and especially those derived from the new biology and from microelectronics. Adaptation to take advantage of the new possibilities for improvement of the human condition will bring many problems, in the face of the unchanging negative characteristics of human nature such as greed and selfishness, a taboo subject, avoided in all political discussion of the world's future.

The factor of scale is also relevant. Everything is now on a large scale; there are hordes of people everywhere; they possess enormous quantities of material goods and their ambition is to acquire still more; they require a great deal of food from all over the world and they travel extensively and often; they consume large amounts of raw materials and energy to provide their products and maintain their prosperity. Contemporary economy depends on the maintenance of this society of conspicuous consumption. Whether it can be sustained indefinitely or not is another matter.

An alarming aspect of the scale problem results from the world population explosion. Until the present century, the population of the world was doubling every few hundred years. By 1900 it amounted to some 1.8 billion. Suddenly it began to rise rapidly with a doubling now every 30–35 years. It is now over 5 billion and will cross the 6 billion threshold by the end of the century. This means that at present an extra million people are added to the population every four and a half days. By far the greatest rates of increase are in the less developed countries and, although fertility rates are beginning to decrease in some areas, the very low average age in many countries (around 15 years) means that by the end of the century, increase in absolute terms will be greater even than today. World population is expected to level off by the middle of the next century at about 10–12 billion. It is generally accepted that the birth rate decreases as economic prosperity grows and, indeed, population levels in most of the industrialized regions of the world are now more or less stationary. Improvement in the economic conditions of most countries in the Third World is, however, too slow to allow us to expect that it will have a significant effect on population levels in the forseeable future. In some of these countries population increase is outstripping food production. This is especially the case in Black Africa which is expected to have a deficit in food grains of about 20 million tons per annum at the turn of the century.

Population explosion in the less developing countries has many difficult aspects in addition to that of food provision. Most of these countries already suffer a high degree of unemployment and underemployment. Even to maintain the existing level of employment will entail finding work-places for millions of people. In addition, it will be necessary to at least double the infrastructure, to build houses and hospitals, roads and docks to say nothing of the need to provide educational and health facilities for the new millions.

Birth-rate differentials between the high levels of the underdeveloped and the low or negative rates of the developed countries indicate that already in the early years of the next century, the population of industrialized areas of the world – North America,

Europe East and West, Japan and Australia – will account for only some 17% of the global population. It is not possible to envisage a world in which a small minority of the population lives in a rich ghetto, well-fed and protected by sophisticated arms, while outside, the majority are poor, hungry, underemployed, miserable and inevitably resentful. It is clearly in the interest of the rich as well as of the poor countries that greater and more systematic efforts be made to tackle the global poverty problem and create basic conditions which will make development possible in the Third World.

Experience so far is not encouraging. During the 'decades of development', while a few countries, such as the so-called Newly Industrialized Countries (NICS) of South-East Asia have made spectacular advances, progress to close the development gap has generally been slow. In many instances the disparities are still increasing and are likely to do so still more as advanced technologies favour the already rich and impact only slowly on those countries which lack scientific and industrial infrastructure to profit by them.

These disparities are clearly reflected in the *per capita* consumption of energy and materials between countries at different stages of development. In the richest of the industrialized countries the average person may consume about 40 times the quantity of materials and energy used by individuals in the average underdeveloped area. In the extreme, the disparity may be as great as 500:1.

Compounding population numbers with average *per capita* consumption one obtains a rough indication of total human activity. In Europe, before the industrial revolution, *per capita* consumption was little different from that of the least poor Third World countries of today. In the meantime, increase of both population and of economic growth and consumption has resulted in an enormous upsurge of material activity by the human race. I estimate that the totality of such activity may have increased some fortyfold during my own lifetime. In the past, its waste products could be absorbed and transformed by the atmosphere, the soil, the rivers and the oceans. Today this can no longer be relied on. For the first time human activity is making a sizeable and possibly irreversible impact on the environment.

Within this picture of resource (including energy) use, we must sketch in also the criminally wasteful uses of resources – human, material and energy – consumed for military purposes. It is difficult to understand how the peoples of the world can tolerate such waste, in face of extensive hunger, poverty and underdevelopment, conditions which themselves generate war and violence. It is not easy to be precise on the magnitude of military resource consumption. National financial expenditure on defence does, however, give some indication. The apparent world total appears to be about US$ 1000 billion, a fourfold increase since the end of the Second World War and a twentyfivefold escalation since the beginning of the century. Figures of this magnitude are not easy to appreciate in perspective, so some comparisons may be useful. It has been pointed out, for instance, that for many years, annual military expenditure of the world has been comparable to the combined GNP of all the countries of Latin America and Africa; the annual budget of UNICEF is equivalent to about four hours of world military cost; the elimination of smallpox under WHO guidance took ten years to achieve and cost about $100 million – less than the price of a small air-to-air missile.

The impact of human activity on the environment is particularly significant with regard to energy use and to the availability of sufficient 'clean' energy in the future to ensure the maintenance of our present materially-based society. The present dilemma is well illustrated by the potential warming-up of the earth's surface by the accumulation of carbon dioxide in the atmosphere through the so-called 'greenhouse effect'.

It has been noticed that accumulation of carbon dioxide in the air has been increasing since the beginning of the century. This is partly due to the increased burning of the fossil fuels, coal, petroleum and natural gas and partly to the cutting down of the tropical forests resulting in a reduction of Nature's absorption of the gas by photosynthesis through the green leaf.

Carbon dioxide inhibits the reflection of solar radiation from the earth's surface back into space and thus controls the terrestrial temperature. It is estimated that further accumulation of this gas will lead to a significant warming-up of the planet. Great uncertainties persist with regard to this phenomenon within the exceedingly complex climatic system and especially as to the extent to which the oceans are capable of absorbing carbon dioxide and at what rate. However, after a period of controversy, the atmospheric scientists seem to have reached consensus that the effect is real and relatively imminent. A number of different and sophisticated models indicate that a doubling of the concentration of carbon dioxide from the 'steady state' at the beginning of the century would result in an average increase in the surface temperature of the earth of between 1.5° and 4.5°C and that this is likely to be reached by the middle of the next century if present energy use continues. Furthermore, it has been realized quite recently that other 'greenhouse gases', such as methane and oxides of nitrogen, are also showing increased concentrations in the atmosphere which could bring the effect closer in time.

The warming-up effect would be much greater at high latitudes than at the equator and this would greatly alter the thermal gradients of the planet, causing considerable modification of wind and ocean currents and hence of the patterns of precipitation. This would mean profound and, at present, unpredictable changes in the agricultural capacities of the different regions of the earth's surface. In addition, we should have to expect a rise in sea level resulting from both thermal expansion and the melting and off-flow of land-borne ice. This might be of the order of half a metre or more and would threaten low lying coastal areas everywhere. A country such as Bangladesh could hardly exist in such circumstances.

This scenario which is probable, but not yet certain, has enormous implications for the planet – human, economic and political. If allowed to develop to crisis dimensions it would be virtually irreversible, it being estimated that if all burning of fossil fuels were to cease at the point of the doubling of the carbon dioxide concentration, it would take the natural processes some 900 years for the present equilibrium to be reestablished. All this illustrates the difficulty of planning in uncertainty, a situation which we are likely to encounter increasingly. We know too much, yet not enough. The probability of the greenhouse effect and its threats were first announced in a declaration of the International Federation of Institutes for Advanced Study (IFIAS), in 1974. It has thus taken 15 years for the knowledge to be spread, the findings to be refined and public attention to be alerted, before the concern of leading political figures could be obtained and policy implications discussed.

While the environmental impact has deep significance in many policy areas, this is most directly evident in energy and agriculture. It is, of course, quite unrealistic in the light of present evidence to expect governments to abandon or seriously curtail the burning of oil and coal, particularly in the absence of the early hope of viable possible alternatives. Yet, if and when it becomes impossible to ignore the phenomenon, it may be too late to start working on the remedies, in view of the long lead-time necessary to bring the results of initial research, through technological development, to production on a significant scale. Nevertheless many delaying, buffering and insurance measures could be initiated. Firstly there is a need to mount intensive campaigns of fuel conservation and efficiency of use, together with parallel enforcement legislation. Very considerable reductions in fuel consumption and hence of carbon dioxide emission are attainable. Then priority might be given to diversion to natural gas which, consisting mainly of methane, produces much less carbon dioxide per calorie generated than the long-chain hydrocarbon molecules of coal and petroleum. Retention and further development of nuclear fission would have to be contemplated as one of the options in the long transition to a new energy system, seen as less dangerous than the continuing burning of coal. Intensification of research and development of soft energy systems is, in any case, called for and should not be subjected to fluctuating priority of support with short-term variations in oil prices. The great hope that nuclear fusion will provide the final solution in yielding a safe, clean and infinite source of energy still seems distant, despite recent claims to have discovered a cool fusion process.

In addition to greatly strengthened efforts to save energy and develop new forms, there is of course a primary need to stop the devastation of the tropical forests and to increase the green coverage of the planet. While reforestation is taking place in many places, it is nevertheless estimated that at present some nine trees in the world are being felled for every one planted.

Availability of sufficient and cheap energy is fundamental to the sustainability of the industrial economy and society and, in view of the uncertainties we have discussed, it is imperative that energy policies for the early decades of the next century should be devised now and the changing situation monitored constantly. This is essential in view of the fact that construction of a new world energy system might take up to forty years and that we are still far from knowing on what this system would be based. Governments find it difficult to tackle long-term issues. The short electoral cycles force both administrations and oppositions to concentrate on issues seen as immediately relevant to the voters and more distant although often more important questions are neglected until they reach crisis level. In the case of energy and environmental policies, their global dimensions demand international consideration and the mechanisms of inter-governmental negotiation are very long and unsure.

The disruption caused by the petroleum crisis of the last decade demonstrated how vulnerable the industrial countries are to political and military events in distant places beyond their control. Some countries, such as Japan and Denmark, have practically no domestic energy sources and have to rely essentially on imports. Even the United States, which has been a major oil producer, is heavily reliant on imported petroleum. Thus access to oil is a major factor in the foreign policy of many nations.

While there is at present an oil glut and prices are relatively low, this will not last indefinitely. The long-term problems of petroleum availability and cost are serious. Proved reserves are considerable, those of Saudi Arabia, for instance, are expected to last for another fifty years at least. However supplies from many other fields will be exhausted long before then. Exploration in recent years has not been too successful and, in many regions the point may be being approached at which energy expended in exploration and recovery is as great as the energy to be extracted. We shall, in fact, have used up this liquid fossil fuel which represents solar energy trapped by plants over the millennia in the course of two centuries. It has to be remembered also that petroleum will be required indefinitely as the feed stock for the petrochemical industry as a basis for a wide range of essential products.

The obvious alternative to oil is, of course, coal, or at least this was so before the greenhouse effect appeared on the horizon. There is said to be sufficient coal on the planet still, to meet human requirements for at least 500 years. China, for example, which has extensive coal measures, is planning its economic expansion on coal. The effect on world climate of the massive dose of carbon dioxide which would result could be disaster heaped on disaster.

The next most important energy source in the industrialized countries is nuclear fission. Despite the success of nuclear power over a long period now, in countries such as France in providing a substantial input to the national energy grid, there is great public opposition to extension or, in some cases, even continuation of its use. This is due partly to its association in the general mind with the nuclear bomb, and events such as the Chernobyl disaster do not help to reassure. There is a good deal of evidence to indicate that newer nuclear power stations have a very low degree of risk and of course many are now arguing that to go nuclear is much less dangerous than to burn coal. Be that as it may, it would seem sensible in view of the warming-up effect, to keep the nuclear option open for the transitional period before the arising of a new world energy system. Great doubts remain concerning nuclear waste disposal and also it would be unfortunate if we were to leave to our descendents large numbers of 'cathedrals' in the form of spent nuclear power stations.

It is not possible here to discuss the many proposals for soft energy such as geothermal, wind, wave and tidal power. A word should be said, however, about solar energy which seems so alluring. Much more could be done to encourage the use of solar heating and refrigeration etc., especially in tropical countries. But in view of the dispersed nature of solar radiation, capital costs are likely to remain high even if the cost of photo-voltaic cells comes down considerably. It is estimated that by end of the next 20 years, solar energy may account for perhaps 4% of world power requirements. There is, nevertheless great need for a much stronger effort of research and development on this subject.

These considerations neglect, of course, the enormous contribution of continuous solar radiation to energy needs through the burning of fuel wood, which, as already stated, is the sole domestic energy for a large proportion of the world's inhabitants. Here also there are great problems, directly flowing from the population explosion and from the commercial exploitation of the forests. Shortage of fuel wood is acute in many areas, especially in many African countries and on the slopes of the Himalayas. This is a commodity, largely outside the international markets, which is one of the essential elements of life in large areas of the world; scarcity or high cost can bring about great hardship of a type which is hardly noticed in the developed world. Whereas the cost of fuel wood in real terms showed little increase up to 1978, it then increased at about 25% per annum in the years that followed. In many West African cities and towns, typical families may spend as much as one quarter of their earnings on fuel wood or charcoal. As a consequence, the tendency is to switch to the use of kerosene, which often represents a drain on hard currency. This, together with dependence on imported food has led Lester Brown to say that 'many African cities are living from ship to mouth'.

However, the main hardship is suffered in the rural areas where wood is normally the only source of energy. It is estimated that some 1.2 billion people in the Third World are meeting their minimum fuel wood needs by overcutting and hence depleting the forest resource base. This can cause acute conditions of erosion which, as in the case of Nepal, can deposit massive amounts of silt and cause flooding many hundred miles down stream. As woodlands recede from towns and villages and firewood becomes scarce, villagers start using animal dung and crop residues for cooking. This deprives the land of nutrients and organic matter necessary for maintenance of soil structure and productivity, leading again to erosion and lowering of the water-tables. In many countries wood gathering is a woman's task and it is noticeable that this chore, which formerly demanded two hours per day, now requires 5–6 hours. The fuel wood crisis has to be seen as an important element of the world energy situation, related through the *problematique* with land degradation, desertification and diminishing food production.

A few words must be added about world agriculture which is overwhelmingly the most important use by mankind of the sun's radiation. The success of agricultural production since the end of World War II has been phenomenal and it has largely kept up with population increase during the same period. In 1950, world grain production was 623 million tons and it increased to about 1.6 billion tons by 1986, an astonishing addition of about 900 million tons per annum. Especially important was the hybridization of maize and the dwarfing of wheat which were at the heart of the

Green Revolution. But the greatly increased harvest was by no means due exclusively to the sun's bounty. Before 1950, increase of food output came mainly from the extension of land under cultivation and from greater use of irrigation. After that date, new, fertile lands became scarce, but cheap chemical fertilizers became more generally available. Thus agriculture has become increasingly energy-intensive and energy dependent. It takes about a ton of oil to produce a ton of fertilizer. Petroleum is also required for the manufacture of pesticides and weed-killers, essential in the new agricultural technologies, as well as for use in tillage and irrigation equipment. During the period 1950–1986, the average consumption of fertilizers per inhabitant of the planet rose from 5Kg to 26Kg while, at the same time, the area *per capita* of harvested cereals dropped from 0.24 to 0.15 hectares.

Thus, in a crude sense, the great increase in world food production represents the conversion of petroleum to edible cereals via photosynthesis in the green plant. In many vegetable products on general sale, each calorie of food intake has necessitated 5 calories of oil in its production. The intensive agriculture practiced in the main grain-producing regions of the world today is thus heavily dependent on petroleum and could well be highly vulnerable to its scarcity or high cost in the future. The possible consequences of the greenhouse effect on agriculture could be very serious, not only as a result of regional changes in climate, but also, if action is taken to lower emissions of carbon dioxide, to energy shortage.

For many years production of food in the world has been sufficient to provide a sufficient diet to every inhabitant. It is estimated for example that in 1987 there was a 19% surplus of food, beyond total human and animal requirements. Yet, at the same time millions were hungry or undernourished with the intolerable situation where some 40,000 children died each day from starvation or diseases caused by malnutrition. One of the tragedies of contemporary world society is the coexistence of food overproduction with the persistence of hunger. The simplicist view is that continuing and augmenting food aid with the provision of cheap cereals would lessen both the hunger and the surplus. Such an approach could, in practice, worsen the situation, although emergency food aid will certainly be frequently necessary. The abolition of hunger is essentially a matter of politics and economics, to which technological factors are only marginally relevant. Technological advances can greatly improve the quantity, quality and variety of food, but cannot ensure that it reaches the hungry. The hungry are the poor who lack the means to buy the food that exists. The real problem, then, is the abolition of world poverty by the creation and equitable distribution of wealth. This is an issue in which food and energy policies are but elements.

The problem of energy, as one strand of the tangle of the *problematique*, highlights the basic dilemma of contemporary society. Can our present economic system of stimulated consumption and economic growth continue? In 1972 the Club of Rome issued the report, *The Limits to Growth*, a pioneering effort to demonstrate the relationships between a number of quantifiable world trends. The report, which has sold some 10 million copies in 37 languages, generated a heated controversy, being denounced by many economists. The report was seen by many as a forecast of doom to come. Its intention was quite otherwise, namely an attempt to indicate the probable consequences of continuation of existing trends, in the hope of achieving policy changes which would ensure that its forecasts would prove to be wrong. This work triggered off a debate throughout the world – but the policies have not been changed!

There were many weaknesses in this first world model, but I am convinced that its general conclusions are still valid. All the signs suggest that the population explosion together with constantly increasing economic growth and consumption will impact dangerously and possibly irreversibly on the environment to an extent that the existing economic system and the life styles of the rich countries will no longer be possible.

Exponential growth in any system can never continue indefinitely and always, as in the growth of the human body, flattens out. This is obviously the case with economic growth. A simple calculation indicates that, with an economy growing at 5% per annum, it would reach, by the end of the next century, a level of about 500 times greater than the current level. Even if the use of materials were to decline sharply in relation to the rise in economic output, the problems of acquiring, processing and getting rid of the wastes would be staggering. The environment could not possibly absorb the consequences of this level of magnitude of human activity.

The adoption of policies of zero growth would provide no solution, especially since zero population growth is many decades ahead and growth in most of the countries will be needed for many years if a basis for a life of human dignity is to be realized. It is not growth which is at fault, but the nature of our present kind of growth – material and undifferentiated. The need is for the cultivation of a growth of society which is based on quality rather than quantity. There are, of course, indications of some trend in this direction in the gradual emergence of the post-industrial or information society which the development of microelectronics is ushering in. This has already expanded the social and service sectors and is encouraging the rise of new industries, cleaner and safer and less demanding of materials and energy. But this is still dominated by the old consumerism mentality and its human quality attributes are, as yet, mainly unexplored. The concept of quality growth is far from new. As early as 1857 John Stuart Mill wrote, 'It is scarcely necessary to remark that a stationary condition of capital and labour implies no stationary state of human improvement. There would be as much scope as ever for all kinds of mental culture and moral and social progress; as much room for improving the art of living and more likelihood of its being improved.'

The conclusion is that present trends, well illustrated by the energy environment elements of the *problematique*, are leading rapidly to a situation which threatens the continuation of society as we know it. While there is now much discussion of some of the most obvious symptoms of the malaise, political leaders are as yet far from admitting, to say nothing of facing up to, the situation. There is an imperative need to reassess the human situation, its perils and prospects and within this analysis, to identify the critical needs for corrective action if major catastrophe is to be avoided. There are many constructive elements in the *problematique*, but they can only be activated if, through general public awareness of the dangers and wise leadership, a new sense of common self-interest in the survival of society can be generated.

Our present society, as Denis Gabor, the Nobel laureate, has put it, 'is based materially on an enormously successful technology and spiritually on practically nothing.' The limits of growth and expansion do not reside in the material but eventually in the nature of man himself. The chauvinism and striving for domination of the nations is a projection of human greed and egoism; difficulties, including war, between countries are a collectivisation of difficulties and hatreds between individuals. The fundamental problems of every man and woman as of their collectivity, the state, lie deep within human nature; without an intensive knowledge of our inner potentialities and limitations and overt recognition of these, the human approach to problem-solving is restricted to analysis of the symptoms of diseases not yet diagnosed.

Egoism, or the life force, as our Victorian ancestors called it, appears to be a property common to all organic species, which provides the primaeval urge to survive, to reproduce, to prosper and excel; it is the driving force of innovation and material progress. But it also manifests itself constantly in selfish, greedy and anti-social behaviour, brutality, lust for power, however petty, exploitation and domination over others. The struggle between the positive and negative aspects of egoism is the eternal Faustian drama, which all perform, and the achievement of a dynamic equilibrium between the two opposing sides is the central, but seldom admitted, objective of social policy; too much latitude given to exercise of the egoistic urge may produce a dynamic society, but it also generates corruption, lack of social justice and oppression.

Such matters are seldom admitted and, when they are, they are shrouded in taboo. If this analysis is at all valid, there would seem to be a need for lifting the taboos and recognizing the existence and power of the negative aspects of human nature as motivations of collective behaviour and for turning towards an approach based on enlightened and common self-interest which, on the individual level, leads to the just society and on the political level to a safe and harmonious world, since it is overwhelmingly in the interest of every inhabitant of the planet to ensure that sustainable physical and social environments are achieved. If not, 'après nous le déluge'.

This alone might give us a little time to get down to the more serious matter of what to do about human nature.